CENTER FOR ORIGINS RESEARCH

Issues

IN CREATION

Genesis Kinds:
Creationism and the
Origin of Species

EDITED BY TODD CHARLES WOOD AND PAUL A. GARNER

Center for Origins Research Issues in Creation
Number 5
January 16, 2009

WIPF & STOCK · Eugene, Oregon

GENESIS KINDS

ISBN: 978-1-60608-490-8

www.wipfandstock.com

Abstract

A belief in creationism, even in young-age creationism, does not necessitate belief in the unique creation of each species. Instead, many creationists accept a secondary origin of species from ancestors originally created by God. In this view, groups of modern species constitute the "Genesis kinds" that God originally created and beyond which evolution cannot proceed (if it can even be called 'evolution'). In this collection of papers, six scholars examine the species and the Genesis kinds. Topics covered include the history of creationist and Christian perspectives on the origin of species, an analysis of the Hebrew word *mîn* (kind) from the perspective of biblical theology, a baseline of minimum speciation within kinds inferred from island endemics, a comprehensive list of proposed kinds from the mammalian fossil record, the occurrence of discontinuity between kinds, and the origin of new species by symbiosis.

Contents

The Real Debate over Creationism and Species

TODD CHARLES WOOD AND PAUL A. GARNER

As we remember the 150th anniversary of the publication of Charles Darwin's *Origin of Species*, it is appropriate to ponder the intense controversies that his work initiated. Obviously, this volume deals with the particular controversy regarding the Christian response to Darwin's understanding of the origin of species. We are not concerned here with just any Christian response, but with the conservative response signified by the label "creationist."

Throughout *Origin*, Darwin used the doctrine of special creation repeatedly as a contrast for his own theory of adaptation and divergence of species by natural selection. Each time he mentioned it, Darwin emphasized the impotence of special creation in explaining biological phenomena. In this influential book, Darwin established the dichotomy that still very much defines the propaganda of the creation/evolution wars: Species originate by evolution from other species or by special acts of divine intervention. To Darwin, there was no other choice.

But as Wood (2008) has shown, there were other choices, even in Darwin's day. The concept of limited evolution, that is, evolution within limited, taxonomic categories, had been discussed for at least 100 years prior to the publication of *Origin*. To be sure, these proposals were the minority opinion and little known, but they existed. Modern historians would see in them precursors to Darwin's evolution, but only in the sense of the dichotomy that Darwin established in *Origin*.

The primary attitude towards creation in Darwin's day was exemplified by the doctrines of accommodation and natural theology. Under accommodation, popularized by Galileo's *Letter to the Grand Duchess Christina*, the Bible was treated as a source of information about salvation and morality but not science. Since God wished to communicate the message of salvation to all people, He found it necessary to use certain figures of speech regarding the natural world, figures of speech that were not literally true. As a result of the accommodation of revelation to the ignorance of humanity, scientists could not rely on the Bible to reveal reliable information about the natural world.

Natural religion or natural theology was an outgrowth of the doctrine of accommodation. Instead of using biblical revelation to enhance science, the natural theologian used science to bolster religion. Paley's version of natural theology, anticipated more than a century before by John Ray's *Wisdom of God Manifested in the Works of Creation*, emphasized what we now call the design argument: the evidence of God's wisdom, power, and benevolence in the "admirable contrivance" of living things.

Writing in the preface to his *Wisdom of God*, Ray (1717) claimed, "by the Works of the Creation, in the Title, I mean the Works created by God at first, and by Him conserv'd to this Day in the same State and Condition in which they were at first made." Thus at the beginning of natural theology, we find a strong emphasis on the fixity of nature. Indeed, a brief reflection reveals why this fixity was necessary. One could not derive evidence of God's design from the admirable contrivance of the woodpecker's adaptation to retrieving insects from wood, as Ray did, if the woodpecker had developed naturally from some other species (or at the very least, it would require a radical re-imagining of the design argument, which the natural theologians were unwilling to do).

Thus, by Darwin's day, the special creation and fixity of species was insisted upon primarily by the natural theologians, and it is to them that we should look for the identification of Darwin's doctrine of special creation. In our modern culture, the doctrine of special creation has evolved into something quite different. First and most importantly, the modern creationist (*sensu* Numbers 1999) holds that the Bible does contain true and reliable information about science. In particular, the first eleven chapters of the book of Genesis are held to be authoritative revelations of the earliest earth history. The special creationist holds to the reality of a week-long creation, a literal Adam and Eve, the onset of human and animal death as a direct consequence of sin, the global nature of the Flood, and the confusion of language at Babel, all within a 6000-year timescale for the age of the earth. In holding these beliefs, the modern creationist explicitly rejects the doctrine of accommodation popular in Darwin's day and still among modern theistic evolutionists (or "evolutionary creationists," as some of them prefer to be called).

Modern creationists also agree with Darwin in rejecting the special creation of each individual species. Frank Lewis Marsh in particular had rather strong words for those who equate creationists with species fixists:

> In our day the inaccurate portrayal of the position of creationists on this point which evolutionists give, is doubtless due to the opinion of Louis Agassiz. We have referred above to his strange belief that modern animals had been created and placed in the very ecological niches which we find them today. Apparently considering that the whole of the theory of special creation was sealed up in Agassiz, evolutionists commonly teach that creationists are all of Agassiz' opinion. As remarked

several times before, however, those who would know the basic tenets of the doctrine of special creation must go to the Bible and read them for themselves rather than depend on some one scientist's exposition of them (Marsh 1947, pp. 289-290).

Development of the concept of limited evolution preceded Marsh, as evolution preceded Darwin, but Marsh became most closely associated with the opinion due to his lifelong advocacy of the concept of the "Genesis Kind" or baramin (from the Hebrew *bara*, create, and *min*, kind).

For the modern creationist, then, the debate is not over the origin of species *per se*, about which we generally agree with Darwin to a limited extent. Rather, the debate turns on other issues, especially over the limits of speciation. How many species ought we assign to each baramin? There are conservative creationists who would assign to a baramin only a few species, perhaps within a single genus. More liberal creationists accept a great deal of speciation and many species per baramin. Both camps are concerned with the origin of species themselves. The conservative creationists tend to accept conventional speciation mechanisms (e.g., by natural selection), while the liberal creationists look to yet undiscovered mechanisms to produce many species in a short amount of time.

In the public creation/evolution debate, dominated as it is by propaganda, anticreationists continue to define creationism as a kind of species fixity, as Darwin did. These anachronistic "special creationists" have little in common with the creationists of the twenty-first century. Considering the recalcitrance of the nineteenth century definition of creationist, it might seem superfluous to once again attempt to explain modern creationist opinions regarding the origin of species. Why then bother producing this book?

The book of Proverbs counsels, "Flog a mocker, and the simple will learn prudence; rebuke a discerning man, and he will gain knowledge" (Prov. 19:25). We know full well that the mockers, those responsible for the propaganda war, will never be satisfied by any creationist response. For the sake of those who might not understand, the simple still looking for prudence, we offer these papers on creationism and the origin of species. These papers are not simply educational tools, though. We hope that each will advance the creation model of the origin of species. We therefore pray that the discerning man will gain knowledge.

This volume opens with a survey of Christian opinions on the origin of species by Paul Garner. Paul notes that those believing in creation are not in any sort of agreement on the origin of species. Ken Turner then surveys the meaning of the "kind" of Genesis 1, especially in the context of biblical theology. Roger Sanders revisits the issue of endemic species on oceanic islands to establish the minimum speciation that modern creationists should all accept. Todd Wood evaluates the evidence of discontinuity—the separate origin of baramins. Kurt Wise looks at the issue from the fossil record of mammals, developing a new method of identifying created kinds. Joe Francis concludes the volume with a new perspective (for creationists) on the origin of species based on symbiosis.

This book will in no way finish the debate. Mockers will continue to accuse creationists of accepting species fixity, and many poorly informed creationists will likely defend the outmoded nineteenth century "creationist." In the meantime, though, we hope and pray that creationists interested in biological issues will continue to study and develop a uniquely biblical and creationist understanding of the origin of species.

References

Marsh, F.L. 1947. *Evolution, Creation, and Science*, second edition. Review and Herald Publishing Association, Washington, DC.

Numbers, R.L. 1999. Creating creationism: meanings and usage since the age of Agassiz. In: Livingstone, D.N. , D.G. Hart, and M.A. Noll, eds. *Evangelicals and Science in Historical Perspective*. Oxford University Press, Oxford, pp. 234-243.

Ray, J. 1717. *The Wisdom of God Manifested in the Works of Creation*, seventh edition. William Innys, London.

Wood, T.C. 2008. Species variability and creationism. *Origins* 62:6-25.

1. Evolving Christian Views of Species

PAUL A. GARNER
BIBLICAL CREATION MINISTRIES

1.1. Introduction

The historic Christian doctrine of creation emphasizes that God is the source and origin of all that exists. The entire universe of time, space, and matter is the handiwork of this transcendent, eternal, and self-existent God. Unlike the Creator himself, the universe had a beginning; God spoke and it sprang into existence *ex nihilo*. This is the teaching of Hebrews 11:3: "Through faith we understand that the worlds were framed by the word of God, so that things which are seen were not made of things which do appear". Furthermore, the creation doctrine affirms that all that exists continues to be upheld, sustained, and nurtured by God. The universe and everything within it depends utterly upon the will of its Creator for its continued existence.

Thus far, most Christians will agree. However, when we consider the specifics of God's creative activity, in particular its mode and timing, we find much less of a consensus. Christians have held widely divergent views concerning the origin and history of the world and the living organisms that inhabit it. Today the choice facing Christians is often presented as a dichotomy between *creation* and *evolution*. On the one hand, there is the creationist view, according to which the world and all its creatures sprang fully formed from the Creator's hand. On the other, there is the theistic evolutionist view, according to which God worked through solely natural processes to bring about the world and the diversity of living species that we see around us.

Moreover, belief in creation is commonly identified with belief in the immutability of species, the idea that each species was created in precisely the same form that we find it today. This seems to reflect Charles Darwin's own understanding of creationism, since it is the view against which he argued in *The Origin of Species* (1859). By contrast, the evolutionary view is commonly identified with acceptance of the reality of biological change, the idea that species, far from being fixed and immutable, are in a process of change and flux.

However, I want to suggest here that this popularly understood dichotomy between creation and evolution is a false one. It must be recognized that Christians who accept that God has worked through the evolutionary mechanism are usually happy to affirm the basic truths of the historic Christian doctrine of creation outlined earlier and, in this broad sense at least, sometimes regard themselves as creationists. For example, in his recent book *Creation or Evolution: Do We Have to Choose?*, Denis Alexander (2008, pp. 169-190) describes himself as an "evolutionary creationist". However, even within creationism defined in the narrower and more particular sense of belief in some form of *miraculous* creation, the range of views about the mode by which God created, the limits of biological change, and the origin of species is very broad. There is no doubt that the popular perception of creationism as a belief in species fixity makes life easier for its opponents, since it allows any evidence against species fixity to be regarded, *ipso facto*, as evidence against creationism. Nevertheless, this common perception of creationism is incorrect.

In this paper I will review the contributions of sixteen scholars from within the Christian tradition in order to elucidate the range of views that they held on the nature and origin of species. I have included those living before and after the time of Darwin, and will demonstrate that their opinions on this subject encompass a wide spectrum, from a rigid belief in the immutability of species to the acceptance of evolution without any limits whatsoever. I have not sought to be comprehensive in this review, although I have sought to be representative. If my selection displays any bias, it is towards the inclusion of those who accepted the evolution of species within limits, for these scholars represent the often-excluded middle ground. While it is fair to say that the immutability of species was the most widely accepted view by the time of Darwin, I want to suggest that it is unrepresentative of the diversity of opinions expressed by Christians (in general) and creationists (more specifically) since the seventeenth century.

In discussing the matter of species fixity, I will also contend that this doctrine was not derived from the Bible, as popular opinion has it, but must instead be traced to extrabiblical influences, chief among them being the essentialist ideas of Plato and Aristotle, the preformationist view of embryonic development, and the rejection of spontaneous generation, all of which were influential in the developing natural sciences of the seventeenth century.

1.2. Fixity of species

We will begin by considering those scholars associated with the notion of species fixity.

1.2.1. John Ray (1627-1705). One of the first naturalists to systematically describe and classify the then-known species of animals and plants was John Ray, widely regarded as the founder of British natural history and in many ways a precursor to Linnaeus (Tyler 2005). Ray was elected a Fellow of Trinity College, Cambridge, in 1649, where he befriended a very capable student called Francis Willughby (1635-1672). Together, the two men embarked upon an ambitious project to catalogue the living world. They began with a systematic flora of Cambridgeshire (1660), followed ten years later by one encompassing the whole of Britain (1670) which became the standard work for several generations of British botanists. After Willughby's premature death, Ray continued this work with a series of catalogues describing birds (1676), fishes (1686), mammals (1693), and insects (1710–*posthumously*). His *magnum opus* was the *Historia Plantarum*, a three-volume work published between 1688 and 1704, which attempted to provide a comprehensive survey of plant physiology and structure, along with descriptions of all the then-known botanical species.

As well as having keen powers of scientific observation, Ray was also a devout Christian with Puritan sympathies, and his works are peppered with observations on God's handiwork as evidenced in nature. In 1691, he dedicated an entire book to this theme, *The Wisdom of God Manifested in the Works of the Creation*, an early and superior exposition of what would become known as natural theology. According to natural theologians like Ray, God had purposed to display his wisdom and benevolence through every detail and contrivance of the created order. So that this natural revelation might be made manifest to all men, God had preserved his works in nature "in the same State and Condition in which they were first made" (Ray 1701, n.p.). This implied, of course, that species had remained unchanged from the time of their original creation and that none of them had subsequently become extinct. God had finished his work of creation and so the number of species in nature, Ray concluded, must be "fixed and determinate" (Raven 1942, p. 190).

Ray was aware that the fossil record presented a challenge to his views and, in particular, his rejection of extinction. Some fossils seemed to represent types of organisms that were no longer present on the earth. Initially, Ray suggested that this was simply an artefact of our own ignorance and that eventually every fossil species would be found alive somewhere. Later in life, however, he came to a different resolution of the problem, adopting the theory proposed by his friend Edward Lhwyd that fossils were inorganic structures that had somehow grown from seeds inside the earth (Bowler 1984, p. 30).

For most of his life Ray appears to have accepted without question that species were the real and immutable units of nature. He recognized that within any particular species there were varieties that were not identical; however, he believed that they differed only in their non-essential characteristics and were products of nothing more than the local conditions of environment and climate. The problem facing naturalists was how to discriminate between those features that were of a defining nature and those that were transient and insignificant.

Nevertheless, at times, Ray does seem to have entertained doubts about the fixity of species. Raven (1942, p. 174) refers to a preface Ray wrote to his *Catalogus Stirpium in Exteris Regionibus*, in which he says he had been assured by Jacob Bobart the younger (1641-1719), the Oxford botanist, that primroses and oxlips had been raised from cowslip seed. Ray concluded that "a true transformation of species cannot be denied unless we set aside the evidence of first-hand and reliable witnesses." However, in later publications he appears not to have developed this thought, although he did admit in a private letter to Willughby that he had almost become persuaded that plants could change their species "within the limits of their genus or tribe" (cited by Raven 1942, p. 150).

1.2.2. Carolus Linnaeus (1707-1778). The naturalist most popularly associated with the belief in species fixity is the Swedish botanist Carl von Linné, better known by the Latinized form of his name as Carolus Linnaeus. Linnaeus was a prodigious student of nature who laid the foundations of our modern system of taxonomy. He was only 28 years old when the first edition of his most celebrated work, the *Systema Naturae*, was published in 1735, and by 1753 he had developed the binomial system of classification that is still used today.

Like Ray, Linnaeus believed that nature had been constructed to display the wisdom, power and goodness of its Creator. This implied a stability of form that would perpetuate God's revelation through the ages. In harmony with this idea, Linnaeus expressed the view that species were the forms that God had originally made and that they had remained unchanged since the beginning. His belief was summed up in the often-quoted aphorism from *The Fundamenta Botanica* No. 157 (1736): "There are as many species as the Infinite Being created diverse forms in the beginning."

As Glass (1959b, p. 145) has pointed out, however, Linnaeus' productivity during his early career was so great that he had probably devoted little time to considering the problem of variation. Later in life, he would have cause to reflect more deeply upon the nature of species and his views would change dramatically (see section 1.4.1).

1.2.3. Louis Agassiz (1807-1873). A native of Switzerland, Louis Agassiz later settled in the United States where he gained a formidable reputation as a zoologist and geologist. In 1859, he founded the Museum of Comparative Zoology at Harvard University and served as its first director until his death. He is perhaps best known for developing the ice age theory, based on his observations of glacial sediments and landforms in Europe and North America.

Agassiz was a firm believer in the immutability of species, even maintaining that considerable numbers of individuals had been simultaneously created across the whole of each species' observed geographical range. He rejected the idea that species had dispersed from a single centre, or even several centres, saying that he could not see how the animals of the arctic, for example, could have survived their migratory passage through warmer climatic zones (Agassiz 1850, p. 184). What is more, he opined, the animals could not have adapted themselves during their migration, for "this would be ascribing to physical influences as much power as to the Creator himself" (1850, p. 184). Asa Gray characterized Agassiz's view as "theistic to excess" (Gray 1860, p. 156) and contrasted it with the more common view which supposed that each species had originated from a single ancestral pair at a local centre of origin, spreading out later by solely natural means.

It is important to recognize, as Bowler (1984, p. 121) has pointed out, that Agassiz's convictions about species fixity were not the product of religious fundamentalism, despite his broadly theistic outlook, but rather the result of his adherence to the philosophical tenets of idealism. Like other idealists, Agassiz believed that living organisms were constructed according to ideal archetypes or body plans that existed in the mind of the Creator. To Agassiz, this suggested that the forms of living organisms were fixed and unchanging.

In 1874, an essay by Agassiz entitled 'Evolution and permanence of type' was published posthumously in *The Atlantic Monthly*. With respect to the "startling array of facts" adduced by Darwin concerning artificial selection, Agassiz advanced the opinion that these observations simply confirmed what was already well known, "namely, that all domesticated animals and cultivated plants are traceable to distinct species" (1874, p. 95). Slight variations, Agassiz insisted, were unlikely to accumulate; instead species would eventually revert to type or become extinct as a result of degeneration or sterility. The production of new species by such a mechanism, he concluded, had never been observed.

Although Agassiz proposed to discuss the fossil record in some detail in future articles, in order to demonstrate that paleontology provided "no evidence of a direct descent of later from earlier species" (1874, p. 101), the proposed series was cut short by his death in 1873.

1.2.4. Fleeming Jenkin (1833-1885). In 1867, a critique of *The Origin of Species* was published in *The North British Review* which some say caused Darwin to doubt for a time his own mechanism of natural selection. Its author was a remarkable man called Fleeming Jenkin, a professional engineer who was also an actor, author, and artist.

Jenkin was a former freethinker who embraced Christianity later in life, although his concerns about the inadequacy of Darwin's theory appear to have been motivated by scientific, rather than religious, considerations. "Some persons", he wrote, "seem to have thought his theory dangerous to religion, morality, and what not. Others have tried to laugh it out of court. We can share neither the fears of the former nor the merriment of the latter" (1867, p. 279).

Jenkin objected to Darwin's theory on three main grounds: the limits of variability, the efficacy of natural selection, and the amount of time available for evolution to occur. He also addressed the difficulties of classifying organisms in well-defined groups, which had led some to adopt evolutionary theories, and other observed facts used to support Darwin's views. He concluded that the cumulative force of the objections that he had marshalled were fatal to Darwin's evolutionary thesis.

It is obvious from Jenkin's discussion that he accepted that species could vary considerably, but he believed that there were natural limits to what was possible. Artificial breeders had shown that many varieties could be produced from the common rock pigeon within a few generations; Darwin suggested that even more dramatic changes might occur if sufficient time was granted. Jenkin's response was characteristically pithy. It was no more reasonable to conclude that because "a cannon-ball has traversed a mile in a minute, therefore in an hour it will be sixty miles off, and in the course of ages that it will reach the fixed stars" (1867, p. 280).

Jenkin believed that the rate of variation in any particular direction was not constant, but would rather diminish over time. "A given animal or plant appears to be contained, as it were, within a sphere of variation; one individual lies near one portion of the surface, another individual, of the same species, near another part of the surface; the average animal at the centre. Any individual may produce descendants varying in any direction, but is more likely to produce descendants varying towards the centre of the sphere, and the variations in that direction will be greater in amount than the variations towards the surface" (1867, p. 282).

Even the occasional "sport of nature", he argued, which produced an individual falling outside the normal sphere of variation, would be swamped by interbreeding with the rest of the population. He could see nothing in natural selection that would be able to overcome this tendency for organisms to revert to type. "Admitting, therefore," wrote Jenkin (1867, p. 288), "that natural selection may improve organs already useful to great numbers of a species, does not imply an admission that it can create or develop new organs, and so originate species."

1.3. How did the belief in species fixity arise?

1.3.1. The popular view. It is often claimed that the doctrine of the immutability of species arose on essentially biblical grounds. Thus, Edey and Johanson (1990, p. 8) write, "Because of a general acceptance of the biblical account of Creation, almost everybody took it for granted that species were 'fixed.' They had been created by God in their own shape and could not change." Of course it is true that John Ray and his successors in the natural theology movement argued that God's design extended to every imaginable contrivance of every individual species, and it is also without question that this had become the prevailing view by the time of Darwin. However we must question whether this doctrine of immutability was really derived from the Bible or from some other source.

1.3.2. The Bible does not require fixity. Contrary to the received wisdom of Darwin's day, the Bible nowhere teaches that species are fixed and unchanging. In fact, it does not even use the word *species*. Rather, the book of Genesis refers to "kinds" (Hebrew *min*; Genesis 1:11, 12, 21, etc.) and suggests that living things have had a very dynamic history. A straightforward reading of the Bible indicates that some animals became predators and that disease entered into the world subsequent to the Fall of Genesis 3, implying dramatic biological change since the creation. Furthermore, Genesis 6-9 describes a catastrophic Flood, after which the birds and land animals repopulated the world from the single pairs (in the case of the "unclean" animals) or the "sevens" (in the case of the "clean" animals) represented on the ark. The diversity that we observe in their modern descendants must have arisen from these survivors (Genesis 8:17), again implying very significant biological change which gave rise to new species and varieties.

So where did the idea of immutable species come from, if not the Bible? Three strands of thinking came together into a conceptual whole and laid the foundations for this view.

1.3.3. The influence of Platonic and Aristotelian essentialism. The first and most important influence upon the development of the doctrine of fixity came from Greek philosophy (Landgren 1993). The word "species" is a Latin translation of the classical Greek εἶδος (*eidos*), meaning "idea" or "form" (Wilkins 2003, p. 19). Plato and his followers used the term to refer to any category of object, whether organic or inorganic, that possessed an unchanging essence or nature. As such it was part of what Wilkins (2003, p. 20) has called a "universal taxonomy".

When applied to living things, the idea became associated with the notion of reproductive faithfulness. In the fourth century before Christ, Aristotle, in his *Generation of Animals*, wrote, "In the normal course of nature the offspring which a male and a female of the same species produce is a male or female of that same species—for instance, the offspring of a male dog and a female dog is a male dog or a female dog" (quoted in Glass 1959a, p. 31).

This Platonic way of thinking became integrated with the emerging science of biology, leading to the belief that every living species was characterized by an eternal and unchanging set of features or form—its immutable "essence."

Of course, neither Plato nor Aristotle believed in biblical creation, but many of those who later adopted their ideas did. The Platonic view became even more closely associated with the creationist view when the Latin Vulgate, an early fifth century translation of the Bible, rendered the Hebrew word *min* as "species" in the first chapter of Genesis (Wood 2008, p. 8). By the seventeenth century, the concept of the immutability of species had become popularly linked to belief in the separate creation of the biblical kinds.

It was in this way that a Greek philosophical concept became Christianized. But despite the fact that it was given a biblical gloss, the belief that living species were unchanging was really rooted in Platonism and Aristotelianism.

1.3.4. The theory of preformationism. Belief in the fixity of species was also encouraged by a theory of embryonic development that became popular in the seventeenth century.

Long before it took on its more familiar Darwinian connotations, the word "evolution" (from the Latin for "unrolling") was used to refer to a theory of embryo development called preformationism. To many of the early naturalists it seemed inconceivable that the human or animal body could develop in the womb from unformed matter by the action of purely material forces. The alternative was to propose that "the embryo from the very beginning existed as a 'miniature adult' that simply unfolded or 'evolved' during gestation" (Richards 1992, p.xiii). This became known as the theory of pre-existing germs, or preformationism. Taken to its logical conclusion, preformationism implied that the entire human race must have been enclosed within our first mother, Eve, rather like a nested series of Russian dolls, waiting to be unpacked generation after generation.

Odd though this theory sounds to modern ears, it received wide acceptance for more than a century. The relevance to our discussion here is that preformationism proved to be a formidable bulwark against the mutability of species. After all, if every individual that ever lived was "front-loaded" in the first member of the species from the beginning, what mechanism could there be for the transmutation of species over time? It would not be until preformationism was rejected in favour of natural processes of development in the early nineteenth century that the idea of species transformation could be seriously contemplated.

1.3.5. The rejection of spontaneous generation. Belief in species fixity was also given impetus by the rejection in the seventeenth century of the theory of spontaneous generation.

The notion that complex, living organisms could spontaneously arise from non-living matter had been popular from antiquity. It was believed by many that fleas could be produced from rotten clothing, mice from putrefying hay, maggots from decaying meat, and so on.

However, the pioneering experiments of the Italian physician Francesco Redi (1626-1697) showed that maggots failed to appear on decaying meat when flies were prevented from laying their eggs upon it.

Experiments like these served to persuade most people that spontaneous generation was false and that living things came only from other living things. The doctrine of *omne vivum ex ovo* ("life only from an egg") was gradually accepted.

The point here is that while it was believed that entirely new organisms could be spontaneously generated from decaying materials, transformations between *existing* species did not seem so hard to contemplate. However, when belief in spontaneous generation was rejected on experimental grounds, and it became evident that living organisms were derived from parents just like themselves, then the belief in species fixity seemed most in conformity with the known laws of reproduction.

In the words of Redi himself, in his *Experiments on the Generation of Insects* (1668, p. 27), "the Earth, after having brought forth the first plants and animals at the beginning by order of the Supreme and Omnipotent Creator, has never since produced any kinds of plants or animals either perfect or imperfect; and everything which we know in past or present times that she has produced, came solely from the true seeds of the plants and animals themselves, which thus, through means of their own, preserve their species."

1.4. Limited evolution of species

Other Christian scholars, many of them overlooked today, accepted species variability but argued for a more limited kind of change than that proposed by Darwin. Those that preceded Darwin are often regarded as anticipating him, even though they were arguing from a non-evolutionary perspective. Those that came after Darwin have generally been eclipsed by him.

1.4.1. Carolus Linnaeus (1707-1778). Somewhat paradoxically, Linnaeus, whose name is so closely associated with species fixity, actually abandoned the idea later in life. This change of thinking on Linnaeus' part is often forgotten today. The turning point came in 1742, when a student named Magnus Zioberg presented him with a collection of common toadflax (*Linaria vulgaris*) from an island near Uppsala in Sweden. In the collection was a specimen similar to *Linaria* but differing in the form of its flowers. In 1744, Linnaeus described the new plant as *Peloria*, from the Greek for "monster".

Linnaeus was intrigued and excited by it, because its peculiar combination of characteristics suggested that it was a hybrid, a cross between two existing species. Crosses between species were known to occur, but they were invariably sterile and not regarded as valid species in their own right. However, here was a hybrid form that was apparently able to reproduce successfully and, furthermore, had arisen multiple times if reports from other localities in Sweden and Germany were to be believed. This was an evident challenge to the popular notion that species were fixed and immutable.

In the years following the discovery of *Peloria*, many other alleged hybrids came to light. In fact Linnaeus encouraged his students to search them out and even undertake their own hybridization experiments. In order to accommodate the new discoveries, Linnaeus changed his views. In his *Disquisitio de Sexu Plantarum* (1756), Linnaeus argued that the genera were the original units of creation and that the species within them had originated by subsequent hybridization. In 1766, he dropped his famous maxim about the permanence of species from the final edition of the *Systema Naturae*. Glass (1959b, p. 151) summarizes his mature view this way: "In the end he believed in the evolution of the smaller systematic categories, of the species as he knew species, and maybe of the genera. But the original Creation was still that of a multitude of forms, distinct then and forever."

The new views of Linnaeus did not go unchallenged. He was fiercely opposed by the defenders of species constancy. In 1772, Michel Adanson (1727-1806) rejected his claim that new species had arisen by hybridization in the *Histoire de l'Académie Royale des Sciences* (Glass 1959b, p. 151). Joseph Gottlieb Kölreuter (1733-1806) also objected on the basis of his own hybridization experiments (Glass 1959b, p. 158). Indeed, according to Bowler (1984, p. 63), all but one of the examples Linnaeus collected were later shown not to be true hybrids at all. Bowler does not state which of Linnaeus' examples was the exception, but Glass (1959b, p. 149) indicates that it was a cross between two species of *Tragopogon* produced artificially by Linnaeus in his garden in 1757. *Peloria* itself seems to have been a mutant form rather than a true hybrid. The great irony of this is that today we know that Linnaeus was right in principle: new plant species can and sometimes do arise by hybridization. See, for instance, Rieseberg *et al.* (2003) for hybridization as the cause of species divergence in *Helianthus*.

1.4.2. William Herbert (1778-1847). Even in Darwin's time, when species fixity was considered "the ordinary view" (Darwin 1859, p. 446), there were those who were willing to question it from a non-evolutionary perspective. One such figure was William Herbert, the third son of Henry Herbert, First Earl of Caernavon. Herbert was a classical scholar and clergyman who became Dean of Manchester in 1840. He was also an accomplished botanist, achieving considerable success in the hybridization of amaryllids. Today, the International Bulb Society continues to award the Herbert Medal for "meritorious achievement in advancing the knowledge of bulbous plants."

Although Herbert believed in an old earth, he accepted the idea of a global flood, and believed that the modern species had arisen within the created kinds in response to the environmental changes that took place in the aftermath of the deluge. He asserted that, "it is no more essential to believe that individuals of every one of the present species of fox, or antelope, or finch (many of which are more like to each other than the greyhound is to the terrier, though they do not intermingle), entered with their present respective aspects into the ark, than that all the calceolarias on the mountains of Chili, or all the mezembryanthemums on the wastes of Southern Africa, exhibited their present peculiarities in the days of the patriarch" (Herbert 1837, pp. 338-339). Instead, he suggested that the Creator had providentially endowed each group on the ark with "a disposition to branch into diversities" for the purpose of repopulating the world after the Flood.

Darwin was certainly aware of Herbert's views, having corresponded with him about his hybridization experiments (Darwin 1859, p. 268) and referring to them in his notebooks. Writing in the historical sketch prefacing *The Origin of Species*, Darwin summarizes Herbert's views in these words: "The Dean believes that single species of each genus were created in an originally highly plastic condition, and that these have produced, chiefly by intercrossing, but likewise by variation, all our existing species" (Darwin 1859, p. 56).

1.4.3. Erich Wasmann (1859-1931). Another proponent of limited evolution was the German entomologist and Jesuit Erich Wasmann, who was concerned that belief in the permanence of species was being presented by some as the only alternative to a fully-fledged Darwinism. In his book, *Modern Biology and the Theory of Evolution* (1910), Wasmann argued that this was a false dichotomy: "If we wish successfully to combat the modern theory of descent, in so far as it has proved serviceable to atheism, we must carefully distinguish truth and falsehood in it" (1910, p. 278).

Wasmann believed that it was possible to accept some form of evolutionary theory without supposing that all living species must be traced back to a single common ancestor. In fact, he argued that much biological and paleontological evidence favoured the polyphyletic origin of the major groups. He drew a distinction between "systematic species", the species of conventional classification schemes, and "natural species", the original created units from which many "systematic species" might be derived (1910, p. 296).

Wasmann was open-minded about the extent of variation, although he evidently thought it operated within very broad limits: "How many systematic species, genera, and families belong to a natural species, cannot yet be stated with certainty in most cases. Still less are we able to say how many natural species there are, i.e. how many lines of ancestry independent of one another" (1910, p. 297). This, he stated, was a matter to be determined by future phylogenetic research.

1.4.4. Harold C. Morton (ca. 1925). Also advocating a theory of evolution within limits was the English Wesleyan Methodist Harold C. Morton. In his book, *The Bankruptcy of Evolution* (1925), he devoted a chapter to this theory, which he called "parvolution" (from the Latin *parva*, meaning small), or alternatively, "varvolution" (combining the word "varieties" with "evolution").

Like Erich Wasmann, to whom he refers, Morton also makes a distinction between species, in their "broad typal sense" (1925, p. 176), and the narrower species of conventional classification schemes. Within the created types there had been very considerable change, whether by degeneration, recombination, or hybridization. Believers in the Bible, he suggested, should be the last to deny this fact, pointing to "the endless varieties" within the human race which must have come from one original pair.

"Creationism," he wrote (1925, p. 182), "does not postulate a static world." Nevertheless, he denied that change from one basic type to another had ever been observed, or could even be conceived.

1.4.5. George McCready Price (1870-1963). In the USA, similar ideas were being independently developed by a number of young-age creationists. One was the prolific Seventh-day Adventist author, George McCready Price, best known for his advocacy of Flood geology in the early years of the twentieth century.

In his book *The Phantom of Organic Evolution*, published in 1924, he expressed the opinion that wide variation had occurred within the created groups, which he identified with the family or, in some cases, the genus of conventional taxonomy. For instance, he asserted (1924, p. 97), "There are now in existence some 40 or 50 species of cats, of the family of the *Felidae*, scattered throughout almost all the regions of the globe. But there is no doubt in my mind that they have all sprung from a common ancestry." Similarly, Price was willing to accept that the Equidae (horses), Suidae (pigs), Ursidae (bears), and Canidae (dogs) represented created kinds whose members were phylogenetically related to one another (pp. 97-98, 214).

He reiterated these views in a journal article published in 1938, suggesting that, "while we may admit any reasonable evidence of change *within the family*, yet we are on solid scientific ground if we say that these families have remained constant down through all the centuries and have never changed or become transformed into different families" (1938, p. 14).

Later, however, Price was to begin taking a different line, arguing that evolutionists were guilty of the excessive splitting of taxonomic categories. His argument concerning variation was basically the same, except that he now wanted to redefine the biological family as the "true" species. This change of perspective was probably motivated, in part at least, by the feud in which he was engaged with his former pupil, Harold Clark (Wood 2008), of whom more will be said in section 1.4.8.

1.4.6. Douglas Dewar (1875-1957). Douglas Dewar was an accomplished field ornithologist who served with the British government as a civil servant in India. He was also one of the founders of the Evolution Protest Movement (now called the Creation Science Movement), the world's oldest extant creationist organization (Morris 1993, p. 237). Besides his publications on birds and other animals, Dewar also authored several books in which he set out his creationist views, including *Difficulties of the Evolution Theory* (1931), *More Difficulties of the Evolution Theory* (1938), and *The Transformist Illusion* (1957).

In *Difficulties of the Evolution Theory*, he dedicated a short chapter to the changes in organisms effected by artificial selection. "Had Darwin been content to apply his theory of evolution to the origin of new species and genera," he wrote (1931, p. 8), "the operations of breeders would have afforded strong experimental evidence of its correctness." However, Dewar went on to point out that neither artificial nor natural selection had been observed to produce a new variety that could be deemed to belong to a new family. This seemed to be the taxonomic unit which Dewar equated with the created kind.

1.4.7. Dudley J. Whitney (1883-1964). Dudley J. Whitney was a Pentecostal Christian from California, who had obtained an agricultural degree from Berkeley and subsequently developed a career as a rancher and journalist. Influenced by the work of George McCready Price, he became interested in creationism and wrote about it in a number of periodicals.

Whitney accepted that new species had arisen, but not by the accumulation of small variations as proposed by Darwin. Instead, he believed that sudden and dramatic mutations had been responsible. He did not think that new species were forming today by this mechanism, but explained that this was simply because present-day conditions were different from those of the past.

In 1929, Whitney set out his thoughts in an article in *The Bible Champion* entitled 'The Origin of Species'. In an argument reminiscent of Fleeming Jenkin, he argued that any mutations that arise today are simply swamped out by interbreeding with normal individuals. He proposed that such mutant forms could only have become permanently established in small populations in which in-breeding was rife. He related this to the situation after Noah's Flood when, according to the Bible, all the kinds of air-breathing land animals were reduced to a pair or a few pairs (1929, p. 477).

Far from opposing the idea that new species had arisen since the beginning, Whitney wanted to encourage creationists to embrace it. Indeed, he believed that they alone had the mechanism that could explain how it had happened. He had come to the conclusion, "The idea of species change has been fought on the supposition that it was anti-Genesis; yet as science advances, it is pro-Genesis and anti-evolution" (1929, p. 478).

1.4.8. Harold W. Clark (1891-1986). When George McCready Price left his job as professor of science at Pacific Union College in Angwin, California, he was succeeded by a former student, Harold W. Clark. In 1933, Clark obtained a master's degree in ecology from the University of California, Berkeley, becoming the first Seventh-day Adventist to earn a graduate qualification in a biological discipline (Numbers 1992, p. 123).

In 1940, Clark published a book called *Genes and Genesis*, in which he set out to examine "the historical and scientific aspects of the species problem" (1940, p. 6). In his book, Clark rejected what he described as "extreme creationism" (1940, p. 43), or the idea that each species had been separately created and was fixed from the beginning. Rather, he stated, "The creationist viewpoint is one of limitation of the amount of change rather than the disallowance of any change whatsoever" (1940, p. 59).

Clark believed that every species showed "a tendency toward continually fluctuating variation" (1940, p. 46) and fully accepted the reality of natural selection. However, he believed that hybridization was the most common mechanism by which new species of animals and plants were produced in nature (1940, p. 85).

Perhaps the most curious feature of Clark's thesis is his proposal that certain fossil and living species were formed when members of different created kinds hybridized with one another. Clark had come to this view on the basis of some rather controversial and ambiguous statements about "amalgamation" in the writings of the Seventh-day Adventist prophetess, Ellen G. White. Such cross-breeding between kinds had resulted in "confused species" (1940, p. 100), which possessed a combination of characteristics found in more than one group. Among the examples adduced by Clark were *Archaeopteryx*, which he regarded as the hybrid offspring of birds and reptiles, and the duck-billed platypus, which he considered the progeny of reptiles and mammals (1940, pp. 102-104).

This rather idiosyncratic perspective was later to bring him into conflict with his former tutor, George McCready Price. However, like Price, Clark was willing to contemplate broad variation within the created kinds. In Clark's own words, "Whether these original types were equivalent to our present genera, families, or orders may be impossible to say arbitrarily. Probably no single comprehensive formula can be given which would cover all cases, but possibly the present families come nearest to representing the original 'kinds' of Genesis" (1940, p. 143).

1.4.9. Byron C. Nelson (1893-1972). A conservative Lutheran minister, Byron C. Nelson was the author of two well-known creationist books, *After Its Kind* (1927), a critical analysis of evolution, and *The Deluge Story in Stone* (1931), a history of the Flood theory of geology.

In *After Its Kind*, Nelson stated his belief that God had created living things to breed true to form throughout succeeding generations, and referred to these created types as "natural species". In journal articles and private correspondence, Nelson expressed concern that some creationists, in allowing for the origin of new species since the beginning, were conceding too much ground to the evolutionists. The sticking point for Nelson appeared to be the intersterility of some species that had been assigned to the same created group. In a published response to an article by Dudley J. Whitney, Nelson (1929, p. 540) wrote: "If we admit, for example, that domestic cattle (of which there are fifty or sixty distinct known varieties, all inter-fertile) and the bisons have a common ancestry, though they are now sterile toward each other, where are we going to stop admitting things?"

However, Nelson himself defined his "natural species" so broadly that they were equivalent, in some cases at least, to the families of conventional classification, so it might be thought that his disagreement with other creationists amounted to little more than a debate over semantics. It is interesting to note that Nelson drew a distinction between "natural species", which represented the broad created groups, and "systematic species", which were the varieties that had subsequently arisen within them. This is essentially the same terminology used by Erich Wasmann, although there is no hint that Nelson was aware of, or influenced by, Wasmann's writings at the time.

1.4.10. Frank L. Marsh (1899-1992). One of the most significant figures in the development of modern creationist biology and the first to attempt a synthesis of the ideas that were being discussed and debated by his creationist contemporaries was Frank Lewis Marsh (Wood 2008).

In 1940, Marsh obtained his doctorate in botany from the University of Nebraska, and in 1963 he was one of the ten original founders of the Creation Research Society. His most widely-circulated book, *Variation and Fixity in Nature* (1976), helped to popularize his conviction that the species of conventional taxonomy were real entities and that speciation had truly occurred within the boundaries of the created groups. He was willing to accept "the development of new breeds or races, subspecies, species, subgenera, genera, subfamilies, and possibly even families, so long as these are populations of individuals which obviously (morphologically) belong to the same basic type" (Marsh 1976, pp. 119-120).

Marsh also accepted that true interspecific hybridization was possible, although he roundly rejected Harold Clark's proposal that members of different created kinds could hybridize. He wrote: "No forms which are obviously hybrids between kinds occur. The same kinds of plants and animals occur just as clearly demarcated in the fossils as they do in the living forms, oaks, walnuts, ferns, horses, eagles, elephants, and all. If there is any evidence of confusion it is not between kinds but rather among the varieties of a kind" (1947, pp. 168-169). Unlike Clark, Marsh viewed the biblical commands concerning creatures multiplying according to their kinds as a divinely mandated and inviolable law of reproduction. As far as Marsh was concerned, the successful crossing of two species was a certain indication that they belonged to the same created kind.

Marsh is perhaps best known as the originator of the term *baramin*, which he coined in 1941 from two Hebrew words meaning "created kind" (Marsh 1941, p. 100). In this way, he laid the foundations of modern creationist biology, and in particular the major subdiscipline of baraminology (Wood 2006).

1.5. Unlimited evolution of species

After 1859, most biologists quickly accepted evolutionary ideas, among them many Christians, although debate about the mechanism of evolution continued to be heated and the theory of natural selection was by no means universally accepted (Bowler 1984, p.204).

1.5.1. Sir Richard Owen (1804-1892). One of the foremost anatomists of his day, Richard Owen was the founder of the British Museum of Natural History (now the Natural History Museum) in South Kensington, London. He is perhaps most famous for giving the dinosaurs their name and for his vehement opposition to Darwinism. He is also associated with the concept of the archetype, an idealized version of the simplest form of vertebrate structure.

Owen expressed his views on evolution rather opaquely, which means that he is sometimes dismissed as a creationist. However, that would be a misrepresentation. He undoubtedly rejected the theory of natural selection, railing against it in an anonymous review of Darwin's book published in the *Edinburgh Review* in 1860. Owen argued that the mechanism of natural selection was speculative and inadequately supported by the evidence. Among the observations adduced by Darwin, Owen dismissed those that were important and original as "few indeed and far apart" (Anon 1860, p.494).

One of the things to which Owen objected was Darwin's view that species, genera, and families differed from individuals within a species only in degree. He seems to have regarded species as real units of nature (1860, p.532). Nevertheless, Owen did accept a form of evolution that represented the unfolding of a divine plan. He vehemently rejected Darwin's accusation that he was a believer in the immutability of species (Anon 1860, p.501). The fact that species changed could not be denied. He wrote (1860, p.532): "We have no objection on any score to the change; we have the greatest desire to know how it is brought about."

Owen's belief was "that some pre-ordained law or secondary cause is operative in bringing about the change" (1860, p.532). He thought that, in some unspecified way, the Creator had worked through intermediate causes to bring about the diversity of life. He was willing to entertain various hypotheses about what those intermediate causes may have been, and whether they had operated by inward impulses or outward influences. However Owen seems to have been clear on one point: whatever the intermediate cause may have been, it was *not* the natural selection of Charles Darwin.

1.5.2. Asa Gray (1810-1888). Appointed in 1842 as professor of natural history at the prestigious Harvard University, Asa Gray was one of the few naturalists taken into Darwin's confidence before the publication of *The Origin of Species* in 1859. Gray's botanical knowledge, and especially his work on the geographical distribution of plants in North America, was of enormous interest to Darwin in the formulation of his ideas. Gray proved to be an influential advocate for evolution and a collection of his writings on the subject, entitled *Darwiniana*, was published in 1876.

In March 1860, the *American Journal of Science and Arts* published Gray's review of *The Origin of Species*. In it, Gray contrasted Darwin's idea of the transformation of species with the "ordinary and generally received view" which assumed the independent creation of each species and their perpetuation, essentially unchanged, to the present day. Gray rejected this idea, expressing the opinion that, "Thoughtful naturalists have had increasing grounds to suspect that a re-examination of the question of species in zoology and botany...would be likely somewhat to modify the received idea of the entire fixity of species" (1860, p. 163).

As a devout Presbyterian, however, Gray was concerned to retain a role for the Creator in the evolutionary process. He believed that Darwin's mechanism of random variations acted upon by natural selection was inadequate to the task, and proposed instead that new characteristics might have arisen under the direction of God. "If there's a Divinity that shapes these ends," wrote Gray, "the whole is intelligible and reasonable; otherwise, not" (1860, p. 184). However, the notion of purposeful variation was vehemently opposed by Darwin, whose conception of evolution was entirely naturalistic, and who rejected any such teleological compromise.

1.5.3. St George Jackson Mivart (1827-1900). An English biologist with a distinguished career, St George Jackson Mivart was the son of evangelical parents but later converted to Roman Catholicism. When Darwin's theory of natural selection was published in 1859, Mivart accepted it wholeheartedly and even became a dining companion of "Darwin's Bulldog", Thomas Henry Huxley. However, Mivart soon began to have misgivings about the theory, perhaps exacerbated by Huxley's anti-Catholic sentiments. To the consternation of his erstwhile colleagues, Mivart began to express his reservations in various journal articles.

In 1871, Mivart provoked even greater controversy with the publication of a book, *On the Genesis of Species*, in which he completely rejected "Mr. Darwin's fascinating theory" (1871, p. 240). He explained to his readers that his attempts to solve the difficulties of natural selection had persuaded him that the theory "as the leading explanation of the successive evolution and manifestation of specific forms is untenable" (1871, p. 240).

Among the problems perceived by Mivart was the inability of natural selection to account for the incipient stages of useful structures (1871, pp. 35-75), the improbability that unaided variations might give rise to closely similar structures in unrelated lineages (1871, pp. 76-110), and the apparent limits to variability observed by breeders and fanciers (1871, pp. 127-141).

Mivart's alternative to Darwinism was to propose that there was some mysterious and innate tendency, an internal power, which, acting in concert with the external conditions of climate and environment, powered and directed the process of evolutionary change. He believed that the normal variations studied by Darwin were irrelevant to this process. He was a saltationist rather than a gradualist. New species, he proposed, appeared suddenly and then remained stable throughout much of their existence. Each new arrival drove the process of evolution onward under the guidance of God.

To those who objected that his theory of an innate tendency was no explanation at all, but "merely a roundabout way of saying that the facts are as they are, while the cause remains unknown" (1871, p. 243), Mivart replied that, "All physical explanations result ultimately in such conceptions of innate power, or else in that of will-force. The far-famed explanation of the celestial motions ends in the conception that every particle of matter has the innate power of attracting every other particle directly as the mass, and inversely as the square of the distance" (1871, p. 246).

Mivart believed that his theory of directed evolution harmonized perfectly with belief in a supernatural creator: "When the remarkable way in which structure and function simultaneously change, is borne in mind; when those numerous instances in which Nature has supplied similar wants by similar means...are remembered; when also all the wonderful contrivances of orchids, of mimicry, and the strange complexity of certain instinctive actions are considered–then the conviction forces itself on many minds that the organic world is the expression of an intelligence of some kind" (1871, p. 253).

Shortly before his death, however, Mivart was effectively excommunicated by the Roman Catholic Church for expressing views that conflicted with official church dogma.

1.6. Conclusions

This review has suggested that ever since speculations began concerning the origin and nature of species a wide spectrum of views has been expressed by Christian scholars. Opinions ranging from a belief in fixed and unchanging species to acceptance of unlimited variability can all be documented. Even confining ourselves to only those individuals that can be regarded as special creationists or anti-evolutionists (as opposed to theistic evolutionists like Owen, Gray, and Mivart), it is clear that a wide variety of views have been articulated by Christians. Some have held strongly to the notion of immutability, while disagreeing about whether species had been created in the same geographical locations in which they are now found or whether they had spread out naturally from an original centre. Others have held to a form of limited evolution, although often without any consensus on what constituted the limits of variation, some suggesting that the created groups are represented by the genera or families, and others proposing the order or some higher taxonomic category. Still others found their views changing over time based on the evidence that was available to them. The important point to note is that species fixity is clearly only one of a larger range of positions that can be regarded as consistent with biblical teaching, and that, historically speaking, there has been no such thing as a definitive creationist view.

Our survey also calls into question the popularly understood distinction between belief in creation or acceptance of evolution, since it is evident that many special creationists have held, and continue to hold, positions that encompass elements of macroevolution, including the phenomenon of speciation. Indeed, young-age creationist biologists of the twentieth century have, almost without exception, rejected species fixity and embraced species change within wide limits. This review establishes a long historical pedigree for their ideas.

Furthermore, we have seen that the mistaken belief in species fixity was not derived from the Bible, as many popularly suppose, but rather it was an idea derived ultimately from Platonic and Aristotelian philosophy. The influence of essentialism in the nascent period of the natural sciences, along with the widespread belief in preformationism and the rejection of spontaneous generation, led to fixity becoming the dominant view by the time of Darwin. This is yet another sobering reminder that scientific ideas which appear to cohere with the known facts and which achieve the status of accepted dogma, may be completely incorrect. It might even be argued that creationists led the way in rejecting species fixity, since it was those wedded to a more Platonic approach that resisted the idea of species transformation, while creationists like Linnaeus were willing to question the dogma.

Sadly, Darwin and his contemporaries overreacted to the mistaken essentialist view that had come to dominate nineteenth century England, and many quickly adopted their ideas. The result was the triumph of evolutionary thinking in the twentieth century. Modern creationists need to challenge both the unbiblical essentialist ideas that underlie species fixity and the naturalistic ideas that underpin evolution from a universal common ancestor. The truth lies somewhere between these two extremes: yes, species change, but variation has its limits. In the twenty-first century, we face the exciting challenge of re-thinking the history of life from a truly biblical perspective.

Acknowledgement

I would like to thank Kurt Wise, Todd Wood and Roger Sanders for their feedback on an earlier version of this paper.

References

Agassiz, L. 1850. Geographical distribution of animals. *The Christian Examiner and Religious Miscellany* 48:181-204.

Agassiz, L. 1874. Evolution and permanence of type. *The Atlantic Monthly* 33:92-101.

Alexander, D. 2008. *Creation or Evolution: Do We Have to Choose?* Monarch Books, Oxford.

Anonymous [Richard Owen]. 1860. Darwin on the origin of species. *Edinburgh Review* 3:487-532.

Bowler, P.J. 1984. *Evolution: The History of an Idea*. University of California Press, Berkeley, CA.

Clark, H.W. 1940. *Genes and Genesis*. Pacific Press Publishing Association, Mountain View, CA.

Darwin, C. 1859. *The Origin of Species by Means of Natural Selection or the Preservation of Favoured Races in the Struggle for Life*. Penguin Books, London (1985 reprint).

Dewar, D. 1931. *Difficulties of the Evolution Theory*. Edward Arnold and Company, London.

Dewar, D. 1938. *More Difficulties of the Evolution Theory*. Thynne and Company Limited.

Dewar, D. 1957. *The Transformist Illusion*. Dehoff Publications, Murfreesboro, TN.

Edey, M.A. and D.C. Johanson. 1990. *Blueprints: Solving the Mystery of Evolution*. Oxford University Press, Oxford.

Glass, B. 1959a. The germination of the idea of biological species. In: Glass, B., O. Temkin and W.L. Straus, Jr., eds. *Forerunners of Darwin: 1745-1859*. The Johns Hopkins Press, Baltimore, MD, pp.30-48.

Glass, B. 1959b. Heredity and variation in the eighteenth century concept of the species. In: Glass, B., O. Temkin and W. L. Straus, Jr., eds. *Forerunners of Darwin: 1745-1859*. The Johns Hopkins Press, Baltimore, MD, pp.144-172.

Gray, A. 1860. Review of Darwin's theory on the origin of species by means of natural selection. *The American Journal of Science and Arts* Second Series 29(66):153-184.

Gray, A. 1876. *Darwiniana: Essays and Reviews Pertaining to Darwinism*. Dupree, A.H., ed. Harvard University Press, Cambridge, MA (1963 reprint).

Herbert, W. 1837. *Amaryllidaceae*. James Ridgway and Sons, London.

Jenkin, F. 1867. The origin of species. *The North British Review* 46:277-318.

Landgren, P. 1993. On the origin of 'species': ideological roots of the species concept. In: Scherer, S., ed. *Typen des Lebens*. Pascal Verlag, Berlin, pp.47-64.

Marsh, F.L. 1941. *Fundamental Biology*. Self-published, Lincoln, NE.

Marsh, F.L. 1947. *Evolution, Creation, and Science*. Review and Herald Publishing Association, Washington, D.C.

Marsh, F.L. 1976. *Variation and Fixity in Nature*. Pacific Press Publishing Association, Mountain View, CA.

Mivart, St.G.J. 1871. *The Genesis of Species*. D. Appleton and Company, New York.

Morris, H.M. 1993. *History of Modern Creationism*, second edition. Institute for Creation Research, Santee, CA.

Morton, H.C. 1925. *The Bankruptcy of Evolution*, second edition. Marshall Brothers, London.

Nelson, B.C. 1927. *After Its Kind*. Augsburg Publishing House.

Nelson, B.C. 1929. More about the origin of species. *The Bible Champion* 35(10):539-540.

Nelson, B.C. 1931. *The Deluge Story in Stone: A History of the Flood Theory of Geology*. Augsburg Publishing House.

Numbers, R.L. 1992. *The Creationists: The Evolution of Scientific Creationism*. Alfred A. Knopf, New York.

Price, G.M. 1924. *The Phantom of Organic Evolution*. Fleming H. Revell Company, New York.

Price, G.M. 1938. Nature's two hundred families. *Signs of the Times* 65(37):11, 14-15.

Raven, C.E. 1942. *John Ray, Naturalist: His Life and Works*. Cambridge University Press, Cambridge.

Ray, J. 1691. *The Wisdom of God as Manifested in the Works of Creation*. London.

Ray, J. 1701. Preface. *The Wisdom of God Manifested in the Works of the Creation*, third edition. London.

Redi, F. 1668. *Experiments on the Generation of Insects*. The Open Court Publishing Company, Chicago, IL (1909 edition).

Richards, R.J. 1992. *The Meaning of Evolution: The Morphological Construction and Ideological Reconstruction of Darwin's Theory*. University of Chicago Press, Chicago, IL.

Rieseberg, L.H., O. Raymond, D.M. Rosenthal, Z. Lai, K. Livingstone, T. Nakazato, J.L. Durphy, A.E. Schwarzbach, L.A. Donovan, and C. Lexer. 2003. Major ecological transitions in wild sunflowers facilitated by hybridization. *Science* 301:1211-1216.

Tyler, S. 2005. John Ray: founding father of botany and British natural history, pioneer of intelligent design concepts. *Origins* (BCS) 39:2-6.

Wasmann, E. 1910. *Modern Biology and the Theory of Evolution*. Third edition. B. Herder, St Louis, MO.

Whitney, D.J. 1929. The origin of species. *The Bible Champion* 35(9):475-479.

Wilkins, J.S. 2003. *The Origins of Species Concepts: History, Characters, Modes, and Synapomorphies*. PhD Thesis, University of Texas, Austin, TX.

Wood, T.C. 2006. The current status of baraminology. *Creation Research Society Quarterly* 43:149-158.

Wood, T.C. 2008. Species variability and creationism. *Origins* (GRI) 62:6-
    25.

2. The Kind-ness of God: A Theological Reflection of *Mîn*, "Kind"

KENNETH J. TURNER
BRYAN COLLEGE

2.1 Introduction

Baraminology is a modern creationist[1] classification of created organisms. The term, "baramin," first coined in 1941 by Frank Marsh,[2] is made up of two Hebrew words: the verb *bārā'*, "create," and the noun *mîn*, "kind." The term "baramin" may be a bit unfortunate,[3] for one might infer that the biblical "kinds" are to be equated with the creationist categories of genetically unrelated organisms. But such an equation has not been established, nor do all creationists assume it.[4] The present paper seeks to address the significance of the word *mîn* with sensitivity to creationist concerns. The first section addresses the question: based on the more recent word studies of the term, what can be known about the meaning of *mîn* in the Old Testament? The second section addresses the question: how might God's creation of flora and fauna "according

---

1   In this paper I use "creationists" to refer to those who do not believe macroevolution can be reconciled with the Bible. Thus, in this paper, proponents of theistic evolution are excluded from the label "creationists." Neither "creationist" nor "theistic evolutionist" are meant as pejorative terms.

2   Frank L. Marsh, *Fundamental Biology* (published by the author in Lincoln, NE, in 1941).

3   My hesitancy with the label is not intended to dismiss the discipline of baraminology. Analogously, I do not dismiss the theological system of "Calvinism" even though I find the label unfortunate (in part because the theological system neither began with John Calvin nor accurately reflects the beliefs of Calvin at every point).

4   One group of baraminologists recently stated that "there is very little linguistic support for viewing [*mîn*] as a scientific term in the modern sense. For this reason, our refined baramin concept specifically avoids equating the baramin with any Biblical category." See Todd C. Wood et al., "A Refined Baramin Concept," Occasional Papers of the Baraminology Study Group No. 3 (2003), 10. See also the word study of *mîn*, with particular attention to creationist concerns, by Pete J. Williams, "What Does *min* Mean?" *Creation Ex Nihilo Technical Journal* 11(3) (1997): 344-52. Williams concludes that, due to remaining linguistic ambiguities with the term, the *min* in "baramin" may not equate to the biblical *mîn*.

to kinds" contribute theologically to the contexts in which the term is found?

2.2. What Does 'Kind' Mean?

The 31 occurrences of the word *mîn*, "kind," in the Old Testament appear in four different contexts: creation (10x in Gen 1); the flood (3x in Gen 6:20; 4x in Gen 7:14); kosher food lists (9x in Lev 11; 4x in Deut 14); and a vision of the eschatological temple (1x in Ezek 47:10). All references of *mîn* occur in a similar syntactical phrase, "[plant or animal X][5] according to its kind"—reflecting the Hebrew, preposition *l*ᵉ ("according to") + *mîn* ("kind") + pronominal suffix ("its").[6] Only one reference has both the noun *mîn* and its suffix in the plural[7]; the others are consistently singular in both the noun and the suffix. Appendix A provides a list of all these references.

With such general uniformity, one might assume that determining the meaning of *mîn* is easily achieved. A survey of the many studies, however,

---

5 Though I will often use the term "life-form" in this paper, I am noting here that the Bible does not consider plants and trees as "life." See James Stambaugh, "'Life' According to the Bible, and the Scientific Evidence," *Creation Ex Nihilo Technical Journal* 6(2) (1992): 98-121.

6 The pronominal suffix is attached to *mîn*, but refers back the preceding life-form. The suffix, "its," translates four different types of singular suffixes occurring in the references of *mîn* (a fifth suffix, which is plural, occurs in Gen 1:21a, and is discussed in the next note). There exists two forms of the masculine singular and two forms of the feminine singular. The variation between masculine and feminine is due to linguistic necessity: a Hebrew noun is inherently "masculine" or "feminine," and a suffix referring back to a given noun must agree in gender (i.e., the life-form to which "its" refers). According to English grammar and usage, the Hebrew masculine singular suffix and the Hebrew feminine singular suffix are both naturally rendered by "its" when referring to plants and animals. Neither the variation between the two masculine forms nor between the two feminine forms makes any difference in meaning. See J. Barton Payne, "The Concept of 'Kinds' in Scripture," *Journal of the American Scientific Affiliation* 10 (1958): 17f.; Walter C. Kaiser, Jr., " =מין," *Theological Wordbook of the Old Testament*, vol. 1 (Chicago: Moody, 1980), 503.

   The Masoretic Text of the reference in Ezek 47:10 could be read as lacking a suffix on *mîn*, "kind" (which would mean that "its" would be missing). But, following the grammars and commentaries generally, it is best to read an irregular spelling of the suffix—which means this reference follows the same basic syntax as the others. Cf. Daniel I. Block, *The Book of Ezekiel Chapters 25-48*, New International Commentary on the Old Testament (Grand Rapids: Eerdmans, 1998), 689.

7 The one exception is Gen 1:21a, where a plural of *mîn* and a plural suffix are used with respect to water animals. The consonantal text (i.e., without the vowels, which were added later by Jewish scholars, the Masoretes) could suggest that the noun is singular rather than plural. There is disagreement (due to a textual variant) whether this reference is singular or plural (for the noun). But the plural is attested by the Masoretic pointing (i.e., the vowels added by the Masoretes) and the Samaritan and early versions and translations (including Samaritan Pentateuch, Septuagint, and Vulgate). For further discussion of the issues (and differing conclusions) see Kaiser, *TWOT* 1:503; Payne, "Concept of 'Kinds'," 17; Claus Westermann, *Genesis 1-11: A Continental Commentary*, trans. J.J. Scullion (Minneapolis: Fortress, 1994), 137; Williams, "What Does *min* Mean," 351 n. 13.

yields a variety of results.[8] The differences of opinion are due, in part at least, to ambiguities concerning issues such as the term's (1) etymology, (2) number, (3) technical precision and consistency of meaning in the Bible, (4) relationship to the corresponding life-forms, and (5) connection to reproduction. I will briefly summarize the nature of these ambiguities and comment on their relative significance to creationist issues.

2.2.1. Etymology. *Mîn* is glossed universally as "kind" or "type." It has proved difficult to get more specific. The etymology of a word is often drawn upon in order to suggest more specification to a word's definition, especially when the word under investigation is undefined or ill-defined. The etymology of *mîn*, however, is itself uncertain. Many scholars consider a connection between *mîn* and the Hebrew noun *t^emûnâ*, "form, image."[9] If such a connection exists, it remains uncertain what common root the two nouns share; speculations include verbal roots meaning "think out," "invent," "devise," or "discern."[10] Several other scholars opt for a connection to the Arabic root, *myn*, "split (the earth in plowing)."[11] Though attractive, the major problem with this connection is that Arabic texts are very late (beginning in first millennium AD). No other suggestion has gained much acceptance.

The uncertain about the etymology of *mîn* might appear to provide next to nothing about the meaning of the word. However, the search itself yields a potential, positive conclusion. After examining both post-biblical Hebrew texts and all potential etymological connections, Pete Williams concludes,

All the etymological explanation can be explained on the assumption that a meaning of 'biological division' was an early part of the root meaning. This need not have been, but could have been the earliest meaning of the root. This is consistent with the observation above that

---

8   The standard lexical studies include Heinz-Josef Fabry, " ᵊⱮ *mîn*," *Theological Dictionary of the Old Testament*, vol. 8, English trans. (Grand Rapids: Eerdmans, 1997), 288-91; Mark Futato, " ᵊⱮ" *New International Dictionary of Old Testament Theology and Exegesis*, vol. 2 (Grand Rapids: Zondervan, 1997), 934-35; Kaiser, *TWOT* 1:503-04; Ludwig Koehler and Walther Baumgarter, " ᵊⱮ" *The Hebrew and Aramaic Lexicon of the Old Testament*, vol. 2, trans. M.E.J. Richardson (Leiden: Brill, 1995), 577; Payne, "Concept of 'Kinds'," 17-20. For specialized studies concerned with creationist-evolutionist issues, see the arguments and secondary literature referenced in Paul Beauchamp, *Création et séparation* (Paris: Desclée de Brouwer, 1969); Henri Cazelles, "MYN = espèce, race ou ressemblance?" in *Mémorial du Cinquantenaire (1914-1964), École des Langues Orientales Anciennes de L'institut Catholique de Paris*, Travaux de L'Institut Catholique de Paris 10 (Paris: Bloud & Gay, 1969), 105-08; Paul H. Seely, "The Meaning of *Mîn*, 'Kind,'" *Science & Christian Belief* 9 (1997): 47-56; Williams, "What Does *min* Mean," 344-52.

9   Fabry's (*TDOT* 8:288) claim that the connection to *t^emûnâ* is "undisputed" is surely an overstatement, but it does reflect a common position by scholars.

10   See Kaiser, *TWOT* 1:503; Williams, "What Does *min* Mean," 352 n. 29.

11   E.g., Cazelles, "MYN = espèce, race ou resemblance," 105-08; Payne, "Concept of Kinds," 17.

biological meaning predominates in attestations from the earliest stages of the Hebrew language.[12]

Williams' working hypothesis—that "biological division" as a basic meaning of *mîn* accords with all possible etymological options—seems reasonable. The earliest extant clear non-biological uses of *mîn* occur in post-biblical Hebrew texts,[13] even while the biological meaning continues to be used. The only qualification that needs to be made is to note that "biological" is being used above in its modern sense; the Bible does not consider plants as living organisms.

2.2.2. Number. Perhaps the most significant linguistic ambiguity in the study of *mîn* is establishing how many individual entities are being referred to when the grammatically-singular noun *mîn* is used. Often, scholars argue that *mîn* is being used in a collective or distributive sense.[14] Both collectivity and distributivity allow a grammatical singular to refer to a plurality of entities. The phrase, "flock of sheep," contains two types of collectives: a "flock" always includes plural sheep; the word "sheep" (on its own) can refer to one animal or a plurality of animals. An example of distributivity is found in the sentence, "The men wore a suit."[15] The word "suit" is a distributive singular because the clear sense is that many suits are assumed even though a singular noun is used.

Williams offers two reasons for taking *mîn* as a distributive singular in some of its biblical references.[16] First, when a large-scale category (e.g., winged fowl in Gen 1:21b; fish in Ezek 47:10) is created "according to its kind," it seems to demand several "kinds." Second, the addition of *kôl,* "all, every," before certain life-forms demands a plurality of forms—

---

12   Williams, "What Does *min* Mean," 349. Cf. his earlier summary of post-biblical Hebrew texts: "With so few occurrences of the word [*mîn*] we cannot rule out the possibility that non-biological meanings existed for the word even in the Biblical period. However, the fact that even the earliest post-Old Testament occurrences are biological in meaning suggests that the simplest hypothesis is to suppose that the earliest meaning in Hebrew was related to biology" (ibid., 348).

13   The two earliest non-biological uses are from intertestamental (after 400 BC) texts from the Dead Sea Scrolls. One is in the Damascus Document (4:14-18): "Its meaning is the three nets of Belial about which Levi the son of Jacob spoke, in which he traps Israel and presents them in the three guise of three kinds [plural of *min*] of righteousness. The first is lust, the second wealth and the third defiling the sanctuary" (translation from Philip R. Davies, *The Damascus Covenant*, Journal for the Study of the Old Testament Supplement Series 25 [Sheffield: JSOT Press, 1983], 243). The second is in the Rule of the Community (3:13-14): "It is for the Teacher to instruct and teach all the sons of light concerning the generations of all the sons of man, as regards all the kinds [plural of *min*] of their spirits with their signs for their works in their generations" (translation from Williams, "What Does *min* Mean," 347).

14   For a collective sense, see, e.g., Kaiser, *TWOT* 1:503; Payne, "Concept of "Kinds'," 17; Westermann, *Genesis 1-11,* 140 [on Gen 1:25]). For a distributive sense, see, e.g., Beauchamp, *Création et séparation*; Williams, "What Does *min* Mean," 345ff.

15   This example is from Williams, "What Does *min* Mean," 346.

16   Ibid., 345-46.

such as "every creeping thing on the ground according to its kind" (or the like; cf. Gen 1:25c; 6:20c; 7:14c).[17] Williams may be right, but his argument assumes a specification of the meaning of *mîn* that has not been established yet. It is not clear why a singular "kind" is precluded by either of these examples.

A stronger case for a collective or distributive sense can be made from an examination of both post-Old Testament Hebrew texts and early translations of the Old Testament.[18] As noted, the plural of *mîn* occurs only in Gen 1:21a (with reference to sea creatures) in the Old Testament. The plural is more widely attested in later Hebrew texts.[19] The Greek, Aramaic, and Latin translations often use plural equivalents for *mîn* and its suffix, even adding words and phrases that show that the translators are interpreting a plurality of entities. This evidence from post-biblical texts suggests a tendency to "clarify" the understanding of *mîn*; that is, they show that the singular of *mîn* in earlier texts may actual refer to some kind of plurality (whether collective or distributive). English translations do the same thing. For example, the KJV translators use plural "kinds" to translate singular *mîn* in Ezek 47:10 (with respect to fish). The ESV (a modern "literal" translation) translators use plural "kinds" to translate singular *mîn* in nine references.[20] In all these instances, the corresponding plant or animal (always in the singular in Hebrew) is also translated by a plural or a collective singular (collectives include livestock [Gen 1:25b; 7:14b] and fish [Ezek 47:10]). Moreover, the ESV uses the phrase, "any kind" (suggesting a plurality) in all 13 references of *mîn* in the kosher food lists (Lev 11; Deut 14)—yet, the word "any" is not in the Hebrew.

None of the evidence above is definitive, and certainly more linguistic work is needed. But it is reasonable to conclude that we must allow the possibility—perhaps probability—that some biblical uses of the singular *mîn* should be interpreted as referring to a plurality. Assuming

---

17 Williams' (ibid.) full list includes Gen 1:21a, 21b, 25c; 6:20c; 7:14 (4x); Gen 1:21a should be excluded, however, because *mîn* is plural. If this is maintained consistently, then "every raven according to its kind" (Lev 11:15; Deut 14:14) would envisage more than one *mîn* of raven.

18 Ibid., 346-50. Others have made some of the same observations (e.g., Fabry, *TDOT* 8:289-91), but Williams' study is the most comprehensive I found.

19 The Samaritan Pentateuch uses the plural of *mîn* (and a plural suffix) in Gen 6:20c (with respect to crawlers). The three occurrences of *mîn* in texts from the Dead Sea Scrolls are all plural: to the two texts quoted in footnote 13 above (Damascus Document 4:14-18 and Rule of the Community 3:13-14), we can add Damascus Document 12:14-15 ("And all locusts in their kinds [plural of *mîn*] shall enter into fire or water while they are still alive, for that is the ordinance of their creation."). The Mishnah (the Jewish oral law, completed c.a. 200 AD) regularly uses a plura form (see Williams, "What Does *min* Mean," 347-48).

20 The references, including the preceding plant or animal life-forms, are as follows: Gen 1:12a (plants yielding seed); Gen 1:24a (living creatures); Gen 1:24b ([livestock and creeping things and] beasts of the earth); Gen 1:25a (beasts of the earth); Gen 6:20a (birds); Gen 1:25b (livestock [a collective]); Gen 6:20b (animals); Gen 7:14b (livestock [a collective]); Ezek 47:10 (fish [a collective]).

this, no one has yet established an objective method for determining which references are true singulars and which are collective or distributive singulars (one need only to compare different Bible translations). The remaining questions concerning the number of *mîn* must be kept in mind as we look at the last two areas of ambiguity.

2.2.3. Technical Precision and Consistency of Meaning. Unless one can show that *mîn* is a technical term, it is a fallacy to assume that the word carries the same level of precision or specification in all its occurrences. Otherwise, the term's precise meaning in each reference must be determined by context. On a straightforward reading of the texts, I see no reason for taking *mîn* as a technical term.[21] We have yet to discuss the relationship between *mîn* and its corresponding life-form, but it is instructive that a different level of specification exists between the categories of animals in the Genesis texts (broader categories) and those in Leviticus 11 and Deuteronomy 14 (more narrow categories). This suggests (or at least allows the possibility) that the precision of "kind" is relative to the precision of these categories. The ambiguity of number discussed above adds to the ambiguity of precision and consistency here. One implication is that it is a mistake to assume (without argument) that *mîn* generally corresponds to a modern taxonomic level (e.g., "species" or whatever).[22] The issue of applying *mîn* to the modern taxonomy will be further discussed later in this paper.

2.2.4. Relationship to Corresponding Life-Forms. A fundamental issue concerns how *mîn* relates to the corresponding plant or animal. While the existing ambiguities already discussed—especially concerning number—make it impossible to draw a firm conclusion, it is worth reflecting on the possibilities. Using the phrase, "plant according to its kind," as an example, we might spell out the options as follows: (1) the plant "kind" (i.e., plants); (2) types of plants (i.e. a "kind" is a particular

---

21   So also Victor P. Hamilton, *Genesis 1-17*, New International Commentary on the Old Testament (Grand Rapids: Eerdmans, 1990), 126; Futato, *NIDOTTE* 2:934-35; Kaiser, *TWOT* 1:503-04; Douglas F. Kelly, *Creation and Change: Genesis 1.1-2.4 in the Light of Changing Scientific Paradigms* (Ross-Shire, Great Britain; Mentor, 1997), 188; Kenneth A. Matthews, *Genesis 1-11:26*, New American Commentary 1A (Nashville: Broadman & Holman, 1996), 152.

22   Interestingly, an examination of the more recent literature shows that non-creationists are the ones who often use "species" as a gloss for *mîn*; see, e.g., Carl Drews, "Biblical Kind" [last accessed Sept. 29, 2008, at http://www.theistic-evolution.com/kind.html]; Fabry, *TDOT* 8:289; Koehler and Baumgarter, *HALOT* 2:577; Bruce K. Waltke and Cathi J. Fredricks, *Genesis: A Commentary* [Zondervan, 2001], 111; Westermann, *Genesis 1-11*, passim. Seely (a non-creationist) is an example of inconsistency at this point. His own work shows a variety of levels of specification for *mîn* in the biblical texts; yet he states that "the meaning of *mîn* in Gen 1 cannot be separated from its meaning in the rest of Scripture and must refer primarily to the *species* and *genus* level" ("Meaning of *Mîn*," 55 n. 29). An earlier creationist example of inconsistency is Payne ("Concept of 'Kinds'," 17-20), who concludes that *mîn* is "basically species" despite the details of his own study that shows otherwise.

type of plant); (3) "all sorts of plants" (i.e., just referring to variety within plants, not equating a "kind" to a particular type of plant at all); or (4) "all divisions of plants" (i.e., referring to a variety of groups within plants, not equating a "kind" to a particular group of plants).[23] The first option sees "kinds" focusing on the set of characteristics that makes a plant a plant. The other options would assume that recognizable characteristics are involved, but the word "kind" has more to do with subdivisions within the plant category. So we might simplify the possible relationships to two: either *mîn* refers to subdivisions within the corresponding plant or animal type, or *mîn* refers to the quality of the type itself.

I am inclined toward understanding *mîn* as a reference to subdivisions.[24] This seems most consistent with my inclinations on other issues discussed—that *mîn* is a (potential) collective or distributive noun, and that *mîn* is a non-technical word. Of the subdivision options, the sense of "all sorts of plants" (option #3 above) is least likely. It seems significant that all 31 references to *mîn* use the same phrase, "according to its kind," rather than, for example, "every kind of." [25] It is difficult to explain the syntactical consistency if other, more general constructions were available to get the same point across.[26] Between the final two options—seeing *mîn* as types of plants (option #2) or divisions of plants (option #4)—the former is more attractive. It is simpler, which fits with the non-technical nature of the word *mîn*. Also, it is easier to account for the animals divided by "kinds" that correspond to the lower taxonomic levels (such as in Lev 11 and Deut 14, in which nothing broader than genus is in view), for the more complex option (#4) would entail multiple levels of differentiation.

2.2.5. Connection to Reproduction. The connection between *mîn* and reproduction is less debated than assumed.[27] Since the connection

---

23   I want to thank Kurt Wise (through personal correspondence) for assistance in raising helpful questions concerning these ambiguities.

24   So also Futato, *NIDOTTE* 2:934-35; Kaiser, *TWOT* 1:503; Seely, "Meaning of *Mîn*," 49; Payne, "Concept of 'Kinds'," 17-20.

25   Some translate the phrase with something like "all kinds of"; see, e.g., Hamilton, *Genesis 1-17*, passim; cf. various translations of Ezek 47:10. Payne ("Concept of 'Kinds'," 20) calls this type of translation a "shotgun approach" because it does not say anything about the creative unit. Post-biblical Hebrew does, in fact, use *mîn* in phrases like "all kinds of" (without the preposition and suffix); see the texts referenced in Williams, "What Does *min* Mean," 346-48. The Old Testament attests to a phrase like "all sorts of" (cf. Lev 19:19; Deut 22:9), but uses a different word than *mîn*.

26   For various proposals for the exact sense of the introductory preposition in the phrase, "according to its kind," see Fabry, *TDOT*, 8:289; and Futato, *NIDOTTE* 2:934. Futato takes it as a preposition of specification, such that "according to its kind" refers to groups of plants or animals united by common characteristics. Fabry takes the preposition in a distributive sense, such that "according to its kind" means "each kind in turn" or "according to the distinctiveness of the species."

27   Reproduction is assumed or argued for in the majority of lexicons and commentaries. See, e.g., Cazelles, "MYN = espèce, race ou resemblance," 105-08; Hamilton,

is not explicit,[28] a case for it should be set out. The strongest textual argument for connecting *mîn* with the capacity to reproduce is the connection between "kind" and "seed" with respect to plants and trees in Gen 1:11-12. The Jewish scholar, Umberto Cassuto, considers the tenfold use of "seed" in Gen 1:11-12 and 29 significant: "as though it wished to draw the reader's attention to the fact that the plants that were created on the third day were capable of reproducing themselves after their likeness by means of the seed."[29] Another argument is that the concept of "kinds" involves categories of plants and animals that are recognizable by distinct traits.[30] The ability to recognize is particularly important for the animals in the kosher food lists (Lev 11; Deut 14), since one's obedience to God's commands was dependent upon it. This implies that "kinds" were reproducible across generations. Further, if *mîn* is a strictly biological term in the Old Testament,[31] then reproductivity is a live possibility.

Yet, two issues would need to be dealt with. First, since plants are not living according to a biblical perspective, the term "biological" is inadequate and should probably be replaced. Second, it would need to be explained why humans are not stated to be created "according to kind."[32] If "kind" refers to subdivisions, then the explanation is obvious: humanity cannot be subdivided into lower forms and, thus, would not be created "according to kind." Of course, this explanation assumes a premise ("kind" means subdivisions) that is unsure. Later in this paper, we will seek to provide a theological explanation for the absence of *mîn* with respect to humans. Therefore, a full argument for connecting *mîn* to reproduction needs to be delayed.

This section has sought to walk through the major ambiguities that presently exist in the study of the term *mîn*, "kind." Though some attempts were made at taking a stance, no firm conclusions were drawn.

Genesis 1-17, 131; Kelly, *Creation and Change*, 187-88; Matthews, *Genesis 1-11:27*, 121, 144, 152, 160; John H. Sailhamer, "Genesis," in *Genesis-Leviticus*, Expositor's Bible Commentary, vol. 1, rev. ed. (Grand Rapids: Zondervan, 2008), 38; Seely, "Meaning of *Mîn*," 54; Waltke and Fredricks, *Genesis*, 56-57; John H. Walton, *Genesis*, NIV Application Commentary (Grand Rapids: Zondervan, 2001), 113.; idem, *Ancient Near Eastern Thought and the Old Testament: Introducing the Conceptual World of the Hebrew Bible* (Grand Rapids: Baker, 2006), 190; Westermann, *Genesis 1-11*, 88, 138-40.

28   This lack of explicit connection seems to be the basis of the following question by Wood et al.: "If *mîn* indicates reproductive limits, why should it be used only for creation and not for reproduction?" ("Reformed Baramin Concept," 9-10).

29   Quoted in Kelly, *Creation and Change*, 187-88.

30   Cf. Futato's description that *mîn* involves the "language of visual appearance" (*NIDOTTE* 2:934).

31   See Seely, "Meaning of *Mîn*," 48, 54; Williams, "What Does *min* Mean," 349, 351.

32   Fabry (*TDOT* 8:290) infers from the absence of *mîn* with reference to humans that *mîn* has nothing to do with "the capacity of a living being to reproduce itself in a continuing sequence of generations." But one could counter that the inference is a logical fallacy; "if X then Y" does not necessitate "if Y then X" (X = *mîn*; Y = reproductive capacity).

Unless more sustained linguistic work—especially concerning the issue of number—is brought to bear on the topic, the uncertainties will remain. With respect to creationism, however, a couple of implications can be drawn. First, many creationists need to show more awareness of the problems in defining *mîn*. My (admittedly limited) reading of creationist literature reveals that some creationists speak with more certainty on the term than is warranted by the evidence. However, exceptions among creationists do exist, which hopefully signals progression in the field of creation science. Second, some who attack certain creationist positions concerning *mîn* are unfair in their critique. For example, Seely accuses creationists of "forcing the implications of modern [creationist] scientific knowledge into the ancient biblical text"[33] because creationists define *mîn* flexibly at the lower levels of species, genus, and family (rarely to the level of order).[34] Likewise, an internet article states,

> In effect, then, creationists define a "kind" as (1) a group of organisms which do interbreed, or (2) a group of organisms which don't interbreed but which are similar in basic body plans—and then they leave the guidelines extremely fuzzy about what constitutes "similarity in basic body plans". This loophole leaves so much room for manipulation that it is essentially useless. Fish as different from each other as hagfish and lungfish and rainbow trout can all be classified as one "kind", while animals as similar to each other as gorillas and chimpanzees are classified as separate "kinds". A created kind, under this definition, is nothing more than whatever the defining creationist wants it to be.[35]

As the ambiguities above show, however, the flexibility of the connotation of "kind" may actually accord with the biblical data, and not be a "forced interpretation" at all. If *mîn* refers to subdivisions, for instance, then it is quite reasonable to relate the Genesis "kinds" to any taxonomic level lower than order.

The following section seeks to approach the concept of "kinds" from a more theological perspective. The purpose is to show that *mîn*, despite the ambiguities in definition, may offer a positive contribution nonetheless to the contexts in which the term appears.

---

33   Seely, "Meaning of *Mîn*," 55.
34   Ibid., 47-48 nn. 2-4, references the works of creationists Kaiser, Marsh, Jones, Payne, Rehwinkel, Siegler, Gish, Nelson, Whitcomb, and Zimmerman.
35   Lenny Flank, "Creation 'Science' and the Genesis 'Kinds'," found at http://www. geocities.com/CapeCanaveral/Hangar/2437/kinds.htm (last accessed Oct. 31, 2008).

2.3. Theologizing on God's Kind-ness

Before examining the texts and contexts, it is important to preface this section with a couple of points. First, the theological investigation here is admittedly speculative. The intention is to "see" how the concept of "kinds" might contribute to the theological agenda of the texts. It is not meant to be absolute, nor does it suggest that the broader theological points of the texts rest on the conclusions drawn here. Second, it will be impossible to argue for every exegetical decision on which the theological discussions depend. Though none of my exegetical positions are out of the mainstream of evangelical scholarship, debates and varying positions exist on many issues. Readers wanting to study these underlying issues are encouraged to consult the resources in the bibliography.

2.3.1. Genesis 1: God's Kind-ness Created in Flora and Fauna. As we stated in the introduction, the creation account of Genesis 1 (actually Gen 1:1-2:3) is one of four contexts that utilize the word *mîn*. Genesis 1 deserves the most attention because of its canonical priority and because it serves as the most fundamental text for creationism. What may (or may not) be said here will affect our reading of the later texts. The present study does not pretend to answer all the nagging science questions; rather, it attempts to orient the discussion along the lines of biblical theology, focusing on the authorial agenda of the text itself. Given the uncertainties outlined above, this approach should help us say something clear and positive about *mîn*.

Though exegetical difficulties immediately arise concerning the relationship between the first three verses of Genesis 1,[36] there is general consensus that the six days of creation (1:3-31) resolve the "problem" of v. 2: the formless (or unproductive), empty, and dark earth is formed (or made productive), filled, and given light. The six creation days, which witness eight creative acts, are often outlined (correctly, in my view) in a way similar to the following framework[37]:

---

36   The main questions include the following: (1) Is v. 1 a main clause or temporal clause? (2) If v. 1 is a main clause, does it summarize all the events described in vv. 2-31, or simply describing the first act of creation (with vv. 2 and 3 describing subsequent phases)? (3) If v. 1 is a temporal clause, is it subordinate to the main clause in v. 2 or v. 3 (with v. 2 as a parenthetical comment); (4) Does v. 2 describe a state that is chaotic or simply abiotic? (either position assumes a "problem" that has to be overcome in vv. 3-31 in order for humanity to exist and function in the earth [see text above]); (5) Is "creation" speaking more about structure or simply function? Some of the more helpful discussions and resources detailing various positions include Matthews, *Genesis 1-11:26*, 136-44; J. Gordon Wenham, *Genesis 1-15*, Word Biblical Commentary 1 (Waco: Word, 1987), 11-15; Walton, *Genesis*, 67-78; idem, Creation," *Dictionary of the Old Testament: Pentateuch* (Downers Grove: InterVarsity, 2003), 155-68; idem, *Ancient Near Eastern Thought and the Old Testament: Introducing the Conceptual World of the Hebrew Bible* (Grand Rapids: Baker, 2006), 167-68, 179-81.

37   This is an adaptation of three charts: Ernest C. Lucas, "Cosmology," *Dictionary of the Old Testament: Pentateuch* (Downers Grove: InterVarsity, 2003), 136; Matthews,

Days of Forming/Separating the Realms (Unproductive Becomes Productive)		Days of Filling the Realms (Uninhabited Becomes Inhabited)	
Day 1	Light and Darkness	Day 4	Luminaries
Day 2	Sea and Sky	Day 5	**Sea and Sky Animals**
Day 3	(a) Dry Land appears **(b) Vegetation**	Day 6	**(a) Land Animals** (b) Humankind

This schematic shows several things about God's ordered creation. First, the creation days are separated into two triads of three days (Days 1-3 and Days 4-6, respectively). Second, each triad shows a geocentric perspective, as the creative acts progress vertically downward (in the schema) toward the land.[38] Emphasis is put on Day 3 and Day 6 in that each has two creative acts. Third, correspondence is shown horizontally: the luminaries of Day 4 rule the periods of day and night separated on Day 1; the sea creatures and birds created on Day 5 fill the sea and sky separated on Day 2; land animals and humans created on Day 6 inhabit the dry land that appears on Day 3 after the waters are gathered, and enjoy the vegetation created on Day 3. Finally, the items in **bold** represent the things that are created "after its/their kind(s)": seed-yielding plants and fruit trees on Day 3 (Gen 1:11-12); fish and fowl on Day 5 (1:21); domesticated cattle, crawlers, and wild animals on Day 6 (1:24-25).

In setting the broader theological stage, my study and reflection cause me to approach the creation account from three interrelated angles: theocentric, anthropocentric, and Israelite. First, Genesis 1 is "theocentric" in that its ultimate purpose is to reveal God and declare his incomparable glory. Second, the account is "anthropocentric" in that the climax of the six days of creation is the special creation of humanity (more on this later). Not only is humanity the most important creation, the other creative acts of God are also preparatory acts awaiting the arrival of humans. Third, Genesis 1 is "Israelite" in that this text is shaped as an introduction to the Pentateuch (as well as the Old Testament and the whole Bible) rather than an independent account. The nation of Israel is its original audience and it must be interpreted as such.[39] The Creator is none other than Yahweh, Israel's redeemer and covenant Lord.

Genesis 1-11:26, 115-16; Gary Edward Schnitjer, *The Torah Story: An Apprenticeship on the Pentateuch* (Grand Rapids: Zondervan, 2006), 62. The different labels for Days 1-3 and Days 4-6, respectively, reflect the main alternatives of how scholars understand the "problem" of v. 2.

38   See Matthews, *Genesis 1-11:26*, 144; cf. Waltke and Fredricks (*Genesis*, 58): "Each triad progresses from heaven to earth (land) and ends with the earth bringing forth."

39   On the "anthropocentric" and "Israelite" angles, I find the works of John H. Sailhamer some of the most illuminating (even though I disagree with his larger theses regarding both Genesis 1 and the Pentateuch!). See Sailhamer, *The Pentateuch as Narrative*

2.3.1.1. How to Be Kind in a Fight. So, what specific theological contribution does mîn make within this context? I think the concept of "kinds" can add to the now widely recognized contrast between the cosmology of Genesis 1 and the cosmologies of the ancient near East.[40] Thus, alongside the positive theological agenda of glorifying God, Genesis 1 offers an implicit critique of the views of Israel's neighbors.[41] Gerhard Hasel's 1974 article, "The Polemic Nature of the Genesis Cosmology,"[42] popularized these issues (especially for evangelicals), and his basic line of thought is still valid (i.e., scholars have tended to add to rather than subtract from his list). Particularly, Hasel identified five areas of polemic:

> First, in some Near Eastern cosmogonies, dragons *tnn* are rivals whom the Canaanite gods conquer, whereas in Gen 1:21 the great sea monsters are just one kind of the aquatic animals created by God. Second, these cosmogonies describe the struggle of the gods to separate the upper waters from the lower waters; but Gen 1:6-10 describes the acts of separation by simple divine fiat. Third, the worship of the sun, moon, and stars was current throughout the ancient orient. Genesis pointedly avoids using the normal Hebrew words for sun and moon, lest they be taken as divine, and says instead God created the greater and the lesser light. Fourth, Babylonian tradition sees the creation of man as an afterthought, a device to relieve the gods of work and provide them with food. For

---

(Grand Rapids: Zondervan, 1995); idem., *Genesis Unbound: A Provocative New Look at the Creation Account* (Grand Rapids: Questar, 1996); idem., "Genesis," in *Genesis-Leviticus*, Expositor's Bible Commentary, vol. 1, rev. ed. (Grand Rapids: Zondervan, 2008).

40   Whether or not they prefer using the term "polemic" (i.e., deliberate contrast), the general consensus of Old Testament scholars is that Gen 1 is *de facto* a repudiation of pagan ideas about the gods, origins, and humanity. For a very helpful chart comparing and contrasting ancient Near Eastern mythologies with Genesis, see Walton, *Genesis*, 29-31.

41   Ancient Near Eastern texts (including myths about creation and the flood, but also much more) started being discovered and translated in the 19th century. For an evangelical who is one of the top experts in understanding the philosophical, theological, linguistic, and historical contexts of Israel and Israelite literature, see Walton, *Ancient Israelite Literature in Its Cultural Context* (Grand Rapids: Zondervan, 1989); idem, *Ancient Near Eastern Thought and the Old Testament*. See also Kenton L. Sparks, *Ancient Texts for the Study of the Hebrew Bible: A Guide to the Background Literature* (Peabody, MA: Hendrickson, 2005). While most recent Genesis commentaries (including those by evangelicals) show awareness of and support comparing the Bible with ancient texts, the standard is still that by Westermann (*Genesis 1-11*).

42   Gerhard F. Hasel, "The Polemic Nature of the Genesis Cosmology," *Evangelical Quarterly* 46 (1974): 81-102. See also idem, "The Significance of the Cosmology in Gen 1 in Relation to Ancient Near Eastern Parallels," *Andrews University Seminary Studies* 10 (1972): 1-20.

Genesis, the creation of man is the goal of creation and God provides man with food. Finally, Genesis shows God creating simply through his spoken word, not through magical utterance as is attested in Egypt.[43]

Neither Hasel nor anyone else, to my knowledge, mentions a specific polemic concerning the creation of plants and animals (i.e., where *mîn* would be utilized). Part of the reason is that the ancient Near Eastern texts are not true creation accounts, and thus do not provide a thorough treatment of all the details. As Walton summarizes, "A number of documents from the ancient Near East contain extensive treatments of creation. It is questionable whether any of them can be labeled as creation accounts...Instead, these reports are often embedded in other types of literature."[44] To the point, reading through all of the relevant texts (from which pagan creation ideas are derived) reveals that the creation of plants and animals are rarely considered and never given a place of prominence.[45]

But some contrasts can be established even in examining some of the generalized statements in the pagan myths, allowing *mîn* to contribute to the theological agenda. For example, some ancient Near Eastern texts mention the creation of plants and animals for the purpose of feeding mankind (so they can keep up their work for the gods).[46] Genesis 1 agrees that plants (though not animals) are created for human consumption (Gen 1:11-12, 29-30); but in God's order, plants and animals are created prior to and apparently in preparation for humanity—ostensibly to bless man, not as an afterthought or emergency measure. Moreover, if reproductive capacity is implicit in the word *mîn*, then this may support a larger point that God is able to create a "system" that insures ongoing sustenance and life (for humans and animals; cf. vv. 29-30). This point supports Hasel's

---

43   As summarized in Wenham, *Genesis 1-15*, 9.

44   Walton, "Creation," 156. Elsewhere, Walton states, "Mesopotamian literature has no extant literature that systematically recounts the details of creation" (*Ancient Israelite Literature in Its Cultural Context*, 19, after which he also states that Egyptian literature is similar [though three major creation accounts offer rival theologies]). Cf. the summary statements about Sumerian, Akkadian, and Canaanite cosmologies in Lucas, "Cosmology": "There is no known Sumerian creation story, but there are descriptions of creation in a number of Sumerian texts of various genres" (p. 132); "The best-known Akkadian cosmogonies are contained within two lengthy narratives: the Atrahasis Epic and *Enuma Elish*" (p. 132); "there is no undisputed [Canaanite] cosmology" (p. 133).

45   Cf. Tony L. Shetter, "Genesis 1-2 in Light of Ancient Egyptian Creation Myths": "While the cosmogonies of Heliopolis, Memphis, and Hermopolis address the origin of the world, the creation of humans and animals receives little attention. The three main Egyptian cosmogonies primarily focus on the condition of the primordial state, the origin of the gods, and the creation of the heaven, the earth, and the sun" (accessed online at http://www.bible.org/page.php?page_id=2966).

46   E.g., the Egyptian text, "Instructions of Merikare," which calls mankind "god's cattle" (see Walton, *Ancient Israelite Literature in Its Cultural Context*, 33).

contrast concerning the creation of man (i.e., dignified role vs. slave), as well as the larger contrast between a deity who creates in an orderly and intentional fashion and deities who create "on the spot" for selfish reasons (i.e., to maintain the workforce). It also showcases the power of God's word—the word that "grants the means of self-perpetuation" (i.e., "according to its kind") and can still guarantee the intended results.[47]

If *mîn* connotes "biological division" of some sort, and/or if *mîn* involves reproductive limits, then the concept of "kinds" also contributes to the polemic of Genesis 1 by witnessing to a created order with recognizable built-in boundaries.[48] While creationists and non-creationists debate over the relationship of *mîn* to modern biological taxonomy, the issue at hand with respect to ancient Near Eastern cosmologies is at a much different level. Egyptian and Sumerian cosmologies often consider creative acts—of plants, animals, humans, gods, and heaven and earth alike—as births from the gods.[49] In summarizing the Sumerian cosmogonic

---

47   Hamilton, *Genesis 1-17*, 126 (on Gen 1:11-12): "God's creative design is that both the plants and the trees will reproduce themselves by bearing see 'each according to its kind' (AV, RSV). Here the concept of both the supernatural and the natural have their place. What exists exists because of the creative word of God. This spoken word is the ultimate background to all terrestrial phenomena. Yet this same word grants the means of self-perpetuation to various species and orders of creation. Here then is both point and process, with neither eclipsing the other." A similar point can be made with respect to the earth being called upon to be an active agent in God's creation (Gen 1:11, 12, 24).

48   Matthews (*Genesis 1-11:26*, 120-21) describes God as the "authoritative Designer who invokes structure, boundaries, as well as gives life." One of his pieces of evidence is that "Life forms, including vegetation, are instructed to reproduce within the restrictions of their own 'kinds' (vv. 11-12, 21, 24)." Another piece of evidence is the repeated use of certain numbers in the account, whether the numbers themselves or the number of times a word occurs (in descending order of frequency, 7's, 3's, and 10's). Interestingly, *mîn* occurs 10 times on 3 creation days in Genesis 1. Cf. also his comment on *mîn* in vv. 21, 24-25: "Inherently, the created order possesses divinely imposed limitations that establish self-maintained and governed systematic categories" (ibid., 157).

49   For a discussion of the four types of creation in the ancient Near East (i.e., by birth, by struggle, by fashioning/making/forming, and by utterance), see Westermann, *Genesis 1-11*, 26-41. For some specific examples of creation by birth, see the 2nd chapter ("Myths of Origins") in Samuel N. Kramer, *Sumerian Cosmology* (New York: Harper & Brothers, 1961), 30-75. The myth, "Enlil and Ninlil,: The Begetting of Nanna" (ibid., 43-47), is the first known example of the metamorphosis of a god, as Enlil assumes the form of three different individuals in impregnating his wife Ninlil with the three nether world deities. In "Cattle and Grain" (ibid., 53-54, 72), Lahar, the cattle-god, and his sister Ashnan, the grain-goddess, are created so the Anunnaki (heaven-gods) could eat and have clothing; but the Anunnaki were unable to make use of these gods' products, so man was created. In "Enki and Ninhursag: the Affairs of the Water-god" (ibid., 54-59), Uttu, the goddess of plants, was created through a series of divine incestuous acts: the god Enki impregnates his cohort Ninhursag, then his daughter Ninsar, then his daughter and granddaughter Ninkur, begetting Uttu. Enki then impregnates Uttu, producing eight different plants. But Enki eats the plants, receiving a curse from Ninhursag, resulting in eight aches and pains—of which he is later healed.

concepts, Kramer states that "all life [plant, animal, human] seems to have been conceived as resulting from a union of air, earth, and water"—made possible after heaven and earth separated.[50] The union of the air-god, Enlil, and his mother, the earth-goddess Ki (with considerable help from the water-god Enki), produces vegetable and animal life. Humans are the product of the combined efforts of the goddess Nammu (the primeval sea), the goddess Nimnah, and the water-god Enki. How different is the picture in Genesis 1! God does not produce his creations via sexual union; he creates outside himself. Moreover, the creation of plants and animals "according to kinds" is different from the creation of humans in God's image—a contrast not generally recognized outside Israel (see more below).[51]

A final set of ancient Near Eastern texts worth considering contain physiognomic omens, which predict future blessings or calamities based on abnormal births.[52] Some types of births need no special attention: multiple offspring; birth defects, some standard and some bizarre; strange noises from the offspring; strange behavior of the offspring; and others. The relevant births are the impossible ones where one type of life-form gives birth to a different type of life-form. Table 1 gives examples from each major category.

---

50   Kramer, *Sumerian Cosmology*, 74 (the full summary is on pp. 73-75).

51   The pagan "mixing" of gods, humans, and animals is also witnessed within the same entity. As an example, we can look at the famous *Enuma Elish*, the seven-tablet composition that receives the most attention as a parallel to Genesis 1 (For brief description of *Enuma Elish*, a 2nd millennium Akkadian text that was recited on the fourth day of the Babylonian New Year festival, celebrating Marduk's ascension to the head of the Babyonian pantheon, see Lucas, "Cosmology," 132-33; Walton, *Genesis*, 29). Of the 650-plus extant lines of text (about a third of the total 994 lines are missing or severely damaged), 18 of them mention an animal figure (for my counting and translation, I used the text found at http://www.sacred-texts.com/ane/enuma.htm). The majority of these creatures are either hybrids (animal-human or animal-god) or deities that appear in animal form: monster-serpents (I:114; II:20; III:24, 82); dragons (I:121; III:31, 89); scorpion men (I:122; II:28; III:32, 90); fish-men (I:123; II:29; III:33); and monster-vipers (II:23; III:85). Thus, the epic clearly allows for forms not part of God's "normal" creation in the Old Testament (mixed forms are found only with respect to cherubs and in symbolic prophetic texts). Having said all this, however, given the small sample pool and complete absence of any details about the creation of animals (note that the hybrid forms mentioned in *Enuma Elish* never show up in the actual creation portions of the epic [on Tablets IV-VI]), it is difficult to claim an intended polemic simply from this comparison.

52   The largest collection of physiognomic omen texts is the Akkadian series *šumma izbu*, found in the library of Aššurbanipal, that contain omens derived from unusual births. The 24 tablets of more than 2000 omens are given in full in Erle Leichty, *The Omen Series Šumma Izbu*, Texts From Cuneiform Sources, vol. IV (Locust Valley, NY: J.J. Augustin, 1970). The examples in the table are from this source (giving Tablet and number).

Table 1.

Parent	Offspring	Examples
Human	God/ Demon	If a woman gives birth to a "god" who has a face—a despotic king will rule the land. (I:24) If a woman gives birth, and (the child) is a female demon with a male face—the king and his family will disappear. (II:67)
Human	Animal	If a woman gives birth and (the child) has a dog's head—that city will go mad; there will be carnage in the land. (II:3) If a woman of the palace gives birth and (the child) has the face of a lion—the king will have no opponent. (IV:56)
Animal	Human	If a mare bears twins and they have a human head—[...] the prince's army will revolt against him. (XX:13) If the anomaly of a mare has the arm of a human—the owner [...] will die. (XXI:40)
Animal	Animal	If a ewe gives birth to a lion, and it has the body of a ram, and the head of a lion—omen of Sargon who ruled the world. (V:87) If the anomaly of a mare has feet like a lion, a head like a dog, a tail like a pig, (and) no hair—downfall of the prince; the same omen—the king will fall violently. (XXI:11)
Animal	Hybrid	If an anomaly's womb is full of faces, [...] one head of a monkey, one head of a lion, one head of a human, one head of a pig—the land will go mad; [...] the prince [...]; attack of a usurper. (XVII:76) If the anomaly of a mare has the face of a human (and) the tail of a dog—the land will draw near to struggle. (XXI:46)

The biblical view of life and reproduction could never conceive of nor tolerate such births. They represent the most fundamental violations of the created order, particularly the discontinuities established in Genesis 1. The confusion between human and divine denies God as eternal, one, and "wholly other." The confusion between human and animal rejects humanity's special relationship and role as God's image, having dominion over the rest of creation. And the confusion between animals as recognizably different as a sheep and a lion—not to mention body parts from other animals—is inconsistent with God's creation (including reproductive potential) of animals within set boundaries (i.e., "according to kinds").

The purpose of this exploration of some ancient Near Eastern texts and ideas was to see if the concept of creation "according to kinds" contributes in any way to the implicit challenge Genesis 1 makes against pagan notions of origins. My own evaluation is that there is no clear-cut parallel on the level of the specific polemics identified by Hasel and others. On the one hand, the pagan cosmologies contain ad hoc (i.e., non-systematic) accounts, or betray only passing interest in, the creation of plants and animals. On the other hand, the anomalous births, which come closest to establishing the type of foil to the concept of "kinds" in the biblical picture of creation, occur in omen texts rather than creation myths.[53]

But we have not arrived at a stalemate. We can say, at least, that the evidence adduced here does provide added support for the larger polemical point that Israel's God is greater than all rival deities. God's creation, including his creation of vegetation and animals "according to kinds," is due to the agency of the divine word rather than the aftermath of a divine power struggle.[54] Yahweh is a God of order not chaos, of calm not whim. As Matthews puts it, "Neither God nor his world is capricious. He produces an orderly, predictable, and dependable world."[55]

2.3.1.2. Humanity Lacking Kind-ness. The concept of "kinds" also contributes theologically to the exaltation of humanity among all of God's creation. Several textual elements indicate that one of the primary purposes of Genesis 1 is to celebrate humanity as the climax of creation. First, the creation of humanity is the final creative act of God. It is possible to interpret all the other creative acts as preparatory acts so that the earth will be prepared for humanity upon arrival (thus, our earlier description of Gen 1 as "anthropocentric").[56] Second, only the creation of humanity is explicitly described as the product of divine deliberation: "Let us make 'ādam" (v. 26). However the "us" is interpreted, this introduction to the actual creative act presents a pause in the narrative and heightens the anticipation. Third, the description of the actual creation of humanity is more intensive and extensive than any of the others. The poetic intrusion of v. 27 in an otherwise prosaic account enhances the vivid and energetic tone of the text. The diversification of humanity into male and female (v. 27c), as well as the ensuing address (vv. 28-30), adds a level of detail

---

53   Perhaps a wedge should not be driven to far between ritual texts (like the omen texts) and cosmological accounts. Creation epics like *Enuma Elish* were recited at annual festivals, in part to manipulate future events of the nation—not wholly dissimilar to the magical notions undergirding the omens. In fact, Hasel ("Polemical Nature," 90-91) concludes his article by contrasting creation by word in Gen 1 and pagan magic: "In Gen. 1...the notions of a magical word and of animate potentialities inherent in matter are absent. The first chapter of the Bible knows only of creation by an effortless, omnipotent, and unchallengeable divine word...Gen. 1 shows in its view of God's creative word its distance to pagan mythology. In Gen. 1 God's effortless creation by the spoken word...'is given a fundamental significance that is without parallel.' May it not indeed be the purpose of Gen. 1 to attack the idea of creation through magical utterance with a concept of a God who creates by the spoken word....It appears that this is a distinct way of indicating that Israelite faith is liberated from the baneful influence of magic."

54   Westermann (*Genesis 1-11*, 81) identifies this contrast as the main difference between Gen 1 and *Enuma Elish*.

55   Matthews, *Genesis 1-11:26*, 121.

56   See footnote 40; cf. Schnitjer, *Torah Story*, 63-65. Hasel ("Polemical Nature, 90") states, "Gen. 1 combats pagan mythological notions while, at the same time, the man-centered orientation of Gen. 1 and man's glory and freedom to rule the earth for his own needs is conveyed."

that is unique. Fourth, the use of the verb *bārā'*, "create," signals that this is a special creative act of God. Though the verb previously appeared in the prologue (v. 1) and in the creation of the sea creatures (v. 21),[57] its three-fold repetition in verse 27 (cf. Gen 5:1-2) may be singling humanity out as the pinnacle of creation. Fifth, God's evaluation of his own work— "And God saw all that he had made, and behold, it was very good" (v. 31)—modifies the usual formula (cf. vv. 4, 10, 12, 18, 21, 25). Instead of only commenting on the individual acts, God now evaluates the whole creation, "all that he had made." The simple *kî tôb*, "and it was good," is replaced by *wᵉhinnēh tôb mᵉ'ōd*, "and behold, it was very good." These changes emphasize the perfection of the final product—perfect only after humans are created.[58]

Finally, and most significantly, humanity is expressly created in God's image and likeness (Gen 1:26). While God is transcendent over and distinct from all his creation, humanity's status as God's image (individually and corporately) raises them to a mediating position (see Ps 8:3-8). Though the meaning of *imago Dei* continues to be debated,[59] the emphasis in the immediate context is the unique role humankind has to represent God in his creation by ruling and subduing (Gen 1:26, 28). God is king; humans are his vice-regents. The vertical emphasis of this role (under God; over the creation) is consistent with the themes of division, separation, and order throughout the creation account. This dignified position of all humanity is a direct contrast to Israel's neighbors, who saw humans as chattel of the gods. To those outside Israel, only kings (and some priests) could serve as divine images.

If these six indicators are intentional to reveal humankind's special role, then it would seem that what is *not* said may be equally significant. One noticeable absence is the lack of the use of *mîn* for the creation of humanity.[60] It might have been expected. In the creation narrative, all the other creative acts are works of separation (*hiḇdîl*; Days 1, 2, 3a, 4) or

---

57   The use of *bārā'* for sea creatures serves two purposes: (1) to indicate the first creation of a living being; and (2) to be a polemic against the pagan belief in divine sea monsters.

58   The grammar at the end of v. 31 also sets Day 6 apart. Instead of the usual "day, Xᵗʰ" for Days 2-5 (Day 1 uses the cardinal, "one"), Day 6 adds the definite article to the ordinal—"day, *the* sixth" (same with Day 7 in Gen 2:3). See Wenham, *Genesis 1-15*, 34.

59   One's particular position on the image of God is irrelevant for the purposes of this paper (i.e., how *mîn* contributes). For helpful discussions, see Matthews, *Genesis 1-11:26*, 164-72; Wenham, *Genesis 1-15*, 26-34; Westermann, *Genesis 1-11*, 147-55.

60   The term is used for humans in post-Biblical Hebrew (Sir 13:16b; 1QS 3:14); cf. Fabry, *TDOT* 8:289-90; Williams, "What Does *min* Mean," 346-48. This may be due to a generalization or expansion of the term. We know, for instance, that the term is later used for "category" (of righteousness in CD 4:16). Later still, the term comes to include the meaning "heretic" (in Mishnaic Hebrew). But we cannot rule out the possibility that the term theoretically could have been used in Old Testament times; its absence in the Bible could then be due to its intentional absence in Gen 1.

works of differentiation (*mîn*; Days 3b, 5, 6a).[61] Humans are differentiated by gender (Gen 1:27c), but not by "kind." Why not? According to the structure of the six creation days, the three creative acts most closely associated with the creation of humans all use *mîn*: vegetation on the second half of Day 3; fish and fowl on Day 5; and land animals on first half of Day 6 (see the portions in **bold** in the chart on p. 13 above). With this "set up," it is most likely that the absence of *mîn* for humans is intentional.

The most natural explanation for the absence of *mîn* for humans is that it adds further support for the uniqueness and superiority of humanity in God's creation. In particular, it highlights the creation of humankind in God's image and likeness as opposed to "kinds."[62] Four specific points of contrast between the creatures of "kind" and the image-bearers can be outlined. First, it suggests that the discontinuity between humans and animals should be considered greater than whatever discontinuities exist among animals themselves through the division of "kinds." Humans and animals have several things in common: they were both created on the same day; they are both living beings; they are both blessed by God and given the ability to reproduce; and they are both given plants for food. But humans are "like" God,[63] not animals. Second, the unity of the human race is emphasized because it is not differentiated by "kinds."[64] Humans are superior to the rest of creation, but no human is inherently superior to another. This democratization of the image of God leads to dignity and corporate blessing and responsibility. Third, the omission of "kinds" for humans emphasizes the uniqueness of human sexuality. The different descriptions in Genesis 1 of humans in contrast to animals shows, as Matthews comments,

> ...that human sexuality is of a different sort from animal procreation: human procreation is not intended merely as a mechanism for replication or the expression of human passion but is instrumental in experiencing covenant blessing. The

---

61   So Fabry, *TDOT* 8:289: "Just as the immutable works are subjected to the principle of separation (*hibdîl*), so also are the mutable ones subjected to the principle of differentiation (*mîn*; 10 occurrences in Gen. 1:11f.,21,24f.)." Cf. Matthews, *Genesis 1-11:26*, 153: "Just as 'separations' are integral to creation, so are distinctions among living beings as indicated by their 'kinds.'"

62   So also Fabry, *TDOT* 8:290; Matthews, *Genesis 1-11:26*, 167, 174; Sailhamer, "Genesis," 37; Schnitjer, *Torah Story*, 64-65 (but see p. 45), Walke and Fredricks, *Genesis*, 65.

63   Scholars debate the relationship between "image" and "likeness" in Gen 1:26. Three options exist: (1) the terms are synonymous (2) "likeness" qualifies "image" by weakening it (i.e., humankind is only like God, not the exact image of God); (3) "likeness" qualifies "image" by strengthening it (i.e. humankind is a representation, not just a representative). See Hamilton, *Genesis 1-17*, 135-36. These varying views are irrelevant for the point being made.

64   Fabry, *TDOT* 8:290; Matthews, *Genesis 1-11:26*, 174.

union of man and woman as husband and wife is an inclusive oneness.[65]

Finally, vegetation and animals were created for the benefit of humans. God's blessing on humanity includes the privilege of ruling all animals (in sky, land, and sea) and eating from seed-yielding plants and fruit-bearing trees (Gen 1:28-29). Each of these had been created by God "according to its kind" (1:11-12, 21, 24-25). The concept of "kinds" implies reproduction, variety, and abundance—good and necessary gifts for a fertile and multiplying humanity. The human-centered picture explains why the vegetation in 1:11-12 is selective.[66]

2.3.2 Other Texts: God's Kind-ness Continued in Flood and Food

Outside Genesis 1, the word *mîn* appears seven times in two verses related to the animals on the ark prior to the flood (Gen 6:20; 7:14), 13 times across two similar but not identical lists designed to differentiate clean and unclean foods for Israelite diet, and one time with respect to fish in Ezek 47:10. This section presupposes all that has been said concerning Genesis 1. It is not necessary, therefore, to go into the same level of detail. We will restrict our discussion to answering a few related questions. How does each context contribute to the themes and theology of its respective book? How does each context compare and contrast to Genesis 1—both with respect to theme/theology and the concept of "kinds"? The answers to these questions will be brief, but they should provide the necessary additional data (to the results of analyzing Genesis 1) to draw basic conclusions regarding the concept of "kinds."

2.3.2.1. God's Kind-ness and the Great Escape. It is difficult to deal with the flood narrative (Gen 6-9) appropriately without reference to Genesis 1.[67] The flood, which is God's response to pervasive human sinfulness (6:5-7), should be viewed as a reversal of creation—an un-

---

65   Matthews, *Genesis 1-11:26*, 173-74.
66   Sailhamer, "Genesis," 31. Against Westermann, *Genesis 1-11*, 124: "The description in Genesis is on the way to a scientific explanation of the origin of plants. The classification of the plants shows a scientific interest. An objective interest has taken the place of a purely functional interest in plants as nourishment for humans" (cf. pp. 88, 124-26). Following the Documentary Hypothesis, Westermann believes that Gen 1 contains several different (often contradictory) once-independent traditions about creation that the author- redactor P (P = Priestly source in source criticism) stitched together, alongside of which he himself added new material. Westermann considers Gen 1:11-12 to be part of the later stages of the development because it speaks about plants without reference to humans, and because it speaks of the earth as an active agent in creation. He considers v. 29, which connects plants to humans, to be part of the earlier stages of the tradition.
67   Fabry, *TDOT* 8:290; Matthews, *Genesis 1-11:26*, 351-52; Walton, "Flood," *Dictionary of the Old Testament: Pentateuch* (Downers Grove: InterVarsity, 2003), 323-24. For a brief discussion of the polemical nature of the Genesis flood account against the pagan myths, see Wenham, *Genesis 1-15*, 204-05.

creation. The bursting forth of the "great deep" and the opening of the "windows of heaven" (7:11) reverses the first three creation days (1:3-13), returning the earth to a "chaotic" state (cf. 1:2). But due to divine grace (cf. 6:8; 8:1), a re-creation occurs as a wind from God (8:1a; cf. 1:2) allows the land to reappear from the waters (8:1b-19; cf. 1:6-7). Noah may be seen as a new Adam,[68] most notably in the repetition (with qualification) of the original blessing and creation mandate, "Be fruitful and multiply and fill the earth..." (1:28-30; 9:1-7).[69]

It is no surprise then to find conceptual unity in the depiction of animals, including the references that speak of animals "according to their kind." The two relevant verses include one of instruction (Gen 6:20) and one of application (7:14). The significant parts of these verses are listed below with Gen 1:21 and Gen 1:25 for the sake of comparison (of course, no water animals would be on the ark!). The wooden translations intend to cue the reader to the same grammar and vocabulary in Hebrew. Where the text contains the phrase, "according to its kind," it is noted by putting "kind" in parentheses following its corresponding animal.

Gen 1:21	...every bird of wing (kind)
Gen 1:25	...the wild animal (kind)...the *behemah* (kind)...every ground crawler (kind)
Gen 6:20	...the bird (kind)...the *behemah* (kind)...ground crawler (kind)...of every shall come...
Gen 7:14	...every wild animal (kind)...every *behemah* (kind)...every earth crawler (kind)...every bird (kind), every small bird, every winged one

Several minor variations exist: qualifiers (e.g., "every"; "ground" vs. "earth"); consistency in the names of the same animal type, especially with respect to birds (1:21; 7:14d)[70] and larger land animals (1:25ab; 6:20b;

---

68 Matthews (*Genesis 1-11:26*, 351) compares the two succinctly: "both 'walk' with God; both are the recipients of the promissory blessing; both are caretakers of the lower creatures; both father three sons; both are workers of the soil; both sin through the fruit of a tree; and both father a wicked son who is under a curse."

69 Discontinuities with Adam include (1) the introduction of fear as an element in humanity's dominion (9:2); (2) the sanctioning of animal life for food (9:3); (3) the explicit mandate to defend the sanctity of life (9:4-6); (4) The permanence of the new order is guaranteed by a divine covenant and a visible sign (rainbow) of that covenant; (5) While life will go on, the decreasing longevity of the members of the species (cf. Gen 11) indicates that something fundamental has happened in the world.

70 The awkward phrase, "every small bird, every winged one," at the end of 7:14 probably gives a further description of the preceding bird category rather than a separate category.

7:14b)[71]; and the order of the broad categories (birds, land animals [Gen 1; 6:20]; land animals, birds [7:14]). But the overall language suggests that the flood texts are directly echoing Genesis 1.

The problem with such unity, at least for this paper, is that the flood texts do little to clarify the ambiguities with respect to *mîn*. Does it refer to a representational "kind"? Is it collective or distributive?[72] Yet, it is precisely at this point—how to address the number of animals on the ark during a global deluge—where creationists find one of their greatest challenges. The emphasis on "every" in Gen 6:20 and 7:14 only exacerbates the problem.[73] The ark would seem to contain at least the same animals as the original creation—but even this may be disputed.

2.3.2.2. God's Kind-ness and Good Eating. The final texts to consider are lists of food laws in the Sinaitic legislation (Lev 11; Deut 14).[74] Yahweh's goal in redeeming his people and making a covenant with them is to form them into a "kingdom of priests and a holy nation" (Exod 19:6; cf. Deut 4:6-8; 26:16-19). The food laws are based in the motto, "You shall be holy, for I am holy" (Lev 11:44-45; Deut 14:21; cf. Lev 19:2; 20:26). More specifically, the lists differentiate between "clean" and "unclean" animals—some of which are qualified by "according to its kind."[75] In Leviticus, clean-versus-unclean is one of the two polarities (the other is holy vs. common; Lev 10:10) that, along with atonement, form the theological core of the book.[76] Furthermore, Lev 20:24-26

---

71   Gen 1:25 and 7:14 subdivide land animals between wild and domesticated (*behemah*). But Gen 6:20 uses *behemah* to refer to land animals in general.

72   The wooden translations above show that all the animals are referenced by collective nouns, i.e., a singular noun referring to a plurality of individuals. This observation, however, does not settle anything with respect to "kind" (except it explains why the pronominal suffixes are all singular [except for the *pl.* sea creatures in 1:21a]).

73   The ambiguous antecedent to "each, every" at the end of Gen 6:20 ("two of *each* shall come to you to keep them alive") seems clarified by 7:14, where "every" is used for each animal.

74   We will consider Lev 11 and Deut 14 together, and refer to it as Sinai. We will also assume the priority of Lev 11, which explains the more concise list in Deut 14. Technically, however, Deut 14 is part of the covenant at Moab (Deut 29:1). There are significant differences with respect to the larger narrative portrayed in Deuteronomy, but the core (Deut 12-26) is basically a recapitulation of Sinai.

75   Lev 11:14b (falcon), 15 (raven), 16d (hawk), 19b (heron), 22a (locust), 22b (bald locust), 22c (cricket), 22d (grasshopper), 29c (great lizard); Deut 14:13b (falcon), 14 (raven), 15d (hawk), 18b (heron). Identifying the animals has proven to be a notoriously difficult task. I will use the ESV translation, since exact precision at this point is not necessary. For an exhaustive study on the issue, see Edwin Firmage, "Zoology," *Anchor Bible Dictionary*, vol. 6 (New York: Doubleday, 1992), 1109-67; cf. Paul J. N. Lawrence, "Zoology," *Dictionary of the Old Testament: Pentateuch* (Downers Grove: InterVarsity, 2003), 914-18; Jacob Milgrom, *Leviticus 1-16*, Anchor Bible 3 (New York: Doubleday, 1991), 645-91.

76   Richard E. Averbeck, "Leviticus: Theology of," *New International Dictionary of Old Testament Theology & Exegesis*, vol. 4 (Grand Rapids: Zondervan, 1997), 918; Gordon J. Wenham, *The Book of Leviticus*, New International Commentary on the Old Testament (Grand Rapids: Eerdmans, 1979), 18-25.

connects the repetition of clean and unclean animals, as well as the call to holiness, with Israel's social distinctiveness in the world. Thus, though the food lists may appear mundane, they are crucial for the well being of the individual and community. This is probably why the lists are so detailed.

An observation of the food lists (see Appendix B) reveals several things. First, the clean/unclean dichotomy is worked out for the broad regions of habitation we have seen: land, sea, and air—with the air animals further divided between birds and flying insects. This division ties these texts to those in Genesis we have examined. But the further differentiation was needed, in order for the theological to become part of daily practice.[77] Second, the list in Deuteronomy 14 is a more concise list. The greatest differences are the addition of the category of land swarmers in Lev 11:41-43, and the deletion of any clean flying insects in Deuteronomy 14. The reasons for the differences are probably practical[78]; Deuteronomy presupposes Leviticus anyway. Third, all but the category of birds provide a single principle that allows one to distinguish between clean and unclean. Fourth, some of the categories identify specific creatures. Because the birds are not differentiated by a principle, they constitute the longest list in each text. Fifth, of the animals identified by name, there are three types: (1) those with a name only; (2) some birds with a name plus the mîn-phrase[79]; and (3) one (in each list) with "every" preceding the name plus the mîn-phrase ("every raven according to its kind" in Lev 11:15; Deut 14:14). Williams found the last category the most intriguing (only in raising more questions) in considering the possible distribute use of mîn.[80] Sixth, no obvious reason can be discerned for the birds in the food lists that are followed by the phrase, "according to its kind" (those in **bold** in the appendix). Other than the four clean insects in Lev 11:22, no pattern emerges as far as I can tell, nor has any scholar I have read attempted to offer an explanation.

Regarding the animals in the list, including those with mîn, the one thing that seems clear is that they are differentiated by traits recognizable to the common person. The individual's religious and social standing in

---

77   Mary Douglas (*Purity and Danger: An Analysis of the Concepts of Pollution and Taboo* [New York: Praeger, 1966]; cf. idem, *Leviticus as Literature* [Oxford: Oxford University Press, 1999]) has been influential in defining holiness as "wholeness" (i.e., normality). While we cannot go into all the details here, this definition comports well with the detailed laws throughout Leviticus that seem to leave no aspect of life untouched. Cf. Wenham, *Book of Leviticus*, 23-25.

78   For suggestions on explaining the differences, see Houston, "Foods, Clean and Unclean," 328; J. Gordon McConville, *Deuteronomy*, Apollos Old Testament Commentary 5 (Downers Grove: InterVarsity, 2002) 244-45; Jeffrey H. Tigay, *Deuteronomy*, The JPS Torah Commentary (Philadelphia: Jewish Publication Society, 1996), 137.

79   The great lizard in Lev 11:29 also have mîn added, but this is part of a prohibition list against touching not eating.

80   Williams, "What Does *min* Mean," 346.

the community was at stake. So while the detailed lists seem to make the categorization of animals more "scientific," they are not prepared by or for an expert, let alone a 21st century one! Moreover, several details of the lists do not agree with modern scientific taxonomy: the bat is considered a bird (Lev 11:19; Deut 14:18) because it flies like one; the rock badger and hare are among the ruminants (Lev 11:5-6; Deut 14:7) because they appear to chew their food for a long time.[81] In Deut 14:5, wild species (e.g., deer and gazelle) are alongside domesticated animals (cattle, sheep, goats) because of their physical resemblance to flocks and herds.[82] Finally, these types of lists were common to ancient cultures.[83] Therefore, it would be unwise to try and assign any specific meaning to *mîn* other than a general, observable category—a lot like the English, "kind"!

The final issue to consider is the relationship of this text to Genesis 1 (and Gen 6:14; 7:20). We have noted that, despite the detailed categories in the food lists, there is still awareness of the broader creational regions of land, sky, and sea (cf. Lev 20:25). At least three more observations connect the present texts to Genesis theologically. First, the theme of differentiation is reminiscent of the creator's interest in order and boundaries. If Israel is to be a corporate image of God in the earth, she must reflect God's holiness in all of life. As Futato states, these texts articulate "the theme of order through separation by using *mîn* to refer to groups of unclean animals, which are part of a symbolic representation of holiness and unholiness."[84]

Second, the rationale for the food laws may be based in creation. Determining the rationale is heavily debated,[85] but two of the options at least consist with broader biblical and theological considerations. One, given that uncleanness is often associated with coming in contact with death—as in Leviticus 11 (vv. 24-39)—it is possible that animals are considered unclean because they are predatory and/or carnivores. Two, if holiness means wholeness and completeness, as many maintain, then a possible rationale is that clean animals are those that are in conformity with the natural order of creation; the unclean animals are those that seem to confuse boundaries. For example, fish without fins and scales are unclean because they do not fit the "normal" expectation of fish. Or, animals with an indeterminate form of motion (i.e., swarm) are unclean. This, incidentally, would put the concept of "kinds" front and center.

---

81   See Houston, "Foods, Clean and Unclean," 327.
82   Ibid., 327, 330.
83   Cf. Seely, "Meaning of *Mîn*," 47-56.
84   Futato, *NIDOTTE* 9:934.
85   See T. D. Alexander, *From Paradise to Promise Land: An Introduction to the Pentateuch*, 2nd ed. (Grand Rapids: Baker, 2002), 227-31; Douglas, *Purity and Danger*; idem, *Leviticus as Literature*; Houston, "Foods, Clean and Unclean," 327-30.

The problem is that not every animal on the lists fits any of the proposed rationales. In the end, the rationale may be arbitrary: God commands it, and the people obey what he says. Even this alternative is not unlike God creating things and situations by fiat.

The third connection with Genesis is the polarization of clean/unclean, which first occurred in the flood narrative (Gen 7:2-3; 8:20). By looking more panoramically, it seems reasonable that Noah is a prototype for Moses.[86] Noah offered burnt offerings (Gen 8:20), received restrictions concerning "lifeblood" (9:5), received a covenant sign (9:13), and is surrounded by a concentration on the numbers "seven" and "forty." Both Noah and Moses were saved by a tēbâ, "ark" or "basket." And both built "sanctuaries" with complete fidelity (6:22; 7:5; Exod 40:16). While some comparisons are more legitimate than others, it is hard to not read one without thinking of the other. Moses would have seen himself in light of the "heroes" that preceded him, and would have understood that God was accomplishing in him the larger purposes of creation and the Abrahamic promise. And we should understand Israel as a creation of God, who will use this new formed people to accomplish his goal for all humanity (cf. Gen 12:3).

But this raises a larger hermeneutical question: Should Sinai be read in light of Genesis, or Genesis in light of Sinai? We naturally read later texts through the lens of what precedes it. But the converse seems to be legitimate in this case. Israel is the original audience for Genesis, which is why I set out the section on Genesis 1 with an "Israelite" perspective. The parallels we have drawn appear intentional, and many others could be added—such as Abraham keeping God's "commandments, statutes, and instructions" (Gen 26:5), terms elsewhere associated with Sinai. It seems best that the texts should be mutually interpreting.

What does this have to do with understanding mîn? For one, it means that the concept of "kinds" should not be considered completely different between the various texts. Just as the food laws are read with creation as a backdrop, it is difficult to imagine that the creation of "kinds" in Genesis 1 does not anticipate the later revelation. Having said this, theological connections do not necessarily argue for consistency of meaning in word usage. That is, while "kinds" causes the reader to interact with the various texts, it does not mean that the word carries the same level of specificity in each case. Many lexical studies of mîn, I believe, have committed this fallacy, and argue for a scientific explanation of the term without warrant.

2.3.2.3. God's Kind-ness and a Glorious Future. The remaining reference of mîn is Ezek 47:10, which describes the water flowing from the eschatological temple as containing fish "according to its kind, like the fish of the Great Sea." Block describes Ezek 47:8-10 as a literary picture of

---

86   See, e.g., Matthews, *Genesis 1-11:26*, 351-52.

the healing powers of the "river of life" for the waters.[87] Thus, in language reminiscent of Gen 1:20-21 (cf. "swarm" and "every living creature" in Ezek 47:9), the use of mîn in Ezek 47:10 speaks to the abundance and variety of fish in the blessed new order (i.e., new creation). This singular reference does not seem to add any new information about the meaning of mîn.

2.4. Conclusion

This paper has attempted to get beyond the impasse of the study of creation "according to kinds" by seeking to determine what theological contribution the term *mîn* can make, despite the uncertainties about its exact meaning in relation to modern science. After introducing the problem, in which we examined the areas of ambiguity, we turned to the texts that utilize the term. With respect to Genesis 1, we found that "kinds" reinforced two significant aspects of creation theology: the implicit polemic against pagan views of creation; and the unique, supreme standing of humanity in God's creation. We then looked at the other primary contexts, asking how they supported, progressed, or challenged earlier themes. The use of "kinds" in the flood narrative supplemented the idea that, in his grace, God gave a fresh start to his creatures and creation, setting things up for the entrance of Israel. The food laws presented a greater challenge because of the distance from Genesis 1 in time, context, and a progression in the concept of "kinds." We found that texts like Genesis 1 and Leviticus 11 mutually interpret one another theologically, as Israel seeks to live out the creation mandate in the context of covenant.

But through this study, we have also been cognizant of the thorny issues surrounding mîn, including its interest for creationists. The following outline of conclusions seeks to speak specifically to this concern.

1. The main contexts (excluding Ezek 47:10) that utilize mîn are related thematically and theologically. The flood narrative (Gen 6-9) describes an un-creation and re-creation. The food laws (Lev 11; Deut 14) apply the creation themes of life and differentiation at a detailed, practical level. The language of "clean" and "unclean" combines with several themes (e.g., burnt offerings and lifeblood) that show an intentional link between the flood narrative and Sinaitic legislation.

2. However, these thematic links do not mean that the word *mîn* should be defined exactly the same in each text. It is possible that *mîn* bears a precise, technical sense (i.e., is a scientific term); but it is also possible that the word itself is imprecise and general—its exact meaning being determined only within each context it is used.

3. Based on the evidence, it is not possible to demand a precise, technical sense of the term *mîn*. The variance in the level of differentiation

---

87   Block, *Book of Ezekiel Chapters 25-48*, 694-95.

between its use in Genesis and its use in Leviticus-Deuteronomy suggests that the precise nuance of "kinds" varies as well. Thus, it is off the mark to try and determine monolithically what *mîn* "means" with respect to modern biological taxonomy.

4. This fluctuation, however, does not yield a complete openness on the science questions. Rather, it means that larger contextual issues—not technical terminology—must be the deciding factors in making informed judgments.

5. For example, the theological contribution of "kinds" in Genesis 1 assumes certain discontinuities. The primary discontinuity is between humans and animals. Other discontinuities between certain types of animals are also assumed, though the exact line of demarcation is difficult to determine. In both cases, it seems that the language and theology of Genesis 1 precludes macro-evolutionary scenarios of origins.

6. It is impossible, however, to determine from the biblical text how many animals existed in the garden of Eden or at the time of the flood. The biblical concept of "kinds" should not be pressed too far in either direction.

7. The term "baramin" should only be used with awareness that "kinds" examined by creationists may not be equal to the biblical word for "kinds," *mîn*.[88]

8. Based on my experience, some creationists need to assume less and work more diligently with the biblical text. Often, creationist literature labels a specific interpretation of a text as "obvious," "clear," "literal," or the like. Yet, such labels often lack exegetical investigation or any awareness of scholarly debates on said texts (even among evangelical scholars).

It should be emphasized that the desire to interpret the relevant biblical texts as "scientific" does not guarantee orthodoxy. For example, Claus Westermann, whose Genesis commentary remains extremely influential, repeatedly makes statements like the following:

> God creates living things according to species. And so there is yet another trait in P's [= the "Priestly" writer who penned Gen 1] creation account which does not belong either to theological or religious tradition but rather to the tradition of the natural sciences.[89]

> The description in Genesis [concerning Gen 1:11-12] is on the way to a scientific explanation of the origin of plants. The classification of the plants shows a scientific interest. An

---

88   Cf. Williams, "What Does *min* Mean," 351.
89   Westermann, *Genesis 1-11*, 88.

objective interest has taken the place of a purely functional interest in plants as nourishment for humans.[90]

By "natural sciences" and "scientific reading," he is not first and foremost thinking in terms of modern science—an issue on which Westermann appears a bit inconsistent.[91] Rather, he is thinking along higher-critical lines, which seeks to get behind the text as it now stands and reconstruct the perceived layers of tradition. Westermann believes that Genesis 1 combines several different (often contradictory) once-independent traditions about creation that the author-redactor "P" stitched together, alongside of which he himself added new material.[92] The more "scientific" texts (like Gen1:11-12) are part of the last stages of development, and move beyond more primitive understandings of creation that still find echoes in the text (e.g., creation by conflict or creation by birth of the gods). Thus, since Gen 1:11-12 provides no explicit benefit to humanity in the near context, this text is "scientific" in the sense that it is not thinking of plants as food, but the general division of all plants.[93] Westermann is well aware that the human-centeredness of plants is spelled out in verse 29, but he takes verse 29 as stemming from an originally independent tradition.[94] What drives Westermann this direction is an assumption that Israelite cosmology developed like all the others—not in final outcome but in process.

Creationists would rightly reject the approach of Westermann. But if they are not careful, creationists could fall into the same modernist trap of spending more time on getting behind the text and wrestling with scientific reconstructions rather than sitting under the text's authority, being informed and transformed by its message and theology.

---

90   Ibid., 124 (see pp. 88, 124-26); cf. Fabry, *TDOT* 8:289.
91   Westermann (*Genesis 1-11*, 126) initially states that the meaning of *mîn* "is precisely the same as that of the word used today in the natural sciences, namely species or genus"; but soon after adds, "one can speak of a scientific interest, provided one distinguishes it from our idea of 'science.'"
92   Cf. ibid., 85: "P could not say that the only possible and correct way to describe creation is by means of a structure which presents the fulfillment of a command. He must, of course, speak of creation in this way. However, he lets other voices speak which have described creation differently. This decision is of great theological moment. The redactors of the Pentateuch and of the canon made a similar decision when they decided to leave side-by-side very different descriptions of creation. This means that when there is talk of creation there must be preserved a succession of very different voices which add their contribution to what is being said."
93   Ibid., 125.
94   Ibid., 162-63.

Appendix A: Biblical References to *mîn*

Context	Reference	Life-Form (or Vegetation) Preceding "according to its/ their kind(s)"	Other Features
Creation	Gen 1:11	fruit-bearing tree	may also refer to seed-producing plant
	Gen 1:12a	seed-producing plant	
	Gen 1:12b	fruit-bearing tree	
	Gen 1:21a	(all) sea creatures	plural suffix and plural "kinds"
	Gen 1:21b	every winged bird	
	Gen 1:24a	living being [land animal in general]	
	Gen 1:24b	land beast [wild]	might also refer to livestock and crawler
	Gen 1:25a	land beast [wild]	
	Gen 1:25b	livestock [*beḥēmâ*]	*beḥēmâ* refers to domesticated animal here (cf. 6:20b; 7:14a)
	Gen 1:25c	crawler	
Flood	Gen 6:20a	bird	
	Gen 6:20b	animal [*beḥēmâ*]	*beḥēmâ* here includes both domesticated and wild animals (more general than 1:25b and 7:14b)
	Gen 6:20c	every crawler	
	Gen 7:14a	every land beast [wild]	
	Gen 7:14b	every livestock [*beḥēmâ*]	*beḥēmâ* refers to domesticated animal here (as in 1:25b)
	Gen 7:14c	every crawler	
	Gen 7:14d	every bird	
Kosher Foods	Lev 11:14b	falcon	
	Lev 11:15	every raven	
	Lev 11:16d	hawk	
	Lev 11:19b	heron	
	Lev 11:22a	locust	
	Lev 11:22b	bald locust	
	Lev 11:22c	cricket	
	Lev 11:22d	grasshopper	
	Lev 11:29c	great lizard	
	Deut 14:13b	falcon	
	Deut 14:14	every raven	
	Deut 14:15d	hawk	
	Deut 14:18b	heron	
Eschatological Temple	Ezek 47:10	fish	

Appendix B: Food Lists in Leviticus 11 and Deuteronomy 14

		Leviticus 11	Deuteronomy 14	
Land	Clean	2-3 Cloven-hoofed, cud-chewing	4-6 Cloven-hoofed, cud chewing Ox Sheep Goat Deer Gazelle	Roebuck Wild goat Ibex Antelope Mountain sheep
	Unclean	4-8 Camel Rock badger Hare Pig	7-8 Camel Hare Rock badger Pig	
Sea	Clean	9 Fins and scales	9 Fins and scales	
	Unclean	10-12	10	

Group	Subgroup	Status	Column 1	Column 2
Air	Birds	Clean	11 — Eagle, Bearded vulture, Black vulture, Kite, Falcon (13), (every) **Raven** (14), Ostrich, Nighthawk, Sea gull, **Hawk** (15)	13-19 — Eagle, Bearded vulture, Black vulture, Kite, **Falcon** (14), (every) **Raven** (15), Ostrich, Nighthawk, Sea gull, **Hawk** (16)
		Unclean	12-18 — Little owl, Short-eared owl, Barn owl, Tawny owl, Carrion vulture, Cormorant, Stork, **Heron** (18), Hoopoe, Bat	Little owl, Cormorant, Short-eared owl, Barn owl, Tawny owl, Carrion vulture, Stork, **Heron** (19), Hoopoe, Bat
	Flying insects	Clean	20	21-22 — Locust (22), **Bald locust** (22), **Cricket** (22), **Grasshopper** (22)
		Unclean	19 — Winged	20, 23 — Walk not hop
Land Swarmers		Unclean		41-43 — [all]
		Unclean to touch		29-30 — mole rat, mouse, **great lizard** (29), gecko, monitor lizard, lizard, sand lizard, chameleon

References

Alexander, T. D. 2002. *From Paradise to Promise Land: An Introduction to the Pentateuch*. 2nd ed. Baker, Grand Rapids.

Averbeck, R. E. 1997. Leviticus: Theology of. *New International Dictionary of Old Testament Theology & Exegesis*, vol. 4. Zondervan, Grand Rapids, pp. 907-23.

Barr, J. 1961. *The Semantics of Biblical Language*. Oxford University Press, Oxford.

Brueggemann, W. 1982. *Genesis*. Interpretation. John Knox, Atlanta.

Beauchamp, P. 1969. *Création et séparation*. Desclée de Brouwer, Paris.

Block, D.I. 1998. *The Book of Ezekiel Chapters 25-48*. New International Commentary on the Old Testament. Eerdmans, Grand Rapids.

Cazelles, H. 1969. MYN = espèce, race ou ressemblance? In: *Mémorial du Cinquantenaire (1914-1964), École des Langues Orientales Anciennes de L'institut Catholique de Paris*. Travaux de L'Institut Catholique de Paris 10. Bloud & Gay, Paris, pp. 105-108.

Davies, P.R. 1983. *The Damascus Covenant*. Journal for the Study of the Old Testament Supplement Series 25. JSOT Press, Sheffield.

Douglas, M. *Purity and Danger: An Analysis of the Concepts of Pollution and Taboo*. Praeger, New York.

Douglas, M. 1999. *Leviticus as Literature*. Oxford University Press, Oxford.

Drews, C. "Biblical Kind." Accessed Sept. 29, 2008, at http://www.theistic-evolution.com/kind.html.

Fabry, H. 1997. *mîn*. In: *Theological Dictionary of the Old Testament* (Eng. trans.), 8:288-91. Eerdmans, Grand Rapids.

Firmage, E. 1992 Zoology. *Anchor Bible Dictionary*, vol. 6. Doubleday, New York, pp. 1109-67.

Flank, L. Creation 'Science' and the Genesis 'Kinds.' Accessed Oct. 31, 2008, at http://www.geocities.com/CapeCanaveral/Hangar/2437/kinds.htm.

Futato, M. 1997 *mîn*. In: *New International Dictionary of Old Testament Theology and Exegesis*, 2:934-35. Zondervan, Grand Rapids.

Hamilton, V.P. 1990. *Genesis 1-17*. New International Commentary on the Old Testament. Eerdmans, Grand Rapids.

Hasel, G.F. 1972. The Significance of the Cosmology in Gen 1 in Relation to Ancient Near Eastern Parallels. *Andrews University Seminary Studies* 10:1-20.

Hasel, G.F. 1974. The Polemic Nature of the Genesis Cosmology. *Evangelical Quarterly* 46:81-102.

Houston, W.J. 2003. Foods, Clean and Unclean. *Dictionary of the Old Testament: Pentateuch*. InterVarsity, Downers Grove, pp. 326-36.

Kaiser, W.C., Jr. 1980. *mîn*. In: *Theological Wordbook of the Old Testament*, 1:503-04. Moody, Chicago.

Kelly, D.F. 1997. *Creation and Change: Genesis 1.1-2.4 in the Light of*

Changing Scientific Paradigms. Mentor, Fearn, UK.

Koehler, L. and W. Baumgarter. M.E.J. Richardson, trans. 1997. מין. In: *The Hebrew and Aramaic Lexicon of the Old Testament.* 2:577. Brill, Leiden.

Kramer, S.N. 1961. *Sumerian Cosmology.* Harper & Brothers, New York.

Lawrence. P.J.N. 2003. Zoology. In: *Dictionary of the Old Testament: Pentateuch.* InterVarsity, Downers Grove, pp. 914-18.

Leichty, E. 1970. *The Omen Series Šumma Izbu.* Texts From Cuneiform Sources, vol. IV. J.J. Augustin, Locust Valley, NY.

Lucas, E.C. 2003. "Cosmology." *Dictionary of the Old Testament: Pentateuch.* InterVarsity, Downers Grove, pp. 130-39.

Matthews, K.A. 1996. *Genesis 1-11:26.* New American Commentary 1A. Broadman & Holman, Nashville.

McConville, J.G. 2002. *Deuteronomy.* Apollos Old Testament Commentary 5. InterVarsity, Downers Grove.

Milgrom, J. 1991. *Leviticus 1-16.* Anchor Bible 3. Doubleday, New York.

Payne, J.B. 1958. The Concept of 'Kinds' in Scripture. *Journal of the American Scientific Affiliation* 10:17-20.

Sailhamer, J.H. 1995. *The Pentateuch as Narrative.* Zondervan, Grand Rapids.

Sailhamer, J.H. 1996. *Genesis Unbound: A Provocative New Look at the Creation Account.* Questar, Grand Rapids.

Sailhamer, J.H. 2008. Genesis. In: *Genesis-Leviticus,* Expositor's Bible Commentary, vol. 1, rev. ed. Zondervan, Grand Rapids.

Schnitjer, G.E. 2006. *The Torah Story: An Apprenticeship on the Pentateuch.* Zondervan, Grand Rapids.

Seely, P.H. 1997. The Meaning of *Mîn,* 'Kind.' *Science & Christian Belief* 9:47-56.

Shetter, T.L. Genesis 1-2 in Light of Ancient Egyptian Creation Myths. Accessed at article: http://www.bible.org/page.php?page_id=2966..

Sparks, K.L. 2005. *Ancient Texts for the Study of the Hebrew Bible: A Guide to the Background Literature.* Hendrickson, Peabody, MA.

Stambaugh, J. 1992. 'Life' According to the Bible, and the Scientific Evidence. *Creation Ex Nihilo Technical Journal* 6(2):98-121.

Tigay, J.H. 1996. *Deuteronomy.* In: The JPS Torah Commentary. Jewish Publication Society, Philadelphia.

Waltke, B.K. and C.J. Fredricks. 2001. *Genesis: A Commentary.* Zondervan, Grand Rapids.

Walton, J.H. 1989. *Ancient Israelite Literature in Its Cultural Context.* Zondervan, Grand Rapids.

Walton, J.H. 2001. *Genesis.* In: NIV Application Commentary. Zondervan, Grand Rapids.

Walton, J.H. 2003. Creation. In: *Dictionary of the Old Testament: Pentateuch.* InverVarsity, Downers Grove, pp. 155-68.

Walton, J.H. 2003. Flood. In: *Dictionary of the Old Testament: Pentateuch.* InterVarsity, Downers Grove, pp. 315-26.

Walton, J.H. 2006. *Ancient Near Eastern Thought and the Old Testament:*

Introducing the Conceptual World of the Hebrew Bible. Baker, Grand Rapids.

Wenham, G.J. 1979. *The Book of Leviticus.* New International Commentary on the Old Testament. Eerdmans, Grand Rapids.

Wenham, G.J. 1987. *Genesis 1-15.* Word Biblical Commentary 1. Word, Waco.

Westermann, C., J.J. Scullion, trans. 1994. *Genesis 1-11: A Continental Commentary.* Fortress, Minneapolis.

Williams, P.J. 1997. What does *min* mean? *Creation Ex Nihilo Technical Journal* 11(3):344-52.

Wood, T.C., K.P. Wise, R. Sanders, and N. Doran. 2003. A Refined Baramin Concept. *Occasional Papers of the Baraminology Study Group,* 3:1-14.

3. Oceanic Islands and Their Plants as a Test of Post-Flood Speciation

ROGER W. SANDERS
CENTER FOR ORIGINS RESEARCH

3.1. Introduction

During the eighteenth and early nineteenth centuries at the height of Natural Theology's influence, biologists accepted species fixity and special creation of every living species without regard to the historicity of the Noachian Flood and how it might influence species distributions and origins (Wood 2008a). As a young naturalist, Darwin held the Natural Theology position until he visited the Galápagos Islands and contemplated the patterns of similarity in specimens collected there (Desmond & Moore 1994, pp. 159-160, 208). When he learned that multiple species per group existed in the archipelago, he realized that each species' closest relatives were on islands within the archipelago and that the next closest relatives, even if the island species were strikingly distinct from them, were on the American continents (Darwin 1839 pp.474-475; 1859 p.349, 478). This pattern led him to make a paradigm-shifting conclusion: God did not specially create each species in place but that a continental species immigrated and diverged into several species within the archipelago (Darwin, 1859 pp.350, 390-410). Conventional science continues to provide evidence in support of Darwin's conclusions: species do vary and change, the process now recognized as speciation.

Because the Bible does imply that change in composition of created kinds (i.e., baramins; see Wood et al. 2003; Wood 2008b)has occurred (Gen. 3, Gen. 6-9) and will occur (Isaiah 11; Rev. 20-21), speciation is consistent with Scripture. What is at odds with the biblical record, though, is the evolutionary extrapolation of speciation back in time such that there is a single great "Tree of Life." Therefore, the question for biblical neocreationists becomes, "How much speciation should we accept?" and "Does that amount of speciation corroborate the number of species estimated to compose baramins?" If we understood the limits of the air-breathing baramins with certainty, knowing how many modern species originated by speciation would be easy: Merely counting the known living and post-Flood fossil species in each baramin would provide an accurate assessment of speciation for those baramins. Although statistical baraminology has increased our confidence in assessing the limits of baramins, there are still problems with the holism and completeness of available data sets for most groups. In non-air-breathing baramins, the problem is compounded by greater uncertainty of the history of the baramin. Challenging questions include: How many intrabaraminic lineages survived the Flood? Can these lineages be recognized? How many individuals of each lineage survived?

The pattern of similarities of species in archipelago and adjacent mainland areas that Darwin observed is actually a very good rationale for understanding the capacity of intrabaraminic speciation. It gives us a baseline of species diversity and divergence that does not require previous knowledge of the limits of those species' holobaramin or phylogenetic relationships. Biogeographic proximity and underlying similariy (even in the face of radiation and divergence in particular traits) within archipelagos argues for both monobaraminic and monophyletic status of the group of similar species. Of course, for these conclusions to hold, the archipelagos must be post-Flood. Islands that predate the end of the Flood or broke from continents during post-Flood residual catastrophes could be inhabited by species that landed there from the Flood waters or that had already diversified on the continent prior to separation. Therefore, this study seeks to sample oceanic archipelagos to establish minimum amounts of speciation among higher plants that are consistent with a biblical history of the world.

Because species diversity on islands was first modeled mathematically in the equilibrium theory of island biogeography by MacArthur and Wilson (1967), one might ask if their model is directly relevant to the present study. They examined species immigration and extinction as affected by island size and distance from source areas under time constraints that exclude conventional evolutionary or speciation events. The present study incorporates the factors of island size and distance. Given the unknown history of all of these archipelagos, total immigration and extinction cannot be known. The number of introductions estimated for each of the archipelagos simply represents the supposed equilibrium—total immigration minus extinction. In addition, the present study incorporates, climate, number of islands, and time—age of the archipelagos, as well as time of introduction (for which, see discussion). Stuessy et al. (1998, pp. 129-130) reviewed the various critiques and modification to MacArthur and Wilson's model and provided refinements of their own to account for diversity on the Juan Fernández Islands. Yet they were not able to model speciation. They still needed to estimate the amount of speciation from outside phylogenetic studies. To counter this shortcoming, the present study incorporates published phylogenetic and baraminological studies and assumptions to estimate monophyly of congeneric endemic species in cases lacking published studies.

3.2. Methods

3.2.1. Estimation of biblical timescale in relation to conventional radiometric dates. In accord with Austin et al. (1994) and Wise (2009), the Flood/post-Flood boundary is accepted as the Cretaceous-Tertiary (Lower Paleocene) boundary (ca. 65 million radiometric years [Ma]). Wise (2005) pointed out that the lowest human fossils are *Homo erectus*, which occur on three continents from the Lower to Upper Pleistocene (1.8 Ma-10 Ka, fossils as recent as 18 Ka) sediments. Since these humans would have to be descended from people who dispersed from Babel (Gen. 11:1-9), this places Babel somewhat earlier, probably in the Lower to Upper Pliocene (5.3 to 1.8 Ma). The context of the Babel passages (Gen. 10-11) places the Babel event during the life of Peleg, who lived from 101 to 310 years after the Flood (Gen10: 25, 11: 10-19), placing the end of the Upper Miocene (5.3 Ma) between about 100 and 300 years after the Flood, and an upper limit of the Upper Pliocene at approximately 310 years after the Flood.

In his paper on mammal baramins in this volume, Wise (2009) uses evidence that the combined Lower and Upper Paleocene (65-55 Ma) took only a few years to few decades to complete and that the entire Lower Paleocene to Upper Eocene (65-34 Ma) took 8.6 times longer than the Lower Paleocene. Given the exponential (or at least decelerating) decrease in geologic activity after the Flood (Austin et al. 1997, slide 58; Austin 1998; Wise 2002, p. 210-212), I provisionally estimate the remaining Tertiary (Lower Oligocene [34 Ma] to Upper Pliocene,) as taking twice this long and the Pleistocene taking about three to four times as long. This accords well with the biblical record if the Pleistocene began at least by the death of Peleg 310 years after the Flood and ended with the drought of Joseph in the Near East (Gen. 41-47) at about 650 years after the Flood. Values ranging from 8 to 25 years for the Paleocene (4 to 12.5 years for the Lower Paleocene) yield a range of 102 to 315 years for completion of the entire Tertiary, a close match for the upper and lower limits of the end of the Tertiary set by the birth and death of Peleg. Comparison of this range with radiometric dates suggests that the Upper Pliocene (3.6 Ma) began in the range of about 95to 300 years after the Flood, the Lower Pliocene (5.3 Ma) began about 90 to 260 years after the Flood, the Upper Miocene (11.2 Ma) began about 80 to 250 years after, and the Middle Miocene (16.4 Ma) began about 70 to 210 years after. Other dates are less pertinent for oceanic islands. Admittedly these estimates are mathematically unsophisticated and geologically naive, but I believe they are reasonable enough to properly bracket the dates

Genesis Kinds

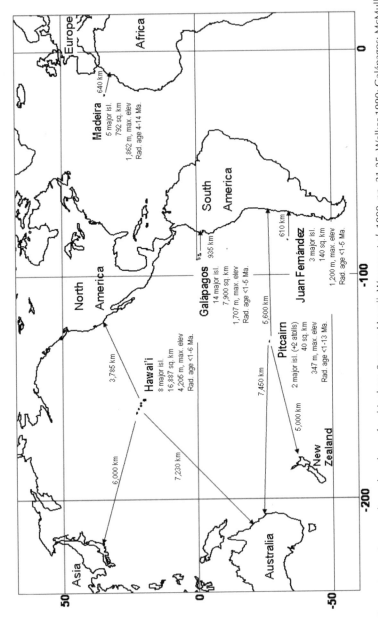

Figure 1. Comparisons of geography and geology of archipelgos. Sources: Hawaii: Wagner et al. 1990, pp. 21-25; Walker 1990; Galápagos: McMullen 1999, pp.12-14; Wood 2005, pp. 23-36; Madeira: Press & Short 1994, p. 1; Geldmacher et al. 2006; Klügel & Klein 2006; Juan Fernández: Pilger 1984; Stuessy et al. 1984;Yáñez et al. 2002; Pitcairn: Spencer 1989;.Göthesson 1997.

of interest and provide consistent comparisons for the purposes of this paper.

3.2.2. Choice of archipelagos sampled and control for physical factors. Choice of archipelagos is constrained largely by two factors—suitable floristic data and geologic and geographic suitability. Geologically, the archipelagos must have had a subaerial origin in the Neogene (Miocene or Pliocene) and must have been oceanic for their entire history. Geographically, they must have been sufficiently distant from continents (ca. 600 km or more) not to be easily colonized and must have sufficient relief to provide a diversity of habitats. The following archipelagos fulfill these criteria (see Figure 1): in the Pacific Ocean —Galápagos, Hawaii, Juan Fernández, Pitcairn, Samoa; in the Indian Ocean—Reunion; in the Atlantic Ocean— Madeira, Saint Helena, and Tristan da Cunha (references in Figure 1, as well as Baker *et al.* 1964; Gillot *et al.* 1994; Cronk 2000, p. 13.; Skogseld 2001; Koppers *et al.* 2008).

All of these archipelagos are less than 15 Ma (Middle Miocene, estimated 72-215 years post-Flood), mostly less than 6 Ma (Upper Miocene, estimated 88-255 years post-Flood). In most cases the mantle plumes, submarine rises, and other tectonic structures associated with the islands originated 110-50 Ma (Cretaceous to Oligocene), which places them in the last phases of the Flood or during the early post-Flood catastrophes, respectively. Furthermore, these islands are associated with lines of submarine seamounts that follow movements of ocean plates over magma plumes ("hot spots") that generate volcanoes. It is likely that any subaerial "proto-islands" generated between the end of the Flood and the appearance of the present islands were 1) not significantly closer to continental masses than the present islands, and 2) sufficiently volcanically active, eroded, and/or submerged to prevent continuous survival of plants groups during early post-Flood catastrophes.

Of these archipelagos, published floras are available for all but Tristan da Cunha. However, the flora for Reunion Island has not been updated for over 110 years, and the floras for St. Helena and Samoa lack sufficient comparative information. Because of inadequate floral information, these four island groups are excluded from the study.

In terms of qualitatively assessing the physical factors, the five included archipelagos are adequate. Hawaii, the Galápagos, Madeira, Juan Fernández, and Pitcairn differ in isolation and number of islands (correlated with size), allowing size comparisons among both isolated archipelagos (Hawaii *vs.* Pitcairn) and those closer to continents (Galápagos *vs.* Juan Fernández and Madeira), as well as isolation comparisons among similarly sized archipelagos (Hawaii *vs.* Galápagos; Pitcairn *vs.* Juan Fernández and Madeira)

3.2.3. Data Acquisition and Analysis. The following published floras and checklists were consulted (in descending order by size): Hawaii:

Wagner et al.1990; Galápagos: Wiggins & Porter (1971), Lawesson et al. (1987); Juan Fernández: Sanders (1979); Madeira: Press & Short (1994); and Pitcairn: Göthesson (1997). Because wind-blown spores might allow for dispersion that violates the assumptions of this study, pteridophytes, bryophytes, and lichens were not considered.

The initial data extracted from the published floras consisted of hand-tallied tables of all genera having native species. Each genus was scored for: 1) the total number of species present in the archipelago, 2) number of native but non-endemic species, 3) whether the genus is endemic, 4) number of endemic species, 5) number of endemic infraspecies (i.e., subspecies and varieties), 6) highest rank of endemic taxa, and 7), lower limit of natural introductions required to explain the presence of the species in the flora, i.e., one for each group of endemic species (in monophyletic groups of genera, only the first listed genus was scored for introductions as 1, the others as 0), and one for each native, non-endemic species.

To determine the lower limit of natural introductions, I consulted relevant phylogenies (Hicks & Mauchamp 1996; others summarized in Wagner et al 1990) and baraminological studies (Cavanaugh & Wood 2002; Wood 2005, pp. 159-162; Wood 2008b), collectively covering only 20 genera. Each monophyletic group, whether consisting of several endemic genera or only a species group within a widespread genus, was designated one introduction from which all the species of the group have speciated. In the remainder of genera, the number of introductions is based on the following assumptions:

1. It is assumed that all congeneric species endemic to an archipelago form a monophyletic group. Therefore, all of the endemic species of a particular genus are assumed to be the result of one natural introduction. Since more than one species of a given genus might have generated endemic species on an island, this assumption will tend to underestimate the number of introductions.

2. It is assumed that none of the native non-endemic species (i.e., species native both to the archipelago and external areas) of a particular genus gave rise to any other species of that genus on that island. Each native, non-endemic species is, thus, the result of a separate introduction from its respective source area. In other words, the ancestor of each monophyletic endemic group is assumed extinct on the mainland, on the island, or both. This acts to counterbalance the first assumption by overestimating the number of introductions.

3. It is assumed that species arise only once, not at two or more different times or in two or more different locations.

4. It is assumed that speciation equals the number of endemic species. That is, divergence points between current species and the

ancestor are not counted, and radiation directly from ancestor is assumed.

In the absence of detailed understanding of each genus, it is my hope that these assumptions will generate a good approximation of an average number of speciations per natural introduction that has actually taken place.

Within each plant family having one or more naturally occurring species, the initial data were summed to determine: 1) the number of native genera (genera having one or more naturally occurring species), 2) the number of native species (number of endemic species plus non-endemic native species), 3) the lower limit of natural introductions, 4) the number of endemic genera, 5) the number endemic species + infraspecies in endemic genera, 6) the number of endemic species, 7) the number of endemic infraspecies. This table, including the highest taxonomic rank of endemism is found in the Appendix. Species introduced or probably introduced by humans were excluded from consideration at this stage. During the data acquisition phase, it became clear that taxonomic ranking of infraspecies versus species is inconsistent among authors of floras. The fact remains that a subspecies or variety denotes character divergence that has occurred since colonization. Whether the populations bearing the divergences are reproductively isolated (and, hence, represent completed speciation as opposed to incipient speciation) is rarely known. The published rank is, thus, dependent on the opinion of the researcher, based on circumstantial evidence, and may be incorrect. Because of this, species and infraspecies numbers are combined and referred to as species henceforth in this analysis.

These data were summed for each archipelago to analyze four different aspects of divergence: the number of native and endemic genera and specieis and percent species endemism (Table 1); percent of families exhibiting endemism at the familial, generic, and species levels (Table 2); the total introductions and average number of endemic genera and species per introduction (Table 3); similar calculations for the subset of endemic genera plus the maximum number per introduction of endemic species for endemic genera (Table 4); and similar calculations for the subset of non-endemic genera containing endemic species plus the maximum number per introduction of those species (Table 5).

From the original data sheets, the number of endemic species per introduction was tallied by archepelago and frequency distributions were obtained for the following categories: all genera (i.e., endemic, non-endemic with endemic species, and non-endemic without endemic species), non-endemic genera with endemic species, and endemic genera. These calculations were graphed to compare among archipelagos the frequency of numbers of speciations per introduction for endemic genera (Figure 2) and for non-endemic genera (Figure 3). Within each

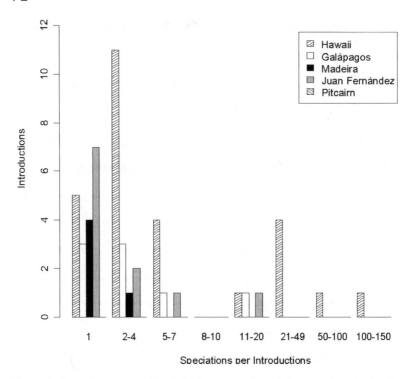

Figure 2. Comparison among islands in frequency of speciations per introduction for endemic genera.

island group, these calculations were graphed to compare the frequency of numbers of non-endemic species along with the numbers of endemic species per introduction for both endemic and non-endemic genera (Figures 4-8).

Data in Figure 1 and Tables 1-5 are graphed to examine the effect of physical parameters on the numbers of total minimum introductions per archipelago (Figure 9) and total speciations in each island flora (Figure 10). To determine if different methods of measuring introductions and speciations would show different degrees of correspondence with the physical parameters the following were plotted: introduction indices against archipelago size (Figures 11), isolation distance (Figure 12), and age of the oldest high island in each archipelago (Figure 13); number of native and endemic species against size (Figure 14), isolation distance (Figure 15), and age of the oldest high island in each archipelago (Figure 16); speciation indices (species per introductions) against archipelago size (Figure 17); and speciation per unit area against archipelago size (Figure 18).

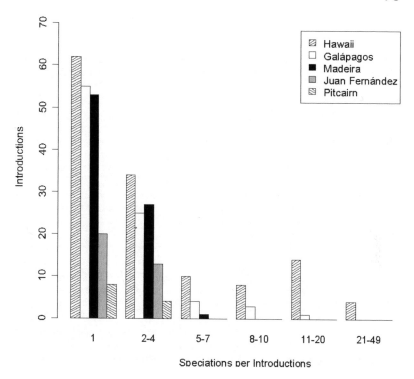

Figure 3. Comparison among islands in frequency of speciations per introduction for non-endemic genera.

3.3. Results

3.3.1. Overview. The bottom line of this study is that significant levels of speciation have been attained by certain groups on Hawaii (20 to 110 species from a single introductions), the Galápagos (19 spp.), and Juan Fernández (11 spp.). On each of these three archipelagos, the genera with the most endemic species are themselves endemic. That is, all the species from a given introduction show divergence to the point of no longer being recognizably part of a mainland genus (which presumably gave rise to the island genus). The majority of new species on all the islands, however, has not diverged to that level, and the island-unique species are classified within more-widespread continental genera. Speciation rates during the short time that oceanic islands have been available for habitation can reach 50 to 100 or more speciations per introduction; generally some cases reach rates of 5-20 speciations per introduction; and all the islands have at least some cases with 2 to 4 speciations per introduction. Widespread species that do not speciate after introduction are often those that occupy weedy, disturbed sites or coastal habitats that are likewise widespread in oceanic areas.

Hawaii

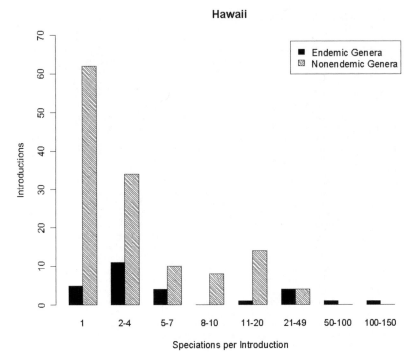

Figure 4. Frequency of number classes of speciation per introduction in Hawaiian Islands; 101 introductions led to no speciation.

Aside from this bottom line, the results suggest that the total number of natural introductions are not strongly positively corrected with any of the physical factors examined because competing factors interfere with one another. For example, introductions generally increase with decreasing distances from continents, although the small size of Juan Fernández may be contributing to its low number of introductions and/ or extant species (Figure 9 ,10, 11, 12; Tables 1, 3). On the other hand, speciation appears to be correlated with archipelago size, but not with other physical factors (Figure 10, 14-17; Tables 1-5).

3.3.2. Divergence in relation to genera. Divergence within genera is variable (Figures 3-8; Tables 1, 3-5). Many introductions have not lead to the divergence of new species, particularly on Madeira and Pitcairn, where nearly 85 percent of the floras consists of widespread species and only a few introductions have resulted in two to six new species. On the other hand, only 26 and 11 percent of the species of the Juan Fernández and Hawaii, respectively, are widespread. In general the widespread species are adapted to disturbed or coastal habitats, as opposed to the more unusual habitats that develop on islands away from the shoreline. About one-quarter of the introductions into the Galápagos and the

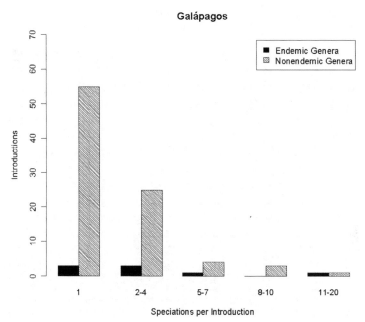

Figure 5. Frequency of number classes of speciation per introduction in the Galápagos Islands; 267 introductions led to no speciation.

majority of those of Hawaii and the Juan Fernández have led to at least one new species (Figure 4-6). Hawaii has the highest rates of speciation per introduction, with one introduction resulting in 110 new species (the Hawaiian lobelioid alliance, Campanulaceae), nine resulting in 22 to 54 new species, and 15 resulting in 10-20 new species. The highest rate of speciation in the Galápagos is 19 species per introduction (*Scalesia*, Asteraceae), whereas speciation rates are predominantly in the one-to-four species range. The same holds true for Juan Fernández where the maximum rate is 11 species per introduction (*Dendroseris*, Asteraceae). Interestingly, the frequency of speciation is weakly bimodal in Hawaii and the Juan Fernández.

Endemism at the generic level is much less than the specific (Table 1, 4), ranging from 0 to 18 percent. Conventional studies often refer to this as anagenesis, sequential modification of an unbranched lineage, as opposed to the branching into species, cladogensis. The values for Hawaii and Juan Fernández (16 and 18 percent, respectively) may be exceptional, and the typical value may be closer to 3 percent. In some cases, the species that originally diverged to represent a new genus undergoes no further speciation. However, the introductions leading to endemic genera usually have the highest rates of speciation per introduction.

3.3.3. Divergence in terms of speciation averages. Averaged over all introductions(Table 3), the number of endemic species ranges from

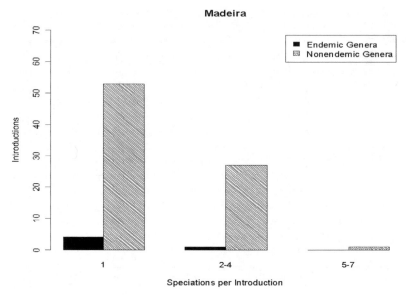

Figure 6. Frequency of number classes of speciation per introduction in Madeira archipelago; 597 introductions led to no speciation.

one for every five introductions (Madeira and Pitcairn) to almost four per introduction (Hawaii), varying by a factor of over 20. As expected the number of genera per introduction is much lower than for species (one in six introductions to one in 100 introductions, varying by factor of 16).

Averaged over only the introductions leading to speciation in non-endemic genera (Table 5), speciation ranges from nearly one-and-one-half (Pitcairn and Juan Fernández) to over 4 per introduction (Hawaii). Averaged over only introductions leading to speciation in endemic genera (Table 4), typically the values are higher—over 14 (Hawaii) to over 3 (Juan Fernández) per introduction. However, Madeira is low with only slightly over 1 per introduction, and Pitcairn has no endemic genera.

3.3.4. Divergence compared among families. (Table 2) The occurrence of endemic families on oceanic islands is rare. In the sample, only one endemic family, Lactoridaceae, occurs on only one archipelago, the Juan Fernández. This may be the only case of an endemic family on a young oceanic island and is discussed below under the Juan Fernández Islands.

Except for Pitcairn which lacks endemic genera, the number of families having immigrants that diverged to the level of endemic genus is generally low ranging from 5 to 26 percent of the families. On each island, the fraction of families in which immigrants diverged only to the level of species is much greater, ranging from 27 percent to 65 percent of the families in the flora.

Juan Fernández

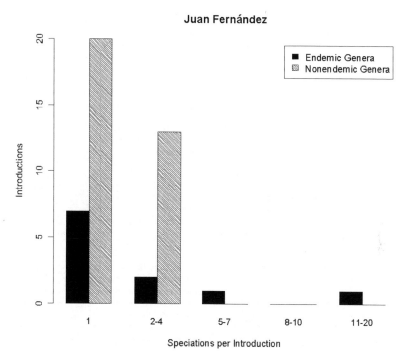

Speciations per Introduction

Figure 7. Frequency of number classes of speciation per introduction in the Juan Fernández Islands; 29 introductions led to no speciation.

3.3.5. Hawaii. Though well isolated in the central Pacific, Hawaii is the largest archipelago in area and number of islands and has the greatest topographic relief (Figure 1). Hawaii has the most species-rich flora and the highest percent endemism of the five archipelagos (34 endemic genera, Table 1). This appears to be related to the large average number of endemic species (and even genera) per introduction (over four each and one in eight, respectively), even though the number of introductions is moderate (Table 3). When the number of endemic species per introduction is limited to just endemic genera (Table 4), this number jumps to 14. The diversity at the family level is typical of islands with the largest number of families having endemic species as the highest taxonomic level. However, it may be unusual in having almost two-thirds of the families in this category and having almost one-fifth of the families having the genus rank as the highest endemic taxonomic level (Table 2).

3.3.6. Galápagos. This archipelago also has a large area and number of islands but is much closer to land than is the Hawaiian archipelago (Figure 1). The flora, level of endemism, and the number of families having endemic species (but not genera) are moderate in size (Table 1). It has the lowest percentage of families containing endemic genera, of which there are only eight (Table 2). The average number of

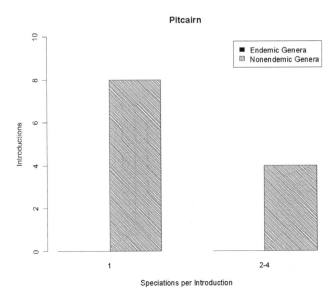

Figure 8. Frequency of number classes of speciation per introduction in the Pitcairn group; 69 introductions led to no speciation.

endemic species per introduction is rather low at about two for every three introductions (Table 3). When the number of endemic species per introduction is limited to just endemic genera, this number rises to over four per introduction (Table 4). The speciation level reaches 19 species in the endemic *Scalesia*.

3.3.7. Madeira. This archipelago is about the same distance from continents as is the Galápagos chain but is considerably smaller with three of its five islands being the remnants of a single ridge reaching only a few hundred meters elevation and covering less than 14 square kilometers together (Figure 1). The flora is fairly large, but the percent endemism, and the number of families having only endemic species are low (Tables 1, 2). The percentage of families containing endemic genera, of which there are only five, is also low. The average number of endemic species per introduction is only one in five introductions (Table 3). When the number of endemic species per introduction is limited to just endemic genera, this number amounts to only slightly over one per introduction (Table 4). Four endemic genera are represented by only one species, and the fifth only has two species. It is interesting to note that several non-endemic genera have as many as four endemic species and one (*Sinapodendron*, Brassicaceae) has six.

3.3.8. Juan Fernández. This archipelago is most comparable to Madeira in size and isolation; it has two main islands and a small third island (Figure 1). The flora is small at 112 species, but the percent endemism is amazingly high, including one endemic family (see in discussion of

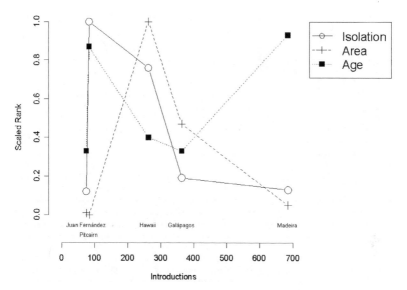

Figure 9. Relationship of the number of total natural introductions (estimated minimum) with the factors of isolation distance, archipelago size, and radiometric age of the oldest high island. To provide a comparable Y-axis, each of the factors are scaled by dividing by the highest value among the island groups.

the archipelago; Tables 1, 2). The percentage of families having endemic species (but not genera) is the highest of any archipelago, as is the percentage of families containing endemic genera, of which there are 11, almost one-third that of Hawaii. On average every introduction led to one endemic species, while every six resulted in an endemic genus (Table 3). When the number of endemic species per introduction is limited to just endemic genera, this number increases to nearly three per introduction (Table 4). The speciation level in *Dendroseris* (11 species) is comparable to that in the Galápagos.

3.3.9. Pitcairn. This archipelago is the smallest of the five examined. Two of the four islands in this archipelago are atolls and do not contribute to goals of the study. Henderson Island is a minimal high island, leaving Pitcairn as the only well developed, young high island. In terms of isolation, it is most comparable to Hawaii, which is the largest of the archipelagos (Figure 1). The flora is quite small with only 87 native species and also has the lowest amount of endemism (Table 1). No endemic genera are found there, and only about every fifth introduction has lead to an endemic species (Tables 3, 4). Other than the divergence of three endemic species arising from the introduction of *Bidens* (Asteraceae), speciation has not taken place in any groups beyond the divergence of the original endemic species (Table 5).

3.3.10. Size and number of islands. Size appears to be reasonably well constrained in the study (Figures 1). Hawaii and the Galápagos

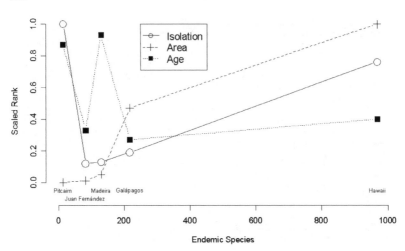

Figure 10. Relationship of the number of total number of speciations (i.e., total number of endemic species) with the factors of isolation distance, archipelago size, and radiometric age of the oldest high island. To provide a comparable Y-axis, each of the factors are scaled by dividing by the highest value among the island groups.

are more or less comparable with one another in size and number of islands, differing markedly from the smaller archipelagos, Madeira, Juan Fernández, and Pitcairn. Figures 9-11, 14, and 17 show that the size of the archipelagos is correlated at least with total number of endemic species, the total number of endemic species in non-endemic genera, the average number of introductions for all genera together, and average number of introductions for non-endemic genera. When speciation *per unit area* is compared among archipelagos (Figure18) it appears that speciation rates are nearly uniform on all but the smallest islands, where other factors may be confounding the results (see below).

3.3.11. Dispersal distance. Hawaii and Pitcairn are comparable in isolation distance from the continents and in contrast sharply from the other three archipelagos (Figure 1). Control appears to be adequate to show that dispersal distance is not well-correlated with either speciation or number of introductions (Figures 12, 15). If Juan Fernández had between 400 and 650 introductions, then dispersal distance would be correlated with introductions, suggesting that other confounding factors possibly are involved (see below).

3.3.12. Age. The most eroded (and presumably oldest) high islands of each archipelago date from less than 4 to 14 Ma (Figures 1, 13, 16). The less eroded (and presumably younger) islands date from about 1 Ma or less. In terms of biblical chronology this difference is not great (probably no more than a few centuries, based on the above calculations). Age is not well correlated with numbers of introductions (Figures 13) or speciations (Figure 16). However, a number of confounding factors, such as geological

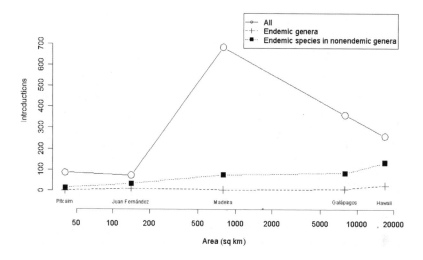

Figure 11. Relationship of various introduction indices with archipelago size ($\log_{10}$ area). Indices include total natural introductions (estimated minimum), number of introductions leading to endemic genera, and number of introductions leading to non-endemic genera containing endemic species.

or tectonic differences, may influence these values, and greater control is needed, either by a larger sample of islands or comparisons made with data from the same archipelago.

3.3.13. Climate patterns. All archipelagos are tropical, and all archipelagos have sufficient topographic relief to have portions that are arid and some that are humid or even wet (Figure 1). The Galápagos are more arid than the others because they are bathed by the cold Humboldt Current, but humid conditions are developed in the upper elevations. Madeira and Juan Fernández are at subtropical latitudes and experience near-freezing cool temperatures at higher altitudes. The Juan Fernández Islands are across the Humboldt Current from South America but are not directly bathed by it (Arana 1979; Sanders *et al.* 1987). Hawaii, Pitcairn, and Madeira are surrounded by predominantly warm waters. All islands are influenced by the prevailing trade winds. Control for these factors would require a much larger sample size, but possible effects are discussed below. However, it is clear that differences in climate and circulation could have a large impact on the number of introductions and speciations.

3.4. Discussion

3.4.1. Hawaii. Due to its large size, number of islands, diversity of habitats, and isolation, the Hawaiian archipelago provides a benchmark by which to compare other archipelagos. The number of introductions is moderate, possibly because isolation distance may be counteracting

Genesis Kinds

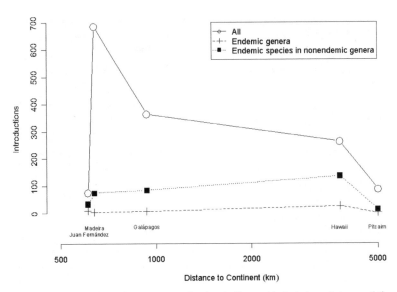

Figure 12. Relationship of various introduction indices with isolation distance of the archipelagos. Indices include total natural introductions (estimated minimum), number of introductions leading to endemic genera, and number of introductions leading to non-endemic genera containing endemic species.

Hawaii's large area and number of islands. However, the amount of divergence following introduction is remarkable with four notable plant radiations of 41 species (silversword alliance, Asteraceae), 47 species (*Pelea*, Rutaceae), 54 species (*Phyllostegia* alliance, Lamiaceae), and 110 species (Hawaiian lobelioid alliance; Campanulaceae).

Appealing to the longevity of the Hawaiian Island hotspot and the frequency with which volcanoes along it emerge from the sea, several authors have posited that the flora's colonizers immigrated to now drowned islands (See Price & Clague 2002; Nepokroeff *et al.* 2003). However, Price and Clague calculated the sizes of previous islands and rates of erosion to determine whether colonists to those islands could persist and migrate to the current islands before their habitats disappeared and they went extinct. They then compared the radiometric age of those islands with molecular clock dates for the most recent common ancestors of endemic groups of plants and animals. They concluded that all flowering plants except the Hawaiian lobelioid alliance immigrated to Hawaii after the current high islands emerged about 6 Ma ago. They proposed that the lobelioid ancestor arrived on Gardner Island about 15 Ma ago. Given the assumptions underlying molecular clocks, this conventional date must be taken cautiously. Even so, a date of 15 Ma translates to fairly late in post-Flood times under assumptions of biblical history. This excludes the possibility that the Hawaiian lobelioids landed on the early proto-islands

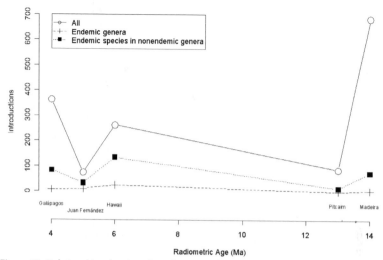

Figure 13. Relationship of various introduction indices with radiometric age of the oldest high island. Indices include total natural introductions (estimated minimum), number of introductions leading to endemic genera, and number of introductions leading to non-endemic genera containing endemic species.

of the Hawaiian archipelago immediately as the Flood waters regressed (see also under "Rates and patterns of diversification").

Another interesting observation that further supports the young age of the Hawaiian biota is that there are no coral reefs in Hawaii-Emperor chain older than 35 Ma (Grigg 1997). This apparently records a significant climatic and biotic shift in the ocean environments in the Middle Tertiary (Upper Eocene), which equates to between 40 and 100 years after the Flood. This suggests that now-drowned "proto-islands" in the mid-Pacific and perhaps elsewhere were not suited at that time to habitation by the organisms there now.

Floristic affinities of the Hawaiian Islands are also intriguing. Today the predominant ocean and wind currents arrive from the northeast, yet only about 20 percent of the flora is related to North American (including the Arctic). About 50 percent is related to Indo-Malaya, Australasia, and Polynesia (Good, pp. 212-213). This is evidence that the Hawaiian Islands were populated by colonizers that benefitted from transport means not currently available.

3.4.2. Galápagos. The Galápagos has a moderately sized flora and level of endemism, and the number of introductions is moderate, though somewhat higher than for the Hawaiian Islands. While it is tempting to relate the higher number of introductions to the shorter dispersal distance, one must ask why there are so many fewer introductions than in Madeira. Clearly a number of competing factors are involved, possibly including the somewhat younger age and the less favorable climate. Also given the lack of nearby tall seamounts on the Cocos and Carnegie Ridges,

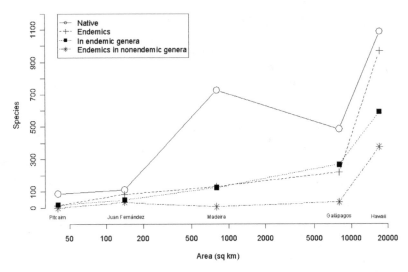

Figure 14. Relationship of the number of native species and various indices of endemic species with archipelago size ($\log_{10}$ area). Indices include total of endemic species in the flora, number of endemic species in endemic genera, and number endemic species in non-endemic genera.

one cannot appeal to colonization of earlier "proto-islands". The aridity also has played a role in attenuating the habitat diversity, which may be related to species diversity.

Floristic affinities of the Galápagos are strongly American, including both western South America and the Mesoamerican portion of North America.

3.4.3. Madeira. Madeira is the most anomalous of the archipelagos in terms of high numbers of introductions and size of flora, as well as low endemism. The two most distinctive features of Madeira, compared to the other two near-continent archipelagos, Galápagos and Juan Fernández, are age and favorable currents. Its oldest island (Porto Santo), now much eroded, is about three times older than the eldest one of the Galápagos. Like the Galápagos, the Madeiran archipelago has no nearby seamounts that could serve as "proto-islands."

Even though the recent literature gives an age of 4-5 Ma for Madeira, the older literature and secondary sources (e.g., Press & Short, 1994) give an age of 60-70 Ma. This discrepancy may be explained by recent geochemical findings. Geldmacher and Hoernle (2000) report that lava making up the island contains recycled, unaltered Paleozoic ocean floor. This results in elevated levels of radiogenic lead isotopes in Madeira compared to lavas generated by typical mantle plumes.

The ocean current bathing Madeira is warm and is accompanied by trade winds. Thus, the climate is favorable for establishment. Combined with the dissected topography and elevation, the climate produces a

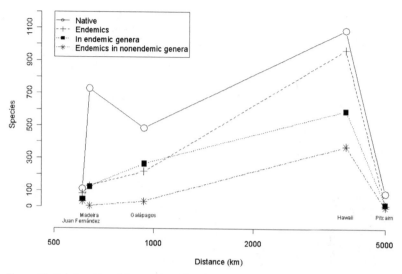

Figure 15. Relationship of the number of native species and various indices of endemic species with isolation distance of the archipelagos. Indices include total of endemic species in the flora, number of endemic species in endemic genera, and number endemic species in non-endemic genera.

diversity of habitats. Perhaps these sufficiently explain the anomalously high number of introductions (that have survived) in Madeira.

The low level of endemism is more difficult to explain. Perhaps this is related somewhat to the older age of the archipelago, redundant immigration via the more favorable migration route and arrival conditions, and/or early competition of numerous mainland colonizers such that selection was not greatly relaxed (see discussion of ecological factors below in "Rates and patternsof diversification"). This could prevent the expression of novel genetic combinations. The flora is strongly related to the Mediterranean and the remainder of Macaronesia (Good, p 197).

3.4.4. Juan Fernández. The Juan Fernández Islands are distinctive because, despite their small size and flora, they have a remarkable degree of endemism and level of speciation. Like, the Galápagos and Madeira, it is unlikely that the present flora could have immigrated from much older "proto-islands." Furthermore, a significant portion of the flora (over 10 percent) has affinity with Australasia and Polynesia (Stuessy et al. 1998). The major endemic genera are probably of American origin. The low number of introductions and high disparity with the American relatives may be largely a consequence of the Humboldt Current, which flows between the islands and South America, acting as a dispersal barrier, making the archipelago effectively more isolated. Another factor that may be distinctive for Juan Fernández is the effect of past erosion and subsidence. It is thought that the major island covers only about 1/20 the area it did when it first emerged from the ocean surface (Stuessy et al. 1998,

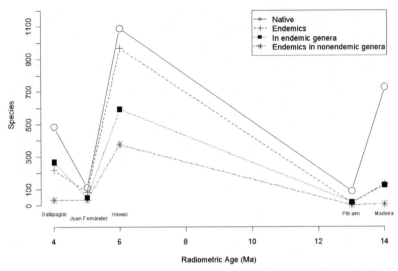

Figure 16. Relationship of the number of native species and various indices of endemic species with radiometric age of the oldest high island. Indices include total of endemic species in the flora, number of endemic species in endemic genera, and number endemic species in non-endemic genera.

pp. 130-132) . Thus, extinction may instead account for the anomalously small flora and number of introductions, while concentration of endemics may account for the high level of speciation per introduction.

The endemic family, Lactoridaceae, does not reflect divergence to the family level on the archipelago. This family has only one known species. It is morphologically isolated and thought to be primitive by conventional biology. Fossilized pollen discovered in Upper Cretaceous strata in Africa (Zavada & Benson 1987) indicates that the family (and possibly the species) is a pre-Flood relict that survived the Flood, landed on a southern hemisphere continent, migrated to the Juan Fernández, then was extirpated from the continent, surviving only on the archipelago.

3.4.5. Pitcairn. As the smallest archipelago and lacking endemic genera and no multispecies divergences, Pitcairn marks a lower bound for the study of island speciation. It is important because, being as isolated as Hawaii, it allows cross comparisons of size and degree of isolation that the other smaller archipelagos do not afford. Its flora is strongly Polynesian in character and shares some species that are found elsewhere only in the Austral Island archipelago and/or Easter Island. It is somewhat different from the other small archipelgos and more like Hawaii in having older islands that have matured into atolls. Therefore it is possible that introductions and speciation could extend back closer to the end of the Flood. If so, however, the species resulting from such hypothetical introductions apparently have not survived to the present. The low degree of endemism and speciations correlate well with the

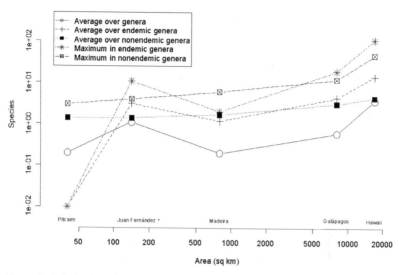

Figure 17. Relationship of the $\log_{10}$ speciation indices of endemic species with archipelago size ($\log_{10}$ area). Indices include: all endemic species averaged over all natural introductions, endemic species in endemic genera averaged over introductions leading to endemic genera, endemic species in non-endemic genera averaged over introductions leading to non-endemic genera. Original Pitcairn values of 0.00 changed to 0.01 in order to be converted to plottable log value.

small size. The fact that there have been dispersal either to or from the Austral Islands, as well as Polynesia, suggest that Pitcairn's isolation is not a major factor in limiting introductions. Conversely, the low numbers may simply reflect extinction as the surface area and habitat diversity shrank. Therefore, it is not clear with which factors the lack of speciation is correlated.

3.4.6. Species diversity and amount of speciation. The amount of speciation on oceanic islands is variable, apparently due to the interplay of parameters (barriers to dispersal, amenability of climate, diversity of habitats, size and number of islands, redundancy of introduction, anomalous community composition, process of community development and ecosystem webs, and effect of addition sequence on competition) that differ from one archipelago to the next. However, the variation is narrow (up to 110 speciations/introduction as compared to all potential speciations in a baramin of large size, e.g., the grass baramin with about 10,000 species; Wood 2002) and consistent with the neocreationist view that diversification to produce new species within baramins since creation has occurred (Wood & Murray 2003; Wise 2002, p. 218, 2006). The evidence here is that given an area suitable for diversification, at least some plants are capable of diverging into 100 or more species from a common ancestor. Because diversification from one founding ancestral population into 5 to 20 species has occurred on most of the islands

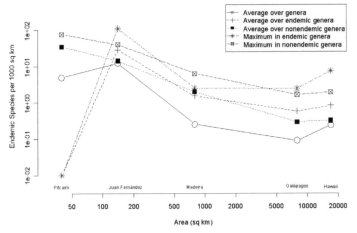

Figure 18. Relationship of the $\log_{10}$ indices of speciation per 1000 square kilometers with archipelago size ($\log_{10}$ area). Indices include: all endemic species averaged over all natural introductions, endemic species in endemic genera averaged over introductions leading to endemic genera, endemic species in non-endemic genera averaged over introductions leading to non-endemic genera. Original Pitcairn values of 0.00 changed to 0.01 in order to be converted to plottable log value.

in this study and in a wide array of families, it may be concluded that diversification is the norm. Wood (2003) and Wood and Murray (2003, pp. 139-143, 173, 178-182) propose a model of intrabaraminic diversification that uses 1) the information resident in or available to a few individuals composing a founding population and 2) mechanisms endowed by the Creator at creation. As applied to founders of monobaramins and rapid diversification on islands over decades or a few centuries, these data are consistent with that model.

Comparisions among archipelagos suggest that speciations per introduction per unit area are more or less uniform (Figure 18). The values are similar for the larger islands but the smaller the area the more erratic the values become. As noted above, Juan Fernández probably was originally about 20 times larger than now (Stuessy et al. 1998). Plotting with non-log values of species per unit area (Figure 19) makes it easy to see that when the speciation values are adjusted for original size of the islands, this would bring the values for Juan Fernández more in line with the other archipelagos. As suggested above, the low number of introductions and endemic species on Pitcairn may be due to extinction, which likewise could be associated with loss of surface area. Therefore, adjusting Pitcairn to former size may also bring it in line with the larger islands. Given the number of mature islands in Hawaii, the original size would have to be enlarged by several fold, reducing its values even closer to the constant value line. The Galápagos are mostly immature and probably were not much larger than now. Based on the bathymetric map in Geldmacher and Hoernle (2000), Madeira was probably only

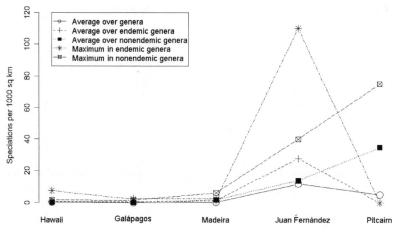

Figure 19. Relationship of the indices of speciation per 1000 square kilimeters with archipelago size rank. Indices include: all endemic species averaged over all natural introductions, endemic species in endemic genera averaged over introductions leading to endemic genera, endemic species in non-endemic genera averaged over introductions leading to non-endemic genera.

about twice its present size. If these data are meaningful, this suggests that above a certain size threshold speciation is not affected by size but is uniform (at about 0.2 to 2 speciations per 1000 sq. km.) and is controlled primarily by other parameters.

Another issue noted by Darwin and closely related to amount of speciation is the disparity between the island descendants and the closest mainland relatives. Carlquist (1974) describes cases for the major archipelagos (e.g., the tree habit of *Scalesia* of Galápagos, and *Dendroseris* and *Robinsonia* of Juan Fernández compared to their herbaceous and low shrubby relatives in South America, not to mention marine iguanas and giant tortoises), and Stuessy *et al.* (2006) documents its significance in island biotas and ascribes it to anagenesis. Wise (this volume) suggests that saltational events may explain disparity better. Although more difficult to quantify than counting endemic species, its occurrence is significant and needs to be addressed in neocreationist diversification models.

3.4.7. Rates and patterns of diversification. The question then is: How do these amounts relate to the total expected since the Flood?

Ever since Wise (1990) introduced the concept of the "creationist orchard" of multiple phylogenies, one for each baramin, to explain current biodiversity, speciation has generally been recognized by young-age creationists. Wood and Murray (2003, pp. 173-176) further pointed out a rapid decay in diversification after the Flood. This is based on biblical evidence (all but one pair of horse-kind individuals and one pair of camel-kind individuals killed in Flood; modern species of horse and camel kinds diversified by time of Abram, about 375 years after Flood) and baraminological evidence (crossability among all members of the

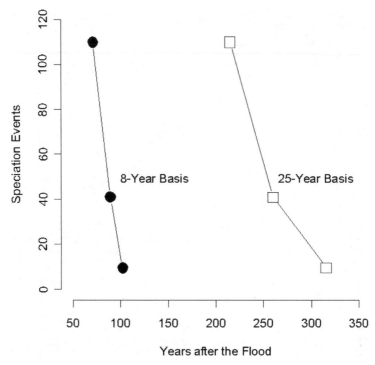

Figure 20. Relationship of number of speciation events in certain Hawaiian plant genera with estimated time of introduction to Hawaii after the Flood. Speciation events are the minimum (one per species) needed to account for endemic species in monophyletic groups for which molecular clock age has been estimated. The two curves give the lower and upper bound of time of the events based on the duration of the Paleocene (see Methods) to obtain lower and upper bounds of the end of the Tertiary to coincide with the birth and death of Peleg.

horse family, as well as all members of the camel family; morphological continuity among living and fossil members of the horse family, and likewise for the camel family). Thus, all members of the horse family are believed to be part of the horse baramin (Cavanaugh *et al.* 2003) and all members of the camel family, the camel baramin (Wood et al. 1999). As a result, Wood and Murray proposed that, in the diversification of most baramins after the Flood, each followed a starburst pattern instead of the growth of a fruit tree. That is, organisms experienced rapid diversification, exponential decline in diversification rates, and subsequent species stasis beginning approximately 300 to 400 years after the flood.

One might argue these proposed patterns would be affected if an alternate model of the Flood/post-Flood boundary is accepted, such as Upper Miocene or Pliocene as advocated by Oard (1990). However, the only effect would be reducing numbers of species within baramins that have to be explained in post-Flood times. This would effect some families, e.g., the horse family (Cavanaugh et al. 2003) with high proportions of fossil species more than other baramins, such as the grass family (Wood 2002) or even cat baramin (Robinson & Cavanaugh 1998) (see Wood 2006, 2008b).

When island speciation is compared to this larger model of diversification, we see that it forms a test of the exponential decline hypothesis. For example, we can test it with the daisy family, Asteraceae, on these islands. If the baramin is close to the family level, then the Galápagos sunflowers (*Scalesia* 19 species), Hawaiian silverswords (41 spp.), and Juan Fernández tree dandelions (*Dendroseris* 11 spp.) and groundsels (*Robinsonia* 7 spp.), all belong to the same baramin, the Asteraceae (25,000 species). In a preliminary baraminological study of the Asteraceae, Cavanaugh and Wood (2002) were unable to find morphological discontinuity separating the tribes Heliantheae and Helenieae from each other or from the representatives of the outgroup tribes, Senecioneae, and Eupatorieae, all of which belong to a much larger subfamily, the Asteroideae. This suggests that the entire subfamily with about 15,000 species, is in one baramin. Since conventional biologists now generally lump the Helenieae into the Heliantheae, only one inclusive tribe was sampled well in the Cavanaugh and Wood study. Therefore, even if one drops the baramin to the tribal level in the Asteraceae, the numbers of species in each tribe of the respective island groups is 4,000 Heliantheae (the 41 Hawaiian silverswords and 19 Galápagos sunflowers), 3,000 Senecioneae (the 7 Juan Fernánadez groundsels), and 2,300 Lactuceae (the 11 Juan Fernánadez dandelions). In another example, the 110 Hawaiian lobelioids belongs to the family Campanulaceae with 1800 species (and the lobelia subfamily of 1200 species).

Thus, conceivably 25,000 species of Asteraceae could have diversified from one survivor (i.e., hermaphoditic individual or single clutch of propagules) of the Flood, although it is more likely that several to many survivors of the Asteraceae established after the Flood so the number of subsequent speciations from each survivor may be only in the few hundreds or thousands, possibly smaller if the holobaramin is closer to the tribal level in the Asteraceae. Wood (2008b) summarizes the known plant mono- and holobaramins. Of the 25 families examined, the holobaramin coincides closely with the family boundaries in 13, above the family level in 4, but below the family in none. Several large families were examined, but the data showed only that the holobaramin was above the tribal level. Based on these ideas, the diversification of a few hundreds to few thousands current plant species (not counting extinct or fossil species) from individual ancestral Flood survivors within 400 years after the Flood is certainly conceivable. Since the numbers diversifying on oceanic islands are less (up to about 100), the island data support the hypothesis of exponential decay in diversification immediately following the Flood.

The molecular clock data cited for Hawaii (Price & Clague 2002) is of interest in this regard. The Hawaiian lobelioids with 110 species supposedly was the first extant plant group to radiate, having been introduced on Gardner Island about 15 Ma. All remaining Hawaiian radiations of plants resulted from introductions to the current high islands of 6 Ma or younger. However, these remaining plant groups can be subdivided based on molecular clock age. The silversword alliance with 41 species is dated at 5 Ma, and the remainder, with an average of 9.5 species, has an average date of 2.2 Ma. Based on the biblical age equivalencies calculated above, the lobelioids arrived roughly between 72 and 215 years after the Flood, the silverswords between 90 and 260 years after the Flood, and the remaining groups between 102 and 315 years after the Flood. None of the speciations date from post-Pleistocene (i.e., post-patriarchal) times. When plotted (Figure 20) these data yield a broad band of potential post-Flood immigration dates suggesting an exponential decrease curve in support of the Wood and Murray's hypothesis. Of the other radiations for which there are no molecular clock data, a few are in the 40 to 50 species range (e.g., phyllostegia alliance with 54 species), but most of the radiations on the younger islands range from 5 to 20 species. Likewise, speciation values of endemic groups from the remaining islands are in the 3 to 19 range and are also consistent with the hypothesis. The plot appears to be in the exponential phase of decrease; extrapolation back to the end of the Flood further suggests that intrabaraminic speciation in the Lower Tertiary could be in the hundreds or thousands and that current speciation is nearly nil.

Another factor that needs to be studied by creation biologists is the establishment of ecological relationships on the ability of groups to speciate. Island biotas do not arrive as intact ecosystem units. Rather, discordant elements arrive from multiple sources over time. These colonizers must adjust to both the previous immigrants and those arriving later. New ecological interactions must be established. This suggests that for early arrivals selection and competition are greatly relaxed. Stored genetic potential to occupy habitats unusual for the group (such as forest-dominating tree traits expressed in otherwise herbaceous groups) possibly can be realized without interference. Perhaps these atypical habitats or island-building catastrophes put the organism's genome under stress as suggested by Wood (2003) and Wood and Murray (2003, p. 180). Furthermore these groups have the longest time available for diversification and exhibit the greatest levels of speciation and disparity. The next groups arriving experience more constraints from selection, competition, and ecological interaction establishment. There would also be less severe catastrophes. Environmental stress would be time-dependent over short time frames. If there is some intrinsic time-controlled factor inhibiting diversification (Wood 2003; Wood & Murray 2003, pp. 174-176), this would exhibit greater control on the later groups. These are the groups that should have one to several, perhaps up to 20, endemic species developed, depending on the size and climate of the archipelago. One would expect that for late arrivals, well established ecological networks, intense selection and competition, and increasingly developed, time-dependent inhibitors of diversification would all work to prevent speciation. Thus the successful immigrants should be widespread oceanic species adapted to disturbed, weedy sites or coastal strands.

Even greater diversification rates would be involved if there has been substantial extinction in the past. Among the horses, for example, there are many times more extinct species than living species (Cavanaugh et al. 2003). If there have been a similar number of extinctions among the plants, this would further increase the number of actual speciation events from each founder on these islands. Extinction might also make it difficult to distinguish different patterns of diversification and numbers of introductions. What appears to be dramatic anagenetic or saltational divergence, for example, might actually be cladogenesis (where all but one descendant becomes extinct). At this time, I see no way to estimate the number of extinctions in the plants on the islands under study.

Irrespective of rates of diversification deduced from baraminological studies or geological placements of the end of the Flood, rates of plant diversification on islands are high. We must accept that post-Flood diversification of a plant baramin can exceed 100 species.

3.4.8. Post-Flood Geology and Geography. Much of the discussion in conventional biogeography centers on the geology and geography during the evolutionary history of particular groups. Likewise, neocreation biologists should incorporate estimates of post-Flood geology and geography into studies of post-Flood diversification and biogeography. Based on the model of Catastrophic Plate Tectonics (CPT) (Austin et al. 1994), most continental land masses were near their current positions by the end of the Flood. However, a limited amount of plate tectonic activity occurred at reduced rates following the Flood, as well as a considerable amount of vertical tectonics and volcanism. Also hypothesized for post-Flood times are high rainfall rates. Therefore, unlike present islands which are largely experiencing geological stasis, "proto-islands" would have developed, eroded, and subsided at higher rates.

Specifically for island biotas, one has to understand where archipelagos were located in relation to the continents, how many islands were subaerial and the area above sea level, and how the post-Flood catastrophes and temperature affected ocean and wind currents. This type of detail has not been worked out but is greatly needed.

3.4.9. Modes of disperal. Conventional biogeography also focuses on dispersal mechanisms—primarily random long-distance dispersal and vicariance. For neocreation biologists, these conventional mechanisms are inadequate because of lack of time and the near completion of continental movement by the end of the Flood.

Wise and Croxton (2003) proposed a neocreation model for post-Flood dispersal based on subcontinental-sized debris rafts that would persist for many decades after the Flood. These rafts would be propelled by the ocean and wind currents and would circulate and repeatedly carry organisms from one land mass to subsequent ones along the circuit. Also, deterioration of the rafts would be exponential—little change at first for several decades, then increasingly rapid disintegration. Thus, rafts initially could carry large land animals but later (when present oceanic islands emerged) could only support smaller ones or ones able to survive on less stable rafts (e.g., salt/desiccation-resistant reptiles and birds, the latter likely to carry seeds both externally and internally) (see also Wood & Murray 2003, pp. 196-201).

Taken together, patterns of speciation, geological/geographical history, and raft dispersal should give a clearer picture of island biogeography as each factor is better modeled. In particular, the floristic connections of Hawaii and the Juan Fernández to the southwestern Pacific need to be explained better. The transequatorial dispersal from far distant continents and other islands to Hawaii may relate to raft dispersal on ocean currents active in the Upper Miocene post-Flood decades. At this time, however, these currents are poorly understood. The weaker southwestern Pacific influence on the Juan Fernández may be related in part to deteriorated rafts on more modern-like currents in the Pliocene decades. The lack of similar floristic connections in the Galápagos may be related to the more arid conditions that would not support most tropical Asian, Australian, or Polynesian plants. Later introductions into archipelagos after the rafts had disappeared would then have to depend on long-distance dispersal (ocean drift, wind-blown, or carried by ocean birds or storm-diverted land birds). Therefore getting a clear picture of the timing of geological events is critical to understanding pattern and subsequent history of the introduction of organisms into archipelagos.

3.5. Conclusions

3.5.1. General conclusions. Plants on oceanic islands give us a window into past earth history from possibly as little as 70 years (Lower-Middle Miocene under a rapid scenario or as late as 210 years under a slower scenario) to perhaps 650 years (end of Pleistocene related to Joseph's drought) after the Flood. During that time period, many groups of flowering plants responded to introduction into oceanic islands by diverging from the founding colonizer and diversifying into new groups of species, new genera, or even into groups of related genera, sometimes producing over 40 or even over 100 new endemic species from a single ancestral species. Many of these endemic genera diverged dramatically from the mainland relatives either prior to diversifying or during an early phase of diversifying when most new species went extinct.

The number of introductions is weakly correlated with size and isolation distance, while speciation is much more strongly correlated with size and possibly with isolation. Neither is correlated with age of the islands but rather with time of introduction. When evaluated per unit area, speciation may be more or less uniform regardless of habitat and climatic diversity, which are required for selectionist mechanisms to act.

Thus, the data presented here supports "starburst speciation" of Wood and Murray (2003). Introduction into the islands probably involved modes not available today, although larger islands would intercept more colonists. Introductions to the islands appear to have triggered (by extrinsic environmental stress?) a certain level of activity of speciation mechanisms (intrinsic genomic design and regulation?). In a short time frame, the duration and decay of environmental stress and the genomic mechanisms and regulation would be the major parameters determining speciation rates. Averaged over any given window of time, the speciation rates per unit area should be roughly the same in different archipelagos exhibiting similar volcanic catastrophes and initially barren habitats. Furthermore, because oceanic islands occur relatively late in the decreasing post-Flood catastrophes, we should expect the post-Flood patterns of deteriorating rates of speciation and deteriorating chances for raft dispersal. Likewise, the amounts of migration and speciation on oceanic islands should be relatively minor compared to that experienced by actual Flood survivors; the data are consistent with this. We would expect the monobaramins on the continents to which the island groups belong to have undergone even greater rates of speciation and world-wide dispersal immediately following the Flood and prior to the advent of the archipelagos. Certainly one does not need to expect for plants that all species in a holobaramin resulted from speciation from a single ancestral pair because multiple surviving propagule clusters or even self-fertile individuals could found entire monophyletic monobaramins at distant locations on the early post-Flood continents. Even so, speciation from each of the founding Flood survivors could number in the hundreds or even thousands in some groups.

3.5.2. Future Prospects. Research into speciation and diversification of plants and other organisms both on oceanic islands and on continental areas will be improved as geology, climates, and ecosystem establishment are modeled in greater detail. Also, detailed studies identifying holobaramins and monophyletic groups to which these organisms belong should better clarify the rates and patterns of speciation. Therefore, future research should address these shortcomings in attempts to more fully understand the role of diversification in creation biology.

Acknowledgments

I am indebted Michelle Bleikamp for recording data from the floras of Hawaii, the Galápagos, Madeira, and the Juan Fernández. Various students in my course on biological origins scanned floras for digital retrieval. I thank the Bryan College library for interlibrary loans. Todd Wood, Kurt Wise, Paul Garner offered encouragement and criticism of the earlier drafts.

References

Arana, P.M. 1979. *Juan Fernandez Islands (Chile): Living Marine Resources and Fishery Perspective.* MS. Thesis, Oregon State University, Corvallis. Accessed July 16, 2008, at https://ir.library.oregonstate.edu/dspace/bitstream/1957/6401/1/Patricio_M_Arana.ocr.pdf.

Austin, S.A., J.R. Baumgardner, D.R. Humphreys, A.A. Snelling, L. Vardiman, and K.P. Wise. 1994. Catastrophic plate tectonics: A global flood model of earth history. In: Walsh, R.E., ed. *Proceedings of the Third International Conference on Creationism.* Creation Science Fellowship, Pittsburgh, PA, pp. 609-621.

Austin, S.A., J.R. Baumgardner, D.R. Humphreys, A.A. Snelling, L. Vardiman, and K.P. Wise. 1997. *Catastrophic Plate Tectonics: A Global Flood Model of Earth History* (Slide Collection Version 1.2). Creation Education Materials, Santee, CA.

Austin, S.A. 1998. The declining power of post-Flood volcanoes. *Impact* 302: i-iv.

Baker, P.E., I.G. Gass, P.G. Harris, and R.W. Le Maitre. 1964. The Volcanological Report of the Royal Society Expedition to Tristan da Cunha, 1962. *Philosophical Transactions of the Royal Society of London. Series A, Mathematical and Physical Sciences* 256: 439-575.

Carlquist, S. 1974. *Island Biology.* Columbia University Press, New York, NY.

Cavanaugh, D.P. and T.C. Wood. 2002. A baraminological analysis of the tribe Heliantheae *sensu lato* (Asteraceae) using Analysis of Pattern (ANOPA). *Occasional Papers of the BSG* 1: 1-11.

Cavanaugh, D.P., T.C. Wood, and K.P. Wise. 2003. Fossil Equidae: A monobaraminic, stratomorphic series. In: Ivey, R.L., Jr., ed. *Proceedings of the Fifth International Conference on Creationism.* Creation Science Fellowship, Pittsburgh, PA, pp. 143-153.

Cronk, Q.C.B. 2000. *The Endemic Flora of St. Helena.* Anthony Nelson, Shropshire, England.

Desmond, A and J. Moore. 1994. *Darwin: The Life of a Tormented Evolutionist,* paperback ed. Norton & Co., New York, London.

Geldmacher, J., and K. Hoernle. 2000. The 72 Ma geochemical evolution of the Madeira hotspot (eastern North Atlantic): Recycling of Paleozoic (□500 Ma) oceanic lithosphere. *Earth and Planetary Science Letters* 183: 73-92. (Corrigendum. 2001. *EPSL* 186: 333.)

Geldmacher, J., and five others. 2006. Origin and geochemical evolution of the Madeira-Tore Rise (eastern North Atlantic). *Journal of Geophysical Research* 111: B09206, doi:10.1029/2005JB003931.

Gillot, P.Y., J.C. Lefevre, and P.E. Nativel. 1994. Model for the structural evolution of the volcanoes of Reunion Island. *Earth and Planetary Science Letters* 122: 291-302.

Good, R. 1964. *The Geography of Flowering Plants.* Longman, London.

Göthesson, L. 1997. *Plants of the Pitcairn Islands.* Univ. New South Wales, Sydney.

Grigg, R.W. 1997. Paleoceanography of coral reefs in the Hawaiian-Emperor Chain—revisited. *Coral Reefs* 16 (Suppl.): S33-S38.

Hicks, D.J. and A. Mauchamp. 1996. Evolution and conservation biology of the Galápagos opuntias (Cactaceae). *Haseltonia* 4: 89-102.

Klügel, A. and F. Klein. 2006. Complex magma storage and ascent at embryonic submarine volcanoes from the Madeira Archipelago. *Geology* 34: 337-340.

Koppers, A.A.P. and five others. 2008. Samoa reinstated as a primary hotspot trail. *Geology* 36: 435-438.

Lawesson, J E., H Adsersen, and P Bentley. 1987. An updated and annotated check list of the Vascular plants of the Galápagos Islands. *Reports from the Botanical Institute, University of Aarhus. Ser. 16.*

MacArthur, R.H. and E. O. Wilson. 1967. *The Theory of Island Biogeograhy.* Princeton University Press, Princeton, NJ.

Nepokroeff, M., K.J. Sytsma, W.L. Wagner and E.A. Zimmer. 2003. Reconstructing ancestral patterns of colonization and dispersal in the Hawaiian understory tree genus *Psychotria* (Rubiaceae): A comparison of parsimony and likelihood approaches. *Systematic Biology* 52: 820-838.

Oard, M.J. 1990. *An Ice Age Caused by the Genesis Flood.* Institute for Creation Research, El Cajon, CA.

Pilger, R.H., Jr. 1984. Cenozoic plate kinematics, subduction and magmatism: South American Andes. *Journal of the Geological Society* 141: 793-802.

Press, J.R. and M. J. Short. 1994. *Flora of Madeira.* Natural History Museum, London.

Price, J.P. and D.A. Clague. 2002. How old is the Hawaiian biota? Geology and phylogeny suggest recent divergence. *Proceedings of the Royal Society: Biological Sciences* 296: 2429-2435.

Robinson, D.A. and D.P. Cavanaugh. 1998. Evidence for a holobarminic origin of the cats. *Creation Research Society Quarterly* 35: 2-14.

Sanders, R.W. 1979. Unpublished field guide to the flora of Juan Fernández, extracted from Skottsberg (1922, 1951) with modifications based on herbarium and field studies. Copies at Ohio State University, University of Vienna, and Bryan College.

Skogseld, J. 2001. Volcanic margins: Geodynamic and exploration aspects. *Marine and Petroleum Geology* 18: 457-461.

Skottsberg, C. 1922. The phanerogams of the Juan Fernandez and Easter Islands. *Natural History of the Juan Fernandez and Easter Islands* 2: 763-960.

Skottsberg, C. 1951. Supplement of the pteridophytes and phanerogams of the Juan Fernandez Islands. *Natural History of the Juan Fernandez and Easter Islands* 2: 95-240.

Spencer T. 1989. Tectonic and environmental histories in the Pitcairn group, Palaeogene to present: Reconstructions and speculations. *Atoll Research Bulletin* 322: 1-41.

Stuessy, T.F., D.J. Crawford, C. Marticorena, and R. Rodríguez. 1998. Island biogeography of angiosperms of the Juan Fernandez archipelgo. In: Stuessy, T.F., and M. Ono, eds., *Evolution and Speciation of Island Plants*. Cambridge University Press, Cambridge, UK. pp. 121-138.

Stuessy, T.F., K.A. Foland, J.F. Sutter, R.W. Sanders, and M. Silva. 1984. Botanical and geological significnace of potassium-argon dates from the Juan Fernández Islands. *Science* 225: 49-51.

Stuessy, T.F., and seven others. 2006. Anagenetic evolution in island plants. *Journal of Biogeography* 33: 1259-1265.

Wagner, W.L., D. R. Herbst, and S.H. Sohmer. 1990. *Manual of the Flowering Plants of Hawai'i*, 2 vols. Bishop Museum, Honolulu.

Walker, G.P.L. 1990. Geology and volcanology of the Hawaiian Islands. Pacific Science 44: 315-347.

Wiggins, I.L. and D.M. Porter. 1971. *Flora of the Galápagos Islands*. Stanford Univ. Press, Stanford, CA.

Wise, K.P. 1990. Baraminology: A young-earth creation biosystematic method. In: Walsh, R. E. and C.L. Brooks, eds. *Proceedings of the Second International Conference on Creationism*. Science Creation Fellowship, Pittsburgh, pp. 345-358.

Wise, K.P. 2002. *Faith, Form, and Time: What the Bible Teaches and Science Confirms about Creation and the Age of the Universe*. Broadman-Holman Publ., Nashville, TN.

Wise, K.P. 2006. Baraminology and the post-Flood boundary [Abstract P1]. *Occasional Papers of the BSG* 8: 7-8.

Wise, K.P. and M. Croxton. 2003. Rafting: A post-Flood biogeographic dispersal mechanism. In: Walsh, R. E. (ed.) *Proceedings of the Fifth International Conference on Creationism*. Science Creation Fellowship, Pittsburgh, pp. 465-477.

Wood, T.C. 2002. A baraminology tutorial with examples from the grasses (Poaceae). *TJ*. 16: 15-25.

Wood, T.C. 2003. Perspectives on AGEing: A young-earth creation diversification model. In: Walsh, R. E. (ed.) *Proceedings of the Fifth International Conference on Creationism*. Science Creation Fellowship, Pittsburgh, pp. 479-489.

Wood, T.C. 2005. A creationist review and preliminary analysis of the history, geology, climate, and biology of the Galápagos Islands. *CORE Issues in Creation* 1: 1-250.

Wood, T.C. 2006. The current status of baraminology. *Creation Research Society Quarterly*. 43: 149-158.

Wood, T.C. 2008a. Species variability and creationism. *Origins (GRI)* 62:6-25.

Wood, T.C. 2008b. Animal and Plant Baramins. *CORE Issues in Creation* 3: 1-258.

Wood, T.C. and M.J. Murray. 2003. *Understanding the Pattern of Life*. Broadman & Holman, Nashville, TN.

Wood, T.C., P.J. Williams, K.P. Wise, and D.A. Robinson, D.A. 1999. Summaries of Camel Baraminology. In: Robinson, D.A. and P.J. Williams, eds. *Baraminology '99: Creation Biology for the 21st Century (Proceedings of the Second Conference of the Baraminology Study Group)*. Baraminology Study Group, pp. 9-20. Available at: http://www.creationbiology.org/content.aspx?page_id=22&club_id=201240&module_id=36812

Wood, T.C., K.P. Wise, R. Sanders, and N. Doran. 2003. A refined baramin concept. *Occasional Papers of the BSG* 3:1-14.

Yáñez, G., J. Cembrano, M. Pardo, C. Ranero, and D. Selles. 2002. The Challenger-Juan Fernández-Maipo major tectonic transition of the Nazca-Andean subduction system at 33-34°S: Geodynamic evidence and implications. *Journal of South American Earth Sciences* 15: 23-38.

Zavada, S., and J. M. Bensen. 1987. First fossil evidence for the primitive angiosperm family Lactoridaceae. *American Journal of Botany* 74: 1590-1594.

Table 1. Number of native and endemic taxa at the generic and specific levels and percent species endemism.

	Total Number of Native Genera	Total Number of Endemic Genera	Total Number of Native species	Total Number of Endemic Species.	Percent Species Endemism
Hawaii	216	34	1088	967	89
Galápagos	240	8	485	218	45
Madeira	363	5	727	130	18
Juan Fernández	60	11	112	83	74
Pitcairn	74	0	88	14	16

Table 2. Percent of Families exhibiting endemism at different taxonomic levels.

	Number of Families Present	Percentage of Families that are Endemic	Percentage of Families with Endemic Genera	Percentage of Families with Endemic Species Only
Hawaii	87	0	20	60
Galápagos	83	0	5	45
Madeira	81	0	6	38
Juan Fernández	31	3	26	65
Pitcairn	48	0	0	27

Table 3. Total minimum number of introductions required to account for the flora and number of endemic genera and species averaged over those introductions.

	Total Number of Introductions	Average Number of Endemic Genera per Introduction	Average Number of Endemic Species per Introduction
Hawaii	262	0.13	3.7
Galápagos	363	0.02	0.6
Madeira	685	0.01	0.2
Juan Fernández	74	0.15	1.1
Pitcairn	83	0.0	0.2

Table 4. Subset of endemic genera. The number of introductions to account for the endemic genera and total number of species in those genera are used to calculate the average numbers of species per introduction in this subset of genera. The percent endemic genera are calculated from the total number of native genera and number of endemic genera in Table 1. The maximum number of species per introduction is obtained by direct count within each family in each flora.

	Total Number of Introductions Leading to Endemic Genera	Percent Endemic Genera	Total Species in Endemic Genera	Average Number of Species from Introductions Leading to Endemic Genera	Maximum Number of Species from Introductions Leading to Endemic Genera
Hawaii	26[a]	16	375	14.4	110[b]
Galápagos	8	3	35	4.4	19
Madeira	5	1	6	1.2	2
Juan Fernández	11	18	34	3.1	11
Pitcairn	0	0	0	0.0	0

[a] These 26 introductions represent 34 genera (Wagner et al. 1990).
[b] The largest genus Clermontia is actually part of a larger monophyletic group containing Cyanea, Delissea, and Rollandia (Wagner et al. 1990, p.425).

Table 5. Subset of non-endemic genera containing endemic species and species groups. The number of introductions to account for the endemic species in non-endemic genera and the total number of species in those genera are used to calculate the average numbers of species per introduction in this subset of genera. The maximum number of species per introduction is obtained by direct count within each family in each flora.

	Total Number of Introductions Leading to Endemic Species in Non-endemic Genera	Total Number of Endemic Species in Non-endemic Genera	Average Number of Endemic Species per Introduction	Maximum Number of Endemic Species per Introduction
Hawaii	135[a]	592	4.4	27or 47[b]
Galápagos	85[c]	267	3.1	12
Madeira	75	124	1.7	6
Juan Fernández	34	49	1.4	4
Pitcairn	14	19	1.4	3

[a] Cyrtandra (Gesneriaceae) is thought to have been introduced at least four times (Wagner et al. 1990, p. 739).
[b] Pelea (Rutaceae) with 47 taxa in not endemic because 2 species occur in the Marquesas. If the Hawaiian species originated from an introduction from the Marquesas, the number is properly reported here. If the reverse is true, Pelea should be included with the endemic genera. Bidens (Asteraceae) and Chamaesyce (Euphorbiaceae) each have 27 endemic taxa in Hawaii, apparently arising from single introductions (Wagner et al. 1990, pp. 268, 602,1176)
[c] Opuntia (Cactaceae) is thought to have been introduced twice (Hicks & Mauchamp 1996).

Appendix. Compiled data for each archipelago by family. Families are listed alphabetically within the groups Gymnosperms, Dicotyledonae, and Monocotyledonae, in that order. "*" refers to the presence of a monophyletic group of genera below the rank of subtribe. "!" refers to the presence of multiple introductions in non-endemic genera suggested by published research. F=family G=genus S=species I=infrasp. Number of species and infraspecies as assigned by floristic authors; combined in the text, tables, and figures.

A. Hawaii

Family	Total No. Native Genera	Total No. Native Species	Lower Limit of Natural Introd.	Total No. Endemic Genera	Sp. + Infraspp in End. Genera	Total No. Endemic Species	Total No. Endemic Infraspp.	Highest Rank of Endemic Taxa
Aizoaceae	1	1	1	0	0	0	0	-
Amaranthac.	4	11	4	1	2	11	0	G
Anacardiac.	1	1	1	0	0	1	0	S
Apiaceae	3	6	3	0	0	6	0	S
Apocynaceae	4	8	4	1	2	8	0	G
Aquifoliaceae	1	1	1	0	0	0	0	-
Araliaceae	4	13	4	2	7	13	0	G
Asteraceae	12	91	10	6	70	90	33	G*
Begoniaceae	1	1	1	1	1	1	0	G
Boraginaceae	1	2	2	0	0	0	0	-
Brassicaceae	1	3	2	0	0	2	2	S
Campanulac.	7	110	5	6	116	110	21	G*
Capparaceae	2	2	2	0	0	1	0	S
Caryophyllac.	3	32	3	2	28	32	2	G
Celastraceae	1	1	1	0	0	1	0	S
Chenopodiac.	1	1	1	0	0	1	0	S
Convolvulac.	4	8	8	0	0	2	0	S
Cucurbitaceae	1	14	1	0	0	14	0	S
Cuscutaceae	1	1	1	0	0	1	0	S
Droseraceae	1	1	1	0	0	0	0	-
Ebenaceae	1	2	1	0	0	2	0	S
Elaeocarpac.	1	1	1	0	0	1	0	S
Epacridaceae	1	1	1	0	0	0	0	-
Ericaceae	1	3	1	0	0	3	0	S
Euphorbiac.	6	21	6	0	0	21	12	S
Fabaceae	12	20	15	0	0	14	0	S
Flacourtiaceae	1	2	1	0	0	2	0	S
Gentianaceae	1	1	1	0	0	1	0	S
Geraniaceae	1	6	1	0	0	6	3	S
Gesneriaceae	1	53	4!	0	0	53	2	S
Goodeniaceae	1	9	2	0	0	8	0	S
Gunneraceae	1	2	1	0	0	2	0	S
Hydrangeac.	1	1	1	1	1	1	0	G
Hydrophyllac.	1	1	1	0	0	1	0	S
Lamiaceae	5	54	3	3	54	52	2	G*
Lauraceae	2	2	2	0	0	1	0	S

Family	Total No. Native Genera	Total No. Native Species	Lower Limit of Natural Introd.	Total No. Endemic Genera	Sp. + Infraspp in End. Genera	Total No. Endemic Species	Total No. Endemic Infraspp.	Highest Rank of Endemic Taxa
Loganiaceae	1	15	1	1	17	15	2	G
Lythraceae	1	1	1	0	0	0	0	-
Malvaceae	7	24	10	2	10	19	5	G
Menispermac.	1	1	1	0	0	0	0	-
Moraceae	1	1	1	0	0	0	0	-
Myoporaceae	1	1	1	0	0	0	0	-
Myrsinaceae	2	21	2	0	0	21	0	S
Myrtaceae	3	8	4	0	0	7	7	S
Nyctaginac.	2	8	7	0	0	3	0	S
Oleaceae	1	1	1	0	0	1	0	S
Papaveraceae	1	1	1	0	0	1	0	S
Phytolaccac.	1	1	1	0	0	1	0	S
Piperaceae	1	25	3	0	0	3	0	S
Pittosporac.	1	10	1	0	0	10	0	S
Plantaginac.	1	3	1	0	0	3	3	S
Plumbaginac.	1	1	1	0	0	0	0	-
Polygonaceae	1	3	1	0	0	3	0	S
Portulacaceae	1	4	2	0	0	3	0	S
Primulaceae	1	11	2	0	0	10	0	S
Ranunculac.	1	2	1	0	0	2	0	S
Rhamnaceae	3	6	4	0	0	5	0	S
Rosaceae	4	4	4	0	0	3	1	S
Rubiaceae	8	54	8	1	4	52	10	G
Rutaceae	3	55	3	2	47	55	2	G
Santalaceae	2	7	2	0	0	7	11	S

Family	Total No. Native Genera	Total No. Native Species	Lower Limit of Natural Introd.	Total No. Endemic Genera	Sp. + Infraspp in End. Genera	Total No. Endemic Species	Total No. Endemic Infraspp.	Highest Rank of Endemic Taxa
Sapindaceae	3	4	4	0	0	2	1	S
Sapotaceae	2	2	2	0	0	1	0	S
Scrophulariac.	1	1	1	0	0	0	0	-
Solanaceae	3	9	4	1	4	7	0	G
Sterculiaceae	1	1	1	0	0	0	0	-
Theaceae	1	1	1	0	0	1	0	S
Thymelaeac.	1	12	1	0	0	12	2	S
Urticaceae	7	15	7	2	7	14	1	G
Verbenaceae	1	0	1	0	0	0	0	-
Violaceae	2	11	2	1	4	11	2	G
Viscaceae	1	6	3	0	0	4	0	S
Zygophyllac.	1	1	1	0	0	0	0	-
Agavaceae	1	6	1	0	0	6	0	S
Arecaceae	1	19	1	0	0	19	0	S
Cyperaceae	16	43	34	0	0	17	8	S
Hydrocharitac.	1	1	1	0	0	1	0	S
Iridaceae	1	1	1	0	0	1	0	S
Joinvilleaceae	1	1	1	0	0	0	0	-
Juncaceae	1	1	1	0	0	1	2	S
Liliaceae	2	4	2	0	0	3	0	S
Orchidaceae	3	3	3	0	0	3	0	S
Pandanaceae	2	2	2	0	0	0	0	-
Poaceae	19	48	21	1	1	40	3	G
Potamogeton.	1	2	2	0	0	0	0	-
Ruppiaceae	1	1	1	0	0	0	0	-
Smilacaceae	1	1	1	0	0	1	0	S
Total	216	951	262	34	375	830	137	

Genesis Kinds

B. Galápagos

Family	Total No. Native Genera	Total No. Native Species	Lower Limit of Natural Introd.	Total No. Endemic Genera	Sp. + Infraspp in End. Genera	Total No. Endemic Species	Total No. Endemic Infraspp.	Highest Rank of Endemic Taxa
Acanathac.	5	5	5	0	0	1	0	S
Aizoaceae	2	3	3	0	0	1	0	S
Amaranthac.	6	20	11	0	0	15	9	S
Apiaceae	4	5	5	0	0	0	0	-
Apocynac.	1	1	2	0	0	0	1	I
Asclepiadac.	1	1	1	0	0	1	0	S
Asteraceae	23	48	27	4	28	32	6	G
Avicenniac.	1	1	1	0	0	0	0	-
Balonophorac.	1	1	1	0	0	0	0	-
Basellaceae	1	1	1	0	0	0	0	-
Batidaceae	1	1	1	0	0	0	0	-
Boraginaceae	4	16	10	0	0	10	0	S
Brassicaceae	3	3	3	0	0	0	0	-
Buddlejacec.	1	1	1	0	0	0	0	-
Burseraceae	1	2	2	0	0	1	0	S
Cactaceae	3	8	4!	2	4	8	10	G
Callitrichac.	1	1	1	0	0	0	0	-
Campanulac.	1	1	1	0	0	0	0	-
Caryophyllac.	1	3	3	0	0	1	0	S
Celastraceae	1	1	1	0	0	0	0	-
Ceratophyllac.	1	1	1	0	0	0	0	-
Chenopodiac.	2	2	2	0	0	0	0	-
Combretaceae	2	2	2	0	0	0	0	-
Convolvulac.	7	15	12	0	0	5	0	S
Crassulaceae	1	1	1	0	0	0	0	-
Cucurbitac.	4	4	5	1	1	2	1	G
Ericaceae	1	1	1	0	0	1	0	S
Euphorbiac.	6	15	6	0	0	13	4	S
Fabaceae	21	32	32	0	0	3	0	S
Goodeniac.	1	1	1	0	0	0	0	-
Hydrophyllac.	1	1	1	0	0	0	0	-
Hypericaceae	1	1	1	0	0	0	0	-
Lamiaceae	3	7	5	0	0	4	0	S
Lentibulariac.	1	1	1	0	0	0	0	-
Linaceae	1	2	1	0	0	2	0	S
Loacaceae	2	2	2	0	0	0	0	-
Malvaceae	7	12	11	0	0	4	1	S
Melastomatac.	1	1	1	0	0	1	0	S
Menispermac.	1	2	2	0	0	0	0	-
Molluginaceae	1	5	2	0	0	4	5	S
Myrtaceae	1	1	1	0	0	1	1	S
Nolanaceae	1	1	1	0	0	1	0	S
Nyctaginac.	4	5	5	0	0	1	0	S
Onagraceae	1	3	3	0	0	0	0	-

Family	Total No. Native Genera	Total No. Native Species	Lower Limit of Natural Introd.	Total No. Endemic Genera	Sp. + Infraspp in End. Genera	Total No. Endemic Species	Total No. Endemic Infraspp.	Highest Rank of Endemic Taxa
Oxalidaceae	1	2	2	0	0	0	0	-
Passiflorac.	1	2	2	0	0	2	1	S
Phytolaccac.	1	1	1	0	0	0	0	-
Piperaceae	1	5	3	0	0	3	1	S
Plantaginac.	1	1	1	0	0	1	0	S
Plumbaginac.	1	2	2	0	0	0	0	-
Polygalaceae	1	2	1	0	0	2	1	
Polygonac.	1	4	4	0	0	1	0	S
Portulacac.	3	5	5	0	0	2	0	S
Ranunculac.	1	1	1	0	0	0	0	-
Rhizophorac.	1	1	1	0	0	0	0	-
Rubiaceae	4	12	7	0	0	9	0	S
Rutaceae	1	1	1	0	0	0	0	-
Sapindaceae	3	4	4	0	0	1	1	S
Scrophulariac.	7	8	8	1	2	1	1	G
Simaroubac.	1	1	1	0	0	1	0	S
Solanaceae	10	13	13	0	0	7	1	S
Sterculiaceae	1	1	1	0	0	0	0	-
Tiliaceae	2	2	2	0	0	0	0	-
Ulmaceae	1	1	1	0	0	0	0	-
Urticaceae	4	5	5	0	0	1	0	S
Valerianac.	1	1	1	0	0	0	0	-
Verbenaceae	6	11	10	0	0	5	4	S
Viscaceae	1	1	1	0	0	1	0	S
Vitaceae	1	1	1	0	0	0	0	-
Zygophyllac.	2	3	3	0	0	1	0	S
Bromeliaceae	1	1	1	0	0	1	0	S
Cannaceae	1	1	1	0	0	0	0	-
Commelinac.	1	1	1	0	0	0	0	-
Cyperaceae	7	30	29	0	0	2	1	S
Hypoxidaceae	1	1	1	0	0	1	0	-
Iridaceae	1	1	1	0	0	1	0	-
Juncaceae	1	1	1	0	0	0	0	-
Lamnaceae	1	1	1	0	0	0	0	-
Najadaceae	1	2	2	0	0	0	0	-
Orchidaceae	10	14	14	0	0	2	0	-
Poaceae	21	47	43	0	0	10	2	S
Potomogenton.	1	1	1	0	0	0	0	-
Ruppiaceae	1	1	1	0	0	0	0	-
Total	240	434	363	8	35	167	51	

C. Madeira

Family	Total No. Native Genera	Total No. Native Species	Lower Limit of Natural Introd.	Total No. Endemic Genera	Sp. + Infraspp in End. Genera	Total No. Endemic Species	Total No. Endemic Infraspp.	Highest Rank of Endemic Taxa
Cupressac.	1	2	2	0	0	0	0	-
Ephedrac.	1	1	1	0	0	0	0	-
Taxaceae	1	1	1	0	0	0	0	-
Aizoaceae	2	3	3	0	0	0	0	-
Amaranthac.	2	2	2	0	0	0	0	-
Apiaceae	16	20	20	1	1	4	0	G
Aquifoliac.	1	1	2	0	0	0	1	I
Araliaceae	1	1	1	0	0	0	0	-
Aristolochiac.	1	1	1	0	0	0	0	-
Asclepiadac.	1	1	1	0	0	0	0	-
Asteraceae	45	81	72	0	0	22	2	S
Berberidac.	1	1	1	0	0	0	0	S
Boraginac.	5	11	10	0	0	2	0	S
Brassicac.	24	33	29	0	0	9	3	S
Callitrichac.	1	1	1	0	0	0	0	-
Campanulac.	6	8	7	1	2	2	0	G
Caprifoliac.	1	1	1	0	0	1	0	S
Caryophyllac.	13	24	25	0	0	0	1	I
Celastrac.	1	1	1	0	0	1	0	S
Chenopodiac.	6	15	15	0	0	1	0	S
Cistaceae	1	1	1	0	0	0	0	-
Clethraceae	1	1	1	0	0	0	0	-
Clusiaceae	1	8	8	0	0	0	0	-
Convolvulac.	3	10	10	0	0	0	0	-
Crassulac.	7	13	8	0	0	9	0	S
Dipsacac.	3	3	3	0	0	0	0	-
Ericaceae	2	4	4	0	0	2	1	S
Euphorbiac.	2	14	13	0	0	2	0	S
Fabaceae	18	83	80	0	0	8	0	S
Frankeniac.	1	2	2	0	0	0	0	-
Gentianc.	1	2	2	0	0	0	0	-
Geraniac.	2	14	12	0	0	3	0	S
Globulariac.	1	1	1	0	0	0	0	-
Lamiaceae	18	27	27	0	0	5	3	S
Lauraceae	4	4	4	0	0	0	0	-
Linaceae	2	4	4	0	0	0	0	-
Lythraceae	1	2	2	0	0	0	0	-
Malvaceae	3	4	4	0	0	0	0	-
Myricaceae	1	1	1	0	0	0	0	-
Myrsinac.	1	1	1	0	0	0	0	-
Myrtaceae	2	4	4	0	0	0	0	-
Nyctaginac.	1	1	1	0	0	0	0	-
Oleaceae	3	3	4	0	0	1	1	S

Family	Total No. Native Genera	Total No. Native Species	Lower Limit of Natural Introd.	Total No. Endemic Genera	Sp. + Infraspp in End. Genera	Total No. Endemic Species	Total No. Endemic Infraspp.	Highest Rank of Endemic Taxa
Orobanchac.	2	5	5	0	0	0	0	-
Papaverac.	5	11	12	0	0	0	1	I
Pittosporac.	1	1	1	0	0	1	0	S
Plantaginac.	1	7	7	0	0	1	1	S
Plumbaginac.	2	2	4	0	0	1	2	S
Polygonac.	4	13	14	0	0	0	2	I
Portulacac.	1	1	1	0	0	0	0	-
Primulaceae	3	3	3	0	0	0	0	-
Ranunculac.	4	10	11	0	0	1	1	S
Resedaceae	1	1	1	0	0	0	0	-
Rhamnaceae	2	2	2	0	0	0	0	-
Rosaceae	11	18	17	1	1	5	0	G
Rubiaceae	4	12	12	0	0	1	0	S
Rutaceae	1	1	1	0	0	0	0	-
Salicaceae	1	1	1	0	0	0	0	-
Sapotaceae	1	1	1	0	0	0	0	-
Saxifragac.	1	2	1	0	0	2	1	S
Scrophulariac.	12	27	25	0	0	7	0	S
Solanaceae	5	8	8	1	1	2	0	G
Theaceae	1	1	1	0	0	0	0	-
Urticaceae	2	6	6	0	0	1	0	S
Valerianac.	2	5	5	0	0	0	0	-
Verbenaceae	1	1	1	0	0	0	0	-
Violaceae	1	4	4	0	0	1	0	S
Zygophyllac.	2	2	2	0	0	0	0	-
Agavaceae	1	1	1	0	0	0	0	-
Alismataceae	1	1	1	0	0	0	0	-
Araceae	3	3	3	0	0	0	0	-
Cyperaceae	8	21	21	0	0	1	0	S
Dioscoreac.	1	1	1	0	0	0	0	-
Iridaceae	2	2	2	0	0	0	0	-
Juncaceae	2	13	12	0	0	2	0	S
Lemnaceae	1	2	2	0	0	0	0	-
Liliaceae	6	10	12	0	0	2	2	S
Orchidaceae	5	5	5	0	0	3	0	S
Poaceae	51	83	82	1	1	5	0	G
Potamogeton.	1	3	3	0	0	0	0	-
Ruppiaceae	1	1	1	0	0	0	0	-
Total	363	707	685	5	6	108	22	

Genesis Kinds

D. Juan Fernández

Family	Total No. Native Genera	Total No. Native Species	Lower Limit of Natural Introd.	Total No. Endemic Genera	Sp. + Infraspp in End. Genera	Total No. Endemic Species	Total No. Endemic Infraspp.	Highest Rank of Endemic Taxa
Apiaceae	1	4	1	0	0	4	0	S
Arecaceae	1	1	1	1	1	1	0	G
Asteraceae	5	24	5	4	24	24	0	G
Berberidac.	1	2	1	0	0	2	0	S
Boraginac.	1	1	1	1	1	1	0	G
Campanulac.	1	3	1	0	0	3	0	S
Caryophyllac.	1	2	2	0	0	1	1	S
Chenopodiac.	1	3	1	0	0	3	0	S
Ericaceae	1	1	1	0	0	1	0	S
Fabaceae	1	2	1	0	0	2	0	S
Flacourtiac.	1	1	1	0	0	1	0	S
Haloragidac.	2	4	2	0	0	3	0	S
Lactoridac.	1	1	1	1	1	1	0	F
Lamiaceae	1	2	1	1	2	2	0	G
Myrtaceae	4	4	4	1	4	4	0	G
Plantaginac.	1	1	1	0	0	1	0	S
Rhamnac.	1	1	1	0	0	1	0	S
Rosaceae	3	3	3	0	0	2	1	S
Rubiaceae	1	2	1	0	0	2	0	S
Rutaceae	1	2	1	0	0	2	0	S
Saxifragac.	1	1	1	0	0	1	0	S
Scrophulariac.	1	1	1	0	0	1	0	S
Solanaceae	2	3	2	0	0	3	0	S
Urticaceae	2	2	2	0	0	2	0	S
Verbenac.	1	1	1	1	1	1	0	G
Winterac.	1	1	1	0	0	0	0	-
Bromeliac.	2	2	2	0	0	2	0	S
Cyperac.	7	14	13	0	0	4	0	S
Iridaceae	1	1	1	0	0	0	0	-
Juncaceae	2	7	7	0	0	1	0	S
Poaceae	10	13	12	1	1	5	0	G
Total	60	110	74	11	34	81	2	

D. Pitcairn

Family	Total No. Native Genera	Total No. Native Species	Lower Limit of Natural Introd.	Total No. Endemic Genera	Sp. + Infraspp in End. Genera	Total No. Endemic Species	Total No. Endemic Infraspp.	Highest Rank of Endemic Taxa
Aizoaceae	1	1	1	0	0	0	0	-
Amaranthac.	1	0	1	0	0	0	1	I
Anacardiac.	1	1	1	0	0	0	0	-
Apiaceae	1	1	1	0	0	0	0	-
Apocynac.	2	3	3	0	0	1	0	S
Araliaceae	1	1	1	0	0	1	0	S
Asteraceae	2	3	2	0	0	2	1	S
Boraginac.	2	2	2	0	0	0	0	-
Brassicac.	2	2	2	0	0	0	0	-
Capparac.	1	1	1	0	0	0	0	-
Cassythac.	1	1	1	0	0	0	0	-
Convolvulac.	2	3	3	0	0	0	0	-
Cucurbitac.	1	1	1	0	0	0	0	-
Euphorbiac.	2	3	2	0	0	2	0	S
Flacourtiac.	2	2	2	0	0	1	1	S
Goodeniac.	1	1	1	0	0	0	0	-
Hernandiac.	1	2	2	0	0	0	0	-
Fabaceae	5	5	5	0	0	0	0	-
Lamiaceae	1	1	1	0	0	0	0	-
Loganiaceae	1	1	1	0	0	1	0	S
Lythraceae	1	1	1	0	0	0	0	-
Malvaceae	2	3	3	0	0	1	0	S
Menispermac.	1	1	1	0	0	0	0	-
Moraceae	1	1	1	0	0	0	0	-
Myoporac.	1	1	1	0	0	0	0	-
Myrsinac.	1	2	1	0	0	2	0	S
Myrtaceae	2	2	2	0	0	0	0	-
Nyctaginac.	2	3	3	0	0	0	0	-
Oleaceae	1	1	1	0	0	0	0	-
Piperaceae	2	5	4	0	0	2	0	S
Pittosporac.	1	1	1	0	0	0	0	-
Portulacac.	1	2	2	0	0	0	0	-
Rosaceae	1	1	1	0	0	0	0	-
Rubiaceae	7	6	7	0	0	0	1	I
Santalaceae	1	0	1	0	0	0	1	I
Sapindac.	2	2	2	0	0	0	0	-
Sapotaceae	1	1	1	0	0	1	0	S
Solanaceae	2	2	2	0	0	0	0	-
Surianiac.	1	1	1	0	0	0	0	-
Tiliaceae	2	2	2	0	0	0	0	-
Ulmaceae	1	1	1	0	0	0	0	-
Urticaceae	1	1	1	0	0	0	0	-
Viscaceae	1	2	2	0	0	0	0	-
Arecaceae	1	1	1	0	0	0	0	-

Genesis Kinds

Family	Total No. Native Genera	Total No. Native Species	Lower Limit of Natural Introd.	Total No. Endemic Genera	Sp. + Infraspp in End. Genera	Total No. Endemic Species	Total No. Endemic Infraspp.	Highest Rank of Endemic Taxa
Cyperac.	1	1	1	0	0	0	0	-
Liliaceae	1	1	1	0	0	0	0	-
Orchidac.	1	1	1	0	0	0	0	-
Poaceae	3	3	3	0	0	0	0	-
Total	74	84	83	0	0	14	5	

4. Natura Facit Saltum: The Case for Discontinuity

TODD CHARLES WOOD
CENTER FOR ORIGINS RESEARCH

4.1. Introduction

Modern historical research has indicated that the initial controversy over Darwin's *Origin of Species* has been exaggerated over the years and that the Darwinian revolution was not so revolutionary after all. Nevertheless, there was a significant contingent of individuals who passionately rejected everything Darwin had to say about evolution (e.g. FitzSimons 1910; Milam 1926; Martin 1938). Previously, I have referred to such individuals by the collective term antievolutionists (Wood 2008a). Antievolutionists are generally characterized by a scornful tone and serious misunderstandings of evolutionary arguments. I distinguish them from creationists by a creationist's willingness to accept or develop an alternative theory of origins, although I admit the distinction is neither sharp nor consistent.

A favorite argument of the antievolutionists is the perceived lack of transitional forms, which is tied directly to Darwin's use of the saying *natura non facit saltum* ("nature makes no sudden leaps"). In his 1860 book *Species Not Transmutable*, Charles Robert Bree wrote,

> But where ... I ask Mr. Darwin, are your intermediate forms? I tell you in the face of the whole world of men who call themselves scientific, that the deduction [evolution] is the wildest, most absurd and visionary, and unwarranted assumption. (Bree 1860, p. 60)

Leaving aside the melodramatic tone, the sentiment expressed was not uncommon. For example, Jesuit entomologist Erich Wasmann (1910, pp. 291ff), while affirming that Darwin was likely correct on speciation, rejected universal common ancestry for lack of evidence of intermediates.

Even T.H. Huxley took issue with Darwin on this question. In his review of *Origin* published in *Westminster Review*, Huxley (1860) claimed that

> Darwin's position might, we think, have been even stronger than it is if he had not embarrassed himself with the aphorism, *"Natura non facit saltum,"* which turns up so often in his pages. We believe ... that Nature does make jumps now and then, and a recognition of the fact is of no small importance in disposing of many minor objections to the doctrine of transmutation.

To be fair to Darwin, he did address nature's "jumps." The oft-cited passage that includes the Latin phrase in question emphasized the necessity of a continuous gradation between species due to the origin of new species from minor variations (Darwin 1859, p. 194). Elsewhere, however, Darwin (1859, p. 206) admitted that the absolute continuity expressed by *natura non facit saltum* was incorrect "if we look only to the present inhabitants of the world." His explanation for this fact was extinction and the "extreme imperfection" of the fossil record.

Ironically, the idea of a perfect gradation between species was not originally an evolutionary idea. As Darwin (1859, p. 194) himself noted, *natura non facit saltum* was already an "old canon in natural history" by the time he used it in *Origin*. An early version of the idea is found in Aristotle (382-322 B.C.),

> Nature proceeds little by little from things lifeless to animal life in such a way that it is impossible to determine the exact line of demarcation.... Indeed, as we have just remarked, there is observed in plants a continuous scale of ascent towards the animal. (1910, p. 264)

It also appeared in the works of Albertus Magnus (ca. 1193-1280) (quoted in Lovejoy 1936, p. 79), John Ray (1627-1705) (Ray 1682), and Carolus Linnaeus (1707-1778) (Linnaeus 2003, p. 40). To these authors, continuity was not considered evidence of actual evolutionary relationship but as evidence of the Creator's design.

Initially, these gradations were seen as linear, leading from inanimate objects to humans (and sometimes all the way to God Himself). With Linnaeus, though, a new conception of continuity began to emerge. Linnaeus understood continuity between species in a two-dimensional way, "like territories on a geographical map" (2003, p. 40). In his influential *Animal Kingdom* (Cuvier 1834), Georges Cuvier (1769-1832) emphasized strictly separated *embranchements* rather than unbroken continuity. As knowledge of natural history increased and classification became more sophisticated, the linear view of earlier ages became untenable.

Thus when Darwin employed the principle of continuity in *Origin*, he was re-interpreting an idea originally used as evidence of design. As noted above, antievolutionists responded by rejecting the principle of perfect continuity altogether and instead emphasized discontinuity. In the words of antievolutionist William Schoeler (1925, p. 66), "nowhere do we find instances of gradual transition from one type into another."

As creationists began to emerge from antievolutionsts, discontinuity continued to function as a refutation of Darwin's gradualism. For example, although Dudley Joseph Whitney claimed to be "disgusted" with antievolutionists (Whitney 1927), he nevertheless employed discontinuity in his own arguments against evolution. "A few links might be missing without discrediting the theory, but the trouble is that virtually *all* the links are missing" (Whitney 1930). According to Flood geologist and ecologist Harold W. Clark, "The problem of evolutionary relationship eventually becomes reduced to the idea that all the different groups are individually and separately distinct, with no good links to join them" (Clark 1929, p. 51).

Creationist Frank Marsh also used the standard antievolution argument from discontinuity, but the form of his argument differed significantly from previous versions. Marsh (1947, p. 101) insisted that "equal with the fact of diversity, is that of *discontinuity*. Organisms cannot be found grading gradually one into the other." From this, Marsh (1947, p. 230) concluded, "it really appears that it is more sensible to assume that the ancestors of our modern groups were not evolved but created."

Rather than just concluding that missing links are still missing, Marsh explicitly argued that the evidence of discontinuity was more readily explained by creation than by evolution. In Marsh's view, the modern species were not unique creations, as many pre-Darwinian scholars had assumed. Instead, Marsh viewed discontinuity as marking off groups of species, which he referred to as "Genesis kinds." These kinds shared a common ancestor (or a population of ancestors) that originated by divine creation. The modern species of each Genesis kind had descended by evolutionary means from these ancestors.

Historically, then, perfect continuity (an unbroken gradation between species) was first viewed as an evidence of design, but after Darwin reinterpreted it as evolutionary, creationists switched to discontinuity as evidence of design, i.e., separate creation. While Darwin emphasized perfect continuity as a necessary outcome of gradualistic evolution by natural selection, he also allowed for a discontinuous outcome due to extinction and the spottiness of the fossil record. Other modern evolutionists have proposed saltational mechanisms to account for discontinuity (e.g. Goldschmidt 1940). It would seem, then, that the presence or absence of discontinuity is not a distinguishing characteristic between creationist or evolutionary models of the origin of life. Advocates of both perspectives have embraced either continuity or discontinuity as evidence of their views.

Intuitively, however, the very real difference between the universal common ancestry of evolution and the origin of separate groups described in Genesis 1 might suggest that discontinuity could be more prevalent under the creationist perspective than the evolutionary. This would be especially true if somehow creationists could demonstrate the consistent presence of discontinuity around Marsh's Genesis kinds (and not at lower taxonomic ranks, which are related to a common, created ancestor). Marsh resisted equating his Genesis kinds with any particular rank of conventional classification, but George McCready Price (1938) and others (e.g., Woodmorappe 1996, p. 6; Jones 2002; Wood 2006) have suggested that the taxonomic rank of family could be roughly equivalent to the Genesis kind.

Given an evolutionary model of gradual species origin, extinction, and random preservation of taxa in the fossil record, there would seem to be no reason to expect discontinuity at any particular taxonomic level. Instead, we might expect to find continuity or discontinuity at any taxonomic level. Consequently, discontinuity could be detected with equal frequency around families as within families. Thus, a distinguishing test between evolutionary claims and those of creationists might be consistent discontinuity roughly around families, and the absence of discontinuity within families.

The presence of discontinuity around or within families can be evaluated by a meta-analysis of published research in statistical baraminology. The methods of statistical baraminology (e.g., Robinson and Cavanaugh 1998a, 1998b; Wood 2005a, 2008b) are purported to be able to detect discontinuity, defined as "significant, holistic difference" (Wood et al. 2003). These methods have been employed in several studies of plants and animals (e.g., Wood 2002; Wood 2005b; Wood 2008c). In general, these studies concluded that discontinuity was detected, but there are important exceptions in cases where evidence was ambiguous. In this work, 73 previously published statistical baraminology studies are examined for successfully predicted discontinuity, based on the assumption that the classification rank of family is approximately equivalent to the Genesis kind.

4.2. Methods

4.2.1. Published Studies and Baraminic Distance.
Statistical baraminology studies were gathered from the published literature and included in this research based on two criteria: 1. The study must include a baraminic distance correlation (BDC) analysis, and 2. The study must

include a multidimensional scaling (MDS) analysis. In the BDC method, baraminic distances (a modified simple matching coefficient) between taxa are calculated from a character set usually derived from the published literature. Next, the standard linear correlation coefficient is calculated for distances from any two taxa. Taxa with significant, positive correlation are thought to be close together in biological character space (i.e., continuous), and significant, negative correlation indicates dissimilarity. The overall pattern of similarity and dissimilarity is then evaluated for evidence of a group of taxa that share significant, positive BDC with each other and significant, negative BDC with outgroup taxa. This pattern is interpreted to be evidence of continuity within the group and discontinuity with the outgroup.

Three-dimensional MDS is then calculated on the baraminic distance matrix, allowing the researcher to observe directly a representation of the baraminic distances between the taxa. This step clarifies patterns of BDC that are difficult to interpret and confirms patterns of BDC interpreted to be continuity and discontinuity. For more details on the methods of statistical baraminology, the interested reader should consult Robinson and Cavanaugh (1998a, 1998b) and Wood (2005a, 2008b). A basic summary of BDC is also given in Wood and Murray (2003).

Statistical analysis of the results was done in R (http://www.r-project.org). Significance of binomial tests was calculated using the proportion test function prop.test(), and resolving power was calculated based on the smaller of the two sample sizes using power.prop.test().

4.2.2. Judging Successful Predictions. Initially, the equation of family with Genesis kind was based entirely on intuition (Price 1938). Wood and Murray (2003, p. 71) argued that the created kind is likely to be somewhere between the ranks of genus and order, based on the separate creations of Genesis 1 and evidence of continuity between species. Furthermore, classification of species into families is often a matter of personal judgment of the expert creating the classification. These imprecisions therefore necessitate some flexibility in the judgment of which analyses should show discontinuity and which analyses.

Any dataset that contained species from more than one family by *any* expert's judgment was considered to contain two different created kinds and therefore should have shown discontinuity in the baraminological analysis. Successful predictions were more difficult to assess and will be discussed on an individual basis below.

Upon examining the results of the statistical baraminology analysis, each dataset was classified as a success or failure, based on the expected discontinuity outcome. In addition, the original author's interpretation of the results of the baraminology study were accepted without change. No attempt was made to reinterpret results.

4.3. Results

4.3.1. Datasets and Successful Predictions. Based on the criteria
described above, 73 statistical baraminology studies were selected
for meta-analysis from five published sources (Cavanaugh et al. 2003;
Wood 2002, 2005a, 2005b, 2008c) (Table 1). The datasets consisted
of 49 animal groups and 24 plants. The majority of the animals were
vertebrates (36), with sixteen mammal groups, eleven bird groups, four
groups each of reptiles and fish, and one amphibian group. The thirteen
invertebrate groups consisted of twelve arthropod and one annelid group.
Seed plants represented the majority of the plant groups (21 of 24). The
remaining plants consisted of one fern and two moss groups. Two groups
(Felidae and Spheniscidae) were each represented by two datasets.

There were eleven datasets that contained taxa from only one family
and four datasets that contained taxa from subfamilial ranks (subfamilies
or tribes). The remaining 58 datasets contained more than one family
and were therefore predicted to show discontinuity in a statistical
baraminological analysis. Of the fifteen datasets predicted to show no
discontinuity, six datasets had evidence of discontinuity.

Of the 58 datasets predicted to contain a discontinuity, 24 were
easily classified as successful: Alseuosmiaceae, Alstroemeriaceae,
Amphipoda, Aristolochiaceae, Coelopidae, Cupressaceae (excluding
Taxodiaceae), Gadidae, Galagonidae, Grammitidaceae, Histeridae,
Ixodidae, Lemnaceae, Leporidae, Mormoopidae, Nymphaeaceae,
Phocidae, Pholcidae, Phyllodocidae, Rapateaceae, Scorpionoidea,
Sironidae, both Spheniscidae datasets, and Theridiidae. Each of these
datasets revealed evidence of discontinuity surrounding a family in the
taxon sample.

Of the remaining 34 datasets, eighteen were easily classified
as failures, due either to evidence of discontinuity within a family
or evidence of continuity between a family and all the outgroup
taxa in the dataset. These eighteen were Bryaceae, Carduelinae,
Celastraceae, Commelinaceae, Curculionidae, Drepanidini, Felidae,
Gasterosteiidae, Moringaceae, Phalacrocoracidae, Phylostomidae,
Pipridae, Rhinocerotidae, Salamandridae, Sarcoptidae, Sulidae, Talpidae,
and Tenrecidae.

Five additional groups were counted as failures. The falconids
showed evidence of discontinuity between the subfamilies Falconinae
and Polyborinae, and the erinaceids had a discontinuity between the
subfamilies Erinaceinae and Hylomyinae. There was evidence of
continuity between one species of Liparidae and all the outgroup
taxa from that dataset. In the case of the Membracidae, discontinuity
was evident between groups of subfamilies, but since these subfamily
assemblages have not been elevated to family rank by a competent

authority (see Deitz and Dietrich 1994; Cryan et al. 2000), this result was counted as a failed prediction.

The remaining eleven datasets were counted as problematic successes. Seven datasets — Cingulata, Hippopotamidae, Viverridae, Iguanidae, Testudines, Olacaceae, and Marsilaceae — showed a discontinuous group that included more than one family. Datasets mentioned above that showed evidence of continuity between a family and outgroup taxa were counted as failure because no discontinuity was detected. Since the key distinction being tested is whether discontinuity occurs within families equally often as between families, datasets that show discontinuous groups of families should be counted as successes.

Four additional problematic families were counted as successes. Zosteraceae was considered a success even though the original baraminological analysis found it inconclusive. Despite the ambiguous application for baraminology, there was no evidence of discontinuity within the family, but there was evidence of discontinuity between some species and the outgroup. Analysis of Lophopidae found discontinuity between two traditional lophopid genera, *Hesticus* and *Silvanana*, and the remaining lophopids. This finding is consistent with Soulier-Perkins's (2001) exclusion of *Hesticus* and *Silvanana* from Lophopidae based on cladistic analysis, thus, the baraminology analysis was considered a success. Two additional families showed discontinuity between a majority of the family's taxa and a much smaller minority of primitive taxa. Analysis of Poaceae excluded the genera *Anommochloa* and *Streptochaeta* (Wood 2002). Since these species encompass only three of the 10,000 known grasses, this result was considered a success. A comparable case in Cunoniaceae was also considered successful.

4.3.2. Summary of Predictions. Using the criteria described above, 45 studies (61.6%) were classified as successes (Table 1). Based on the initial prediction of discontinuity for 58 datasets, 36 datasets were found to exhibit evidence of discontinuity, for a success rate of 62%. Of the 15 datasets not expecting discontinuity, six (40%) showed evidence of discontinuity. According to the evolutionary prediction, the proportion of groups showing discontinuity in these two sets should be equal. Although the proportions are different, they are not significantly different ($p = 0.212$).

Broken down by classification, the plant groups had a higher success rate than animals (75% vs. 55.1%) (Table 2). Of the 21 seed plant groups examined, sixteen were counted as successful discontinuity predictions. The fern group (Grammitidaceae) and one of the moss groups (Marsileaceae) were also successful. Among the animals, invertebrates had a higher success rate than the vertebrates (76.9% vs. 47.2%). The worst success rate occurred among the birds (18.2%), with only two (both Spheniscidae datasets) of the eleven groups exhibiting successful discontinuity predictions. The mammals had a success rate near the overall frequency (62.5%), and the reptiles, amphibians, and fish had a slightly lower success rate (55.6%). The arthropods had the highest success rate among the animals at 75%.

An important factor in interpreting these results is the degree of certainty with which the statistical baraminology results have been interpreted. Some studies give very clear evidence of continuity and discontinuity, while other studies are more ambiguous. For example, in the case of the iguanids (Wood 2005b), significant, negative BDC was observed between some but not all iguanids and non-iguanids, but discontinuity was still concluded since no significant, positive BDC was observed between iguanids and non-iguanids. When classified according to the perceived confidence of the original author, there were 45 studies with certain results and 28 studies with uncertain results. The overall success rate was significantly different between the certain and uncertain groups (80% vs. 32%, p = 1.2 × 10^{-4}).

When counting only the 45 certain studies, there were 37 groups that were predicted to show evidence of discontinuity. Of these, 29 (80.6%) did show evidence of discontinuity. Only one of the remaining eight subfamilial groups showed evidence of discontinuity (12.5%). Contrary to the evolutionary prediction, the proportions of discontinuous groups in the two sets are significantly different (p = 0.001).

Considering only the high confidence studies, the 32 animal studies had a success rate of 75%, while the 13 plant groups had a success rate of 92.3% (Table 3). Nine of ten mammal groups were successfully predicted. Eight of the nine arthropod groups were successes, and five of the six reptile/amphibian/fish groups were successful. As in the full dataset, however, only one of six (16.7%) of the bird groups were successful predictions. Among the twelve plant groups, the only failure observed was the flowering plant family Trilliaceae (Wood 2008c).

4.4. Discussion

In the present sample of 73 groups, the creationist prediction was correct in 61.6% of the groups tested, but the evolutionary prediction could not be rejected at the 5% significance level. In the smaller sample of 45 studies with certain results, the creationist prediction was correct in 80% of cases, which was significantly different from the evolutionary prediction (p = 0.001). Interpretation of these results is hampered by a lack of statistical power. For the larger sample of 73 groups, the statistical power is 0.22, given the present proportion of successful predictions. Given a success rate of 62.1%, 212 groups would need to be analyzed (106 familial and 106 subfamilial) in order to achieve a statistical power of 0.9. The smaller sample of high confidence studies had a much greater power (0.82), but the classification of groups as "certain" and "uncertain" is problematic. Some judgments on certainty are influenced by the conformity to the creationist prediction (e.g., the phalacrocoracids in Wood 2005b), thus introducing bias into the results.

At present then, we can only note qualitatively that discontinuity for 62.1% of the groups was successfully predicted. This may sound quite bad, but several mitigating factors should be kept in mind. First, the statistical baraminology methods used are novel and generally untried. Second, the data used for the statistical baraminology studies came almost entirely from the published literature with no modification. As yet, it is still unclear what type of data is preferable for baraminology studies or what type of characters best reveal discontinuity. It could be that the data used in many studies (both successes and failures) were in some way unsuitable. Third, the restrictions on "success" or "failure" in this study were not observed in the original analyses. For example, the analysis of the Erinaceidae was considered a failure in this study because of discontinuity between the two subfamilies, but in the original analysis, Wood (2008c) merely referred the subfamily Erinaceinae to a single created kind (holobaramin). Fourth, the intuitive prediction of "family is kind" may in fact be wrong (see Wise's paper in this volume) or may be wrong for particular taxonomic groups. The created kind may be family for some groups but a more or less inclusive rank for other groups. Taken together, it should perhaps be more surprising that the success rate was not worse than it was.

Furthermore, when examined by taxonomic classification, not all taxonomic groups had similar success rates. In particular, the bird groups had an exceptionally poor success rate, even among the groups with high confidence results. If the birds are unusual by having discontinuity at a different taxonomic level than the family, then it would be appropriate to analyze the results omitting the birds from the overall sample. This would give 62 total groups, 50 of which are expected to show discontinuity and 12 of which are not. Only three of the subfamilial groups in the non-bird sample show discontinuity, and 34 of the familial groups show discontinuity, a proportion (25% vs. 68%) that is significantly different (p = 0.02) with a power of 0.57.

Though these present results are suggestive that the creationist prediction of discontinuity approximately at the taxonomic rank of family may be correct, additional studies should be done, especially at the subfamilial level, in order to statistically distinguish between the evolutionary and creationist predictions of discontinuity. It would be especially helpful to analyze additional bird groups to clarify why these groups have such a poor record of successful predictions.

Given the larger theme of this work, the origin of species, the present results suggest that any model of the origin of species should accommodate a discontinuous distribution of organisms. Darwin argued that such a distribution would be expected, given extinction and the imperfection of the fossil record, despite the general continuity expected by his own gradualist understanding of speciation.   In a creationist model where organisms appear suddenly as described in Genesis 1, it should come as no surprise that discontinuity is a predominant pattern of life.   Unlike Darwin, it is unnecessary to posit other explanations for why we do not observe what our theory predicts.   Organisms appear discontinuous because they were created separately. *Natura facit saltum*: Nature does make leaps.

References

Aristotle. 1910. *History of Animals.* Trans. D.W. Thompson. Clarendon, Oxford.

Bree, C.R. 1860. *Species Not Transmutable.* Groombridge and Sons, London.

Clark, H.W. 1929. *Back to Creationism.* Pacific Union College Press, Angwin, CA.

Cavanaugh, D.P., T.C. Wood, and K.P. Wise. 2003. Fossil Equidae: a monobaraminic, stratomorphic series. In: Ivey, R.L., ed. *Proceedings of the Fifth International Conference on Creationism.* Creation Science Fellowship, Pittsburgh, PA, pp. 143-153.

Cryan, J.R., B.M. Wiegmann, L.L. Deitz, and C.H. Dietrich. 2000. Phylogeny of the treehoppers (Insecta: Hemiptera: Membracidae): evidence from two nuclear genes. *Molecular Phylogenetics and Evolution* 17(2):317-334.

Darwin, C. 1859. *On the Origin of Species.* John Murray, London.

Deitz, L.L. and C.H. Dietrich. 1994. Superfamily Membracoidea (Homoptera: Auchenorrhyncha). I. Introduction and revised classification with new family-group taxa. *Systematic Entomology* 18(4):287-296.

Goldschmidt, R. 1940. *The Material Basis of Evolution.* Yale University Press, New Haven, CT.

[Huxley, T.H.] 1860. Darwin on the origin of species. *Westminster Review* 17:541-570.

FitzSimons, S. 1910. *Revised Darwinism or Father Wasmann on Evolution.* P.J. Kenedy & Sons, New York.

Jones, A. 2002. The identity and nature of the created kind—speciation among cichlid fish. *Genesis Agendum Occasional Papers* 7:1-12.

Linnaeus, C. 2003. *Philosophia Botanica.* Trans. S. Freer. Oxford University Press, Oxford.

Lovejoy, A.O. 1936. *The Great Chain of Being.* Harvard University Press, Cambridge, MA.

Martin, J.L. 1938. *Monkey Mileage from Amoeba to Man.* Wm. B. Eerdmans, Grand Rapids, MI.

Milam, J.W. 1926. *Specie Permanata: Opposed to Evolution.* Self-published, Nashville, TN.

Price, G.M. 1938. Nature's two hundred families. *Signs of the Times* 65(37):11,14-15.

Ray, J. 1682. *Methodus Plantarum Nova.* Impensis Henrici Faithorne & Joannis Kersey, London.

Robinson, D.A. and D.P. Cavanaugh. 1998a. A quantitative approach to baraminology with examples from the catarrhine primates. *Creation Research Society Quarterly* 34(4):196-208.

Robinson, D.A. and D.P. Cavanaugh. 1998b. Evidence for a holobaraminic origin of the cats. *Creation Research Society Quarterly* 35:2-14.

Schoeler, W.   1925.   *The Truth about Evolution.*   The Book Concern, Columbus, OH.

Soulier-Perkins, A.   2001.   The phylogeny of the Lophopidae and the impact of sexual selection and coevolutionary sexual conflict.   *Cladistics* 17(1):56-78.

Wasmann, E.   1910.   *Modern Biology and the Theory of Evolution.* B. Herder, St. Louis, MO.

Whitney, D.J.   September 14, 1927.   Letter to George McCready Price.   Box 1, folder 3, George McCready Price Collection.   Center for Adventist Research, James White Library, Andrews University, Berrien Springs, Michigan.

Whitney, D.J.   1930.   Evolution and uniformitarian geology.   *The Bible Champion* 36(5):259-263.

Wood, T.C., Wise, K.P., Sanders, R., and Doran N.   2003.   A refined baramin concept. *Occasional Papers of the BSG* 3:1-14.

Wood, T.C.   2002.   A baraminology tutorial with examples from the grasses (Poaceae). *TJ* 16(1):15-25.

Wood, T.C.   2005a.   Visualizing baraminic distances using classical multidimensional scaling. *Origins* 57:9-29.

Wood, T.C. 2005b. A creationist review of the history, geology, climate, and biology of the Galápagos Islands. *CORE Issues in Creation* 1:1-241.

Wood, T.C.   2006.   The current status of baraminology. *Creation Research Society Quarterly* 43(3):149-158.

Wood, T.C. 2008a. Species variability and creationism. *Origins* 62:6-25.

Wood, T.C.   2008b.   Baraminic distance, bootstraps, and BDISTMDS. *Occasional Papers of the BSG* 12:1-17.

Wood, T.C.   2008c.   Animal and plant baramins. *CORE Issues in Creation* 3:1-258.

Woodmorappe, J.   1996.   *Noah's Ark: A Feasibility Study.*   Institute for Creation Research, Santee, CA.

Table 1. Studies used in this meta-analysis.

Group	Discontinuity Predicted?	Observed?	Certainty	Reference
Mammals				
Brontotheriidae	No	No	Certain	Wood 2008c
Cingulata	Yes	Yes	Uncertain	Wood 2008c
Equidae	No	No	Certain	Cavanaugh et al. 2003; Wood 2005a
Erinaceidae	Yes	No	Certain	Wood 2008c
Felidae	Yes	No	Uncertain	Wood 2008c
Felidae	No	No	Certain	Wood 2008c
Galagonidae	Yes	Yes	Certain	Wood 2008c
Hippopotamidae	Yes	Yes	Certain	Wood 2008c
Leporidae	Yes	Yes	Certain	Wood 2008c
Mormoopidae	Yes	Yes	Certain	Wood 2008c
Phocidae	Yes	Yes	Certain	Wood 2008c
Phyllostomidae	Yes	No	Uncertain	Wood 2008c
Rhinocerotidae	Yes	No	Uncertain	Wood 2008c
Talpidae	Yes	No	Uncertain	Wood 2008c
Tenrecoidea	Yes	No	Uncertain	Wood 2008c
Viverridae	Yes	Yes	Certain	Wood 2008c
Birds				
Alcidae	No	Yes	Uncertain	Wood 2008c
Anserinae	No	Yes	Uncertain	Wood 2008c
Ardeidae	No	Yes	Uncertain	Wood 2008c
Carduelinae	Yes	No	Certain	Wood 2008c
Drepanidini	Yes	No	Certain	Wood 2008c
Falconidae	Yes	No	Uncertain	Wood 2008c
Phalacrocoracidae	Yes	No	Certain	Wood 2005b
Pipridae	Yes	No	Certain	Wood 2008c
Spheniscidae	Yes	Yes	Uncertain	Wood 2005b
Spheniscidae	Yes	Yes	Certain	Wood 2008c
Sulidae	Yes	No	Certain	Wood 2005b
Reptiles				
Iguanidae	Yes	Yes	Certain	Wood 2005b
Pygopodidae	No	Yes	Uncertain	Wood 2008c
Testudines	Yes	Yes	Certain	Wood 2005b
Tropidurinae	No	No	Certain	Wood 2005b

Genesis Kinds

Group	Discontinuity Predicted?	Observed?	Certainty	Reference
Fish				
Gadidae	Yes	Yes	Certain	Wood 2008c
Gasterosteiidae	Yes	No	Uncertain	Wood 2008c
Liparidae	Yes	No	Certain	Wood 2008c
Stomiidae	Yes	Yes	Certain	Wood 2008c
Amphibians				
Salamandridae	Yes	No	Uncertain	Wood 2008c
Arthropods				
Amphipoda	Yes	Yes	Certain	Wood 2008c
Coelopidae	Yes	Yes	Certain	Wood 2008c
Curculionidae	Yes	No	Certain	Wood 2005b
Histeroidea	Yes	Yes	Certain	Wood 2008c
Ixodidae	Yes	Yes	Certain	Wood 2008c
Lophopidae	Yes	Yes	Certain	Wood 2008c
Membracidae	Yes	No	Uncertain	Wood 2008c
Pholcidae	Yes	Yes	Certain	Wood 2008c
Sarcoptidae	Yes	No	Uncertain	Wood 2008c
Scorpionoidea	Yes	Yes	Certain	Wood 2008c
Sironidae	Yes	Yes	Certain	Wood 2008c
Theridiidae	Yes	Yes	Certain	Wood 2008c
Annelids				
Phyllodocidae	Yes	Yes	Uncertain	Wood 2008c
Seed Plants				
Alseuosmiaceae	Yes	Yes	Certain	Wood 2008c
Alstroemeriaceae	Yes	Yes	Certain	Wood 2008c
Aristolochiaceae	Yes	Yes	Certain	Wood 2008c
Astereae	No	No	Certain	Wood 2005b
Celastraceae	Yes	No	Uncertain	Wood 2008c
Commelinaceae	Yes	No	Uncertain	Wood 2008c
Cunoniaceae	Yes	Yes	Certain	Wood 2008c
Cupressaceae	Yes	Yes	Uncertain	Wood 2008c
Lemnaceae	Yes	Yes	Certain	Wood 2008c
Moringaceae	Yes	No	Uncertain	Wood 2008c
Nymphaceae	Yes	Yes	Uncertain	Wood 2008c
Olacaceae	Yes	Yes	Uncertain	Wood 2008c
Poaceae	Yes	Yes	Certain	Wood 2002, 2005a
Podocarpaceae	No	Yes	Uncertain	Wood 2008c

Group	Discontinuity Predicted?	Observed?	Certainty	Reference
Pontederiaceae	No	No	Uncertain	Wood 2008c
Rapateaceae	Yes	Yes	Certain	Wood 2008c
Robinieae	No	No	Uncertain	Wood 2008c
Rubiaceae	No	No	Certain	Wood 2008c
Saururaceae	No	No	Certain	Wood 2008c
Trilliaceae	No	Yes	Certain	Wood 2008c
Zosteraceae	Yes	Yes	Uncertain	Wood 2008c
Ferns				
Grammitidaceae	Yes	Yes	Certain	Wood 2008c
Mosses				
Bryaceae	Yes	No	Uncertain	Wood 2008c
Marsileaceae	Yes	Yes	Certain	Wood 2008c

Table 2. Summary of results for all datasets.

Class	Successful Predictions	Failed Predictions	Total Datasets	Percent Successful
Mammal	10	6	16	62.5%
Bird	2	9	11	18.2%
Reptile/Amphibian/Fish	5	4	9	55.5%
Arthropod	9	3	12	75%
Annelid	1	0	1	100%
Seed Plant	16	5	21	76.2%
Fern	1	0	1	100%
Moss	1	1	2	50%

Table 3. Summary of results for datasets with certain interpretations.

Class	Successful Predictions	Failed Predictions	Total Datasets	Percent Successful
Mammal	9	1	10	90%
Bird	1	5	6	16.7%
Reptile/Amphibian/Fish	5	1	6	83.3%
Arthropod	8	1	9	88.9%
Annelid	1	0	1	100%
Seed Plant	10	1	11	90.9%
Fern	1	0	1	100%
Moss	1	0	1	100%

5. Mammal Kinds: How Many Were on the Ark?

KURT P. WISE

SOUTHERN BAPTIST THEOLOGICAL SEMINARY

5.1. Introduction

The great oceanic voyages of the sixteenth and seventeenth centuries brought back hundreds of species unknown to the naturalists of Europe. It became evident that the floral and faunal diversity of Europe and surrounding regions was dwarfed by the diversity of organisms across the entire planet. With this realization arose concern that it may not have been possible to bear this diversity on a single ark as indicated in the biblical account of the Flood.

At about the same time, however, inter-specific hybridization suggested to biologists that the biblical kind might be a more inclusive group than the species. In the course of his lifetime, for example, Linnaeus enlarged his understanding of the biblical kind from the species to the genus and even to the family (compare editions 1 and 12 of Linnaeus 1735). Raising the taxonomic level of the created kind not only explained inter-specific hybridization, but also reduced the number of organisms that had to be included on Noah's ark, as well as the number of animals that Adam had to name on the first day of his existence.

As biology strayed from its biblical moorings, the interest in created kinds waned. However, with the return in some quarters to a biblically-based science, there is renewed interest in this centuries-old question: What were the animal kinds represented on the ark? The purpose of this paper is to apply a new criterion for the identification of ark kinds to the world's mammals and propose a list of created mammal groups.

5.2. The Criterion

Scripture indicates that terrestrial organisms experienced a population bottleneck at the time of the Flood. The kinds of unclean terrestrial animals were represented on the ark by two individuals each, and of clean animals by 'sevens' (either seven individuals or seven pairs).

The text implies that this is a small sample of the number of individuals present in the pre-Flood world. The present number of individual animals around the world would also suggest that this was almost certainly an extremely small percentage of all the animals on the earth at the time. And, since the text makes it very clear that the remainder of the terrestrial organisms perished in the Flood, the Flood involved a shockingly narrow population bottleneck. Furthermore, if the created kind is more inclusive than species, the Flood not only involved a bottleneck in numbers of individuals, but also a bottleneck in numbers of species. The more inclusive the taxonomic level of the created kind, the more substantial the bottleneck in species diversity.

The blessing and command after the Flood to refill the earth is then understood to be a divine sanction of the restoration of pre-Flood diversity–both in terms of individuals and taxonomic diversity. Taxonomic levels below the level of the created kind in the present world had to have been generated after the Flood. If, for example, the level of the created kind in a modern group was identified to be at the level of the family, then all subfamilies, tribes, subtribes, genera, and species within that family must have arisen *after* the Flood. This in turn suggests a criterion for the identification of the animal kinds represented on the ark (hereafter called 'ark kinds'): The lowest taxonomic level which goes back to the Flood for a particular set of organisms identifies the ark kind and its taxonomic level. In taxa with a sufficiently complete fossil record, then, the lowest taxonomic level with a fossil record reaching back to Flood sediments for a particular set of organisms identifies the ark kind and its taxonomic level. This criterion is called the 'Post-Flood Continuity Criterion' (the PFCC) (Wise 2008).

5.3. The Flood/post-flood Boundary

To use the post-Flood continuity criterion, the Flood/post-Flood boundary has to be identified. Various criteria converge on placing it at or near the Cretaceous/Paleogene system boundary. First, as Austin et al. (1994) claimed, this is where the areal distribution of sedimentary packages transitions from a trans-continental to a regional scale. Second, this is where currents transition from consistent basin-ignoring trans-continental direction to scattered, basin-centering directions (Chadwick 2007). These two criteria suggest a transition from trans-continental to regional sedimentation consistent with a transition from Flood to post-Flood sedimentation. Third, a spectrum of criteria (including the last two), suggests that the preponderance of evidence favors the Cretaceous/Paleogene boundary (Whitmore and Garner 2008).

The post-Flood continuity criterion as applied to the mammals also suggests a Flood/post-Flood boundary at or near the same level (Wise 2008). Table 1 illustrates where living mammal taxa listed in McKenna

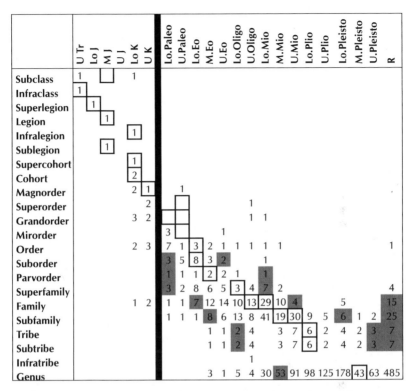

	U.Tr	Lo.J	M.J	U.J	Lo.K	U.K	Lo.Paleo	U.Paleo	Lo.Eo	M.Eo	U.Eo	Lo.Oligo	U.Oligo	Lo.Mio	M.Mio	U.Mio	Lo.Plio	U.Plio	Lo.Pleisto	M.Pleisto	U.Pleisto	R
Subclass	1					1																
Infraclass	1																					
Superlegion		1																				
Legion			1																			
Infralegion				1																		
Sublegion		1																				
Supercohort				1																		
Cohort				2																		
Magnorder				2	1		1															
Superorder					2							1										
Grandorder				3	2							1	1									
Mirorder							3				1											
Order					2	3	7	1	3	2	1	1	1	1	1							1
Suborder							3	5	8	3	2			1								
Parvorder							1	1	1	2	2	1		1								
Superfamily							3	2	8	6	5	3	4	7	2							4
Family					1	2	1	1	7	12	14	10	13	29	10	4				5		15
Subfamily							1	1	1	8	6	13	8	41	19	30	9	5	6	1	2	25
Tribe									1	1	2	4		3	7	6	2	4	2	3		7
Subtribe									1	1	2	4		3	7	6	2	4	2	3		7
Infratribe											1											
Genus										3	1	5	4	30	53	91	98	125	178	43	63	485

Table 1. First Appearance of Mammalian Taxa in the Fossil Record. For each taxonomic level, the number of living mammal taxa having a first appearance at a given stratigraphic level is recorded. Outlined cell indicates the stratigraphic level of the mean first appearance and shaded indicates the stratigraphic level above or below which 5% of the occurrences are confined. Data from McKenna and Bell (1997).

and Bell (1997) first appear in the fossil record. All living mammal suborders (n=22), infraorders (n=17), parvorders (n=9), and superfamilies (n=44) first appear in Lower Paleocene sediments. 95% of the living mammal families (n=124), subfamilies (n=176), tribes (n=142), subtribes (n=42), and genera (n=1179) appear (respectively) by the Lower Eocene, Middle Eocene, Upper Eocene, Lower Oligocene, and Middle Miocene sediments. The exclusion of mammal taxa which are currently restricted to the water–e.g. order Cetacea, superfamily Phocoidea, infraorder Sirenia– does not change any of these results (given that marine mammals account for only 13 of 124 living families, and there are no obvious differences in the first appearance records of terrestrial and marine mammals).

Since studies of living groups have generally identified the created kinds at about the family level and tribes and genera as always *below* that

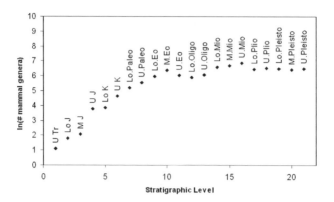

Figure 1. Mammalian Genus Diversity Through Time. Plotted is the natural log of the total genus diversity for Mesozoic subsystems and Cenozoic subseries. The line represents that portion of the data which appears to show logarithmic growth in genus diversity following the Flood. Data from McKenna and Bell (1997).

level, at a confidence $\alpha = 0.05$, the Flood/post-Flood boundary lies below the Upper Eocene. A Flood/post-Flood boundary at the Cretaceous/ Paleogene boundary would place the created kind at the family level or above–a conclusion quite consistent with studies in living taxa. A further confirmation comes if we assume a reasonably complete mammalian fossil record–an assumption we evaluate later in the paper. When the log of the generic diversity is considered (Figure 1) the portion of the graph which is closest to a straight line (and thus the closest to an exponential growth curve) is that which runs from the Lower Paleocene to the Middle Eocene. This is consistent with a Cretaceous/Paleogene boundary. It is also consistent with exponential diversification of mammal genera into the time of deposition of Middle Eocene sediments and with a diversity of mammal ark kinds being approximated by the Upper Cretaceous to Lower Paleocene generic diversity (100-200).

The Flood/post-Flood boundary is thus accepted to be the Cretaceous/Paleogene boundary. Mammal taxa without Mesozoic occurrences are here considered post-Flood taxa and mammal taxa with Mesozoic occurrences are considered to be pre-Flood taxa. Some of these pre-Flood taxa may be ark kinds. However, others may be taxa which were exterminated in the Flood because they were part of a larger group of organisms represented by an ark kind of *another* morphology.

Merely finding a Mesozoic mammal does not suggest that an ark kind has been identified.

The most serious limitation of the post-Flood continuity criterion may be the difficulty of the fossil record to capture representatives of the initially small populations following the Flood–thus making it look like ark kinds actually do not exist all the way back to the Flood. At least two factors would be expected to substantially reduce preservation potential in immediate post-Flood times: very brief geological divisions and low population levels. A special concern regards the Paleocene. According to estimations by Whitmore and Wise (2008), for example, only a few years (a few decades at most) might be involved in the deposition of all Paleocene sediments. On the other hand, using Whitmore and Wise's (2008) methods, the subseries lengths for the Lower Paleocene through Upper Eocene are (respectively) 1.00, 1.08, 1.80, 3.47, and 1.21 times the length of the Lower Paleocene (radiometric lengths are 1.00, 1.00, 1.48, 2.35, 0.68 times the length of the Lower Paleocene), so it is unlikely that differences in subseries lengths are of concern in the Lower Paleogene. A second concern, however, is the lower total volume (and exposed surface area) of Paleocene sediments. Reason for concern may be evidenced by the late first occurrence of mammalian taxa as given in McKenna and Bell (1997). Although the *lowest* first occurrences of living superfamilies through suborders are Lower Paleocene or below, all *mean* first occurrences are above the Paleocene (Table 1). This suggests that the lack of Paleocene occurrences should not be considered evidence against a fossil record continuous with Flood sediments.

By the time of the Lower Eocene, however, the Green River Formation—a half-world away from the landing site of the ark—has a mammalian species diversity on par with, and a family and order diversity twice that of, the present mammalian diversity of the entire state of Wyoming (Whitmore & Wise 2008). This suggests that by the Lower Eocene, anyway, mammalian diversity is high enough to be preserved in the fossil record—at least locally—at levels approaching that of the present. So when does the *global* diversity reach appreciable levels? If the total number of known mammalian genera (4674 in McKenna and Bell 1997) were reported from only one stratigraphic division and were randomly distributed through the stratigraphic divisions, 4.5% of the total diversity would be found in each stratigraphic division. Since many genera are reported from more than one stratigraphic division, the actual average diversity per stratigraphic division is 11%. The lower figure is not exceeded until the Upper Paleocene (6.6%) and the actual average is not approached until the Lower Eocene (10%). It is also in the Lower and Middle Eocene that absolute diversity levels (Figure 1) reach a plateau maintained for most of the remainder of the Paleogene and Neogene. This suggests that by the Lower Eocene, mammalian diversity has achieved

	n	%
U. Pleistocene	559	40%
M. Pleistocene	611	15%
Lo. Pleistocene	416	19%
U. Pliocene	301	21%
Lo. Pliocene	247	23%
U. Miocene	140	20%
M. Miocene	141	6%
Lo. Miocene	76	6%
U. Oligocene	78	17%
Lo. Oligocene	65	13%
U. Eocene	64	13%
M. Eocene	26	4%
Lo. Eocene	22	9%
U. Paleocene	9	0%
Lo. Paleocene	2	0%
U. Cretaceous	1	0%

Table 2. Stratigraphic Completeness. 'n' records the number of times that a particular subseries (or subsystem in the case of Upper Cretaceous) was located between the first and last subseries in the stratigraphic range of a mammal genus. The percent column records that fraction of sandwiched subseries where the genus was not reported. Data is from McKenna and Bell (1997).

'modern' levels, not only at special local sites like the Green River, but also globally.

The Lower Eocene also has a very good sampling of the higher mammalian taxa. Of the living orders, suborders, infraorders, parvorders, and superfamilies, respectively, only 50%, 14%, 6%, 11%, and 7% have appeared by the Lower Paleocene (Table 1). The bulk (66%) of these taxa do not appear until the Lower Eocene (when 67%, 73%, and 65% of the living orders, suborders, and infraorders have appeared). The bulk of the living parvorders is not approached until the Upper Eocene and the bulk of the living superfamilies is not reached until the Lower Oligocene.

Yet another measure of the quality of the fossil record concerns missing subseries in stratigraphic ranges. Of the 4674 genera in McKenna and Bell (1997), 1066 (23%) of them have a stratigraphic range of three or more subseries. A total of 2548 subseries are sandwiched between the first and last subseries in stratigraphic ranges (e.g. a stratigraphic range which runs from the Lower Eocene to the Upper Miocene contains six sandwiched subseries: the Middle and Upper Eocene, the Lower and Upper Oligocene, and the Lower and Middle Miocene). Of these sandwiched subseries, 676 (27%) lack a report of the respective genus. There also does not seem to be appreciable and systematic differences in the percentage of genera missing in a particular subseries (Table 2), so there appear to be approximately constant probabilities across subseries. If anything, Lower Paleogene subseries have a *higher* probability of preserving fossils that later subseries. This suggests that for genera which actually did live through a given subseries, there is a 27% chance that it would not be reported as a fossil in that subseries. This in turn suggests that the probability that a genus might have actually existed one subseries before or after its first or last reported occurrence is about 27%. Similarly the probability that it actually existed for *two* subseries before or after its first or last occurrence is about 7% [$(27\%)^2$], and 2% [$(27\%)^3$] for three subseries. This means that it is conceivable (with a 7% likelihood) that Lower Eocene first appearances could be stretched back to the end of the Flood, but that there is less than a 2% chance that a Middle Eocene first occurrence could be stretched back to the Flood.

All this suggests that whereas Paleocene absence should not be considered a falsification of continuity with Flood sediments, a Lower Eocene absence should be. Thus for the purposes of this study, a taxon which has a presence in Lower Paleocene, Upper Paleocene, or Lower Eocene sediments is considered to be a post-Flood taxon with a presence back to the Flood.

5.4. Preservation Potential

The greatest single limitation of the post-Flood continuity criterion for identifying ark kinds is an incomplete fossil record. And, indeed, several lines of argument lead to the popular opinion that the fossil record is, indeed, very poor. For example, the relative rarity of soft-bodied organisms in the fossil record is argued to be the expected result of mineralized structures giving some organisms (e.g. vertebrates) advantages in preservation. Secondly, Darwin (1859) popularized the idea of an incomplete fossil record in order to explain the absence of the myriad of intermediates which he expected if his evolutionary hypothesis were correct. Thirdly, at present rates of sedimentation, billions of years of earth history should have generated many thousands of times more sediment than we see preserved on our present planet. For this to be true, erosion must have taken away a vast percentage of the sedimentary record and what we have today should be a very small sample of the whole. Finally, if fossil time ranges approximately represent actual taxonomic durations, and radioisotope ages are considered actual ages of the rocks and contained fossils, then the turnover rate of taxa suggests billions of species have come and gone in geologic time. The quarter million or so fossil taxa that we have identified so far would then represent an extremely small percentage of all the species which ever existed.

Not only are most of the arguments for an incomplete fossil record dependent on assumptions which creationists would reject, there are indications that the fossil record might actually be rather good. Among organisms with mineralized structures a large percentage of living taxa have a fossil record. James Valentine (1989), for example, found that 77% of living species of bivalves and snails from the California Province (Point Conception, California southward to Punta Eugenia, Baja California) are known from the fossil record. Similarly Bjorn Kurtén (1968) found 88% of European mammal species are known from the fossil record in Europe. These studies suggest that the fossil record of mammals and mollusks, at least, may be good even down to the level of species—at least in Europe and North America. Indeed, according to data in McKenna and Bell

(1997) 99% of the mammal genera in Europe are known from the fossil record (Figure 2). Even among organisms lacking mineralized structures, such as Burgess, Hunsrich, Mazon Creek, Solenhofen, Santana, and Green River provide amazing preservation regimes–even of soft-bodied organisms. In the Mazon Creek fauna, for example, the most abundant animal fossil is called a 'blob' (*Essexella*)–a jellyfish! Furthermore, ever since Sepkoski published his diversity curves (Sepkoski 1981), numerous studies have wrestled with the question of the reliability (i.e. completeness) of large-scale databases possible with modern technology. Even the conventional paleontological community has concluded that there are numerous reasons to expect that these data sets are very robust and–at least among the 9 animal phyla with mineralized hard parts (including the vertebrates)–rather complete. With the rejection of both conventional geologic dating and the biological intermediates postulated by evolutionary theory, virtually every argument for an incomplete fossil record is invalid (Wise 1991). Combined with the intuitive expectation of high preservability with the rapid deposition involved in both a global Flood and post-Flood catastrophism, there is every reason to believe that the fossil record of mammals is very good.

Though the general fossil record of mammals might be good, there are concerns about some parts of it. First, preservability may be different in different mammal taxa. It might be expected, for example, that flying mammals would have a lower preservation potential than mammals which spend their time closer to environments of burial. Likewise, mammals in the water might have a different chance of preservation than terrestrial mammals. Secondly, even if they were present in equal numbers, small mammals, with their extremely small individual bones, might be less likely to be located by collectors than large mammals. Thirdly, different geographic regions, such as equatorial regions with high chemical erosion rates, might have a poorer fossil record and/or may have been searched less thoroughly than temperate regions.

The percent living taxa *without* a fossil record may confirm some of these concerns. Based on data in McKenna and Bell (1997), a rather large 44% of living mammal genera have no fossil record at all (9% of all genera fossil and modern). That percentage varies by geographic region between 1% and 59% (Table 3) and by taxonomic group between 0% and 100% (Table 3). It does seem to be high for bats, some small mammals, and some tropical localities. However, it is slightly above average (48%) for whales, slightly below average (42%) for rodents, and equally low (13%) for the West Indies and the Arctic Ocean! Perhaps preservation potential is not as important as intuition might expect. Further research is needed to determine whether the absence of a mammalian taxon is due to a poor fossil record or because it really wasn't there. Until that research is done, the number of ark kinds might be underestimated in

	n			n	
Microbiotheria	1	100%	Madagascar	58	59%
Notoryctemorphia	1	100%	East Indies	187	56%
Paucituberculata	3	100%	South America	267	49%
Pilosa	5	80%	New Guinea	81	47%
Scandentia	5	80%	Pacific Ocean	82	44%
Chiroptera	233	64%	Central America	143	41%
Primates	46	61%	Indian Ocean	43	35%
Peramelia	8	50%	Africa	274	32%
Cimolesta	4	50%	Asia	310	30%
Soricomorpha	32	50%	New Zealand	10	30%
Cete	40	48%	Antarctica	7	29%
Rodentia	76	41%	Atlantic Ocean	53	28%
Chrysochloridea	6	33%	North America	161	21%
Carnivora	103	32%	Australia	92	21%
Didelphimorphia	14	29%	Arctic Ocean	15	13%
Dasyuromorphia	15	27%	West Indies	46	13%
Macroscelidea	4	25%	Mediterranean	43	5%
Lagomorpha	12	25%	Europe	92	1%
Erinaceomorpha	15	20%			
Uranotheria	5	20%			
Diprotodontia	34	18%			
Cingulata	9	11%			
Artiodactyla	82	9%			
Platypoda	1	0%			
Tachyglossa	2	0%			
Tubulidentata	1	0%			
Perissodactyla	6	0%			

Table 3. Taxonomic and Geographic Preservability. Percentage of living genera lacking a fossil record according to orders and geographic region. Orders, geographic regions and data from McKenna and Bell (1997).

some groups—especially in the case of groups with a large percentage of genera without a fossil record. In the meantime, for this paper, it is assumed that the lack of fossil record is due to a recent origin rather than inadequacy of the fossil record.

5.5. Taxa, Strata, and Data

Creation biologists have developed phenetic methods of studying organisms—methods which are not dependent upon the veracity of evolutionary theory. These methods have repeatedly confirmed that, for the most part, biological classification tends to reflect actual similarities and dissimilarities among organisms–even when that structure was developed using distinctly evolutionary methods. Thus subtaxa tend to be more phenetically similar to each other than they are to other taxa. This suggests that the classification structure would not only reflect the path of evolution if that did occur, but also that the boundaries of created kinds are likely to correspond to conventional taxonomic boundaries. It also seems reasonable to assume that true phenetic discontinuities will provide bounds which conventional taxonomy will almost be forced to use as taxonomic boundaries. In fact, larger discontinuities might form the bounds of higher taxonomic groups. To identify the mammalian ark kinds, then, it is not unreasonable to begin with a conventional mammalian classification. All creation biology studies so far have identified the created kind at the genus level or above. Thus a conventional taxonomy of genera and above should be a good starting point for identifying created kinds.

Creation geologists accept the stratigraphic column and biostratigraphic terms in lieu of chronological or chronostratigraphic terms (i.e. Lower and Upper rather than Early and Late; System and Series rather than Period and Epoch–see Snelling et al. 1996).

To identify the mammalian ark kinds using the post-Flood continuity criterion, this paper uses the data in McKenna and Bell (1997) because (1) it is a mammalian classification; (2) it includes all mammals; (3) being a single volume, it maximizes the taxonomic consistency; and (4) it contains the highest detail known on the fossil record (Mesozoic subsystem and Cenozoic subseries) and taxonomy (genus level) for all the mammals.

5.6. Methods And Results

Data from McKenna and Bell (1997) was tabulated to indicate generic diversity for all subfamily and higher mammalian groups throughout the stratigraphic column (Appendix A). Occurrences recorded with certainty in a Mesozoic subsystem or a Cenozoic subseries are scored with a 1; uncertain occurrences are scored with a 0.5; and occurrences from a stratigraphic range which cannot be defined as narrowly as a single Mesozoic subsystem or single Cenozoic subseries are scored the fraction of one divided by the number stratigraphic divisions included in that zone of uncertainty. Genera are scored 1 in each subseries from the oldest definite occurrence to the youngest definite occurrence, even when the genus has not been reported from a given stratigraphic range. For an alternative classification system and to tie these figures to modern species diversity, Appendix A also includes generic and species diversity on living mammalian groups from Wilson and Reeder (2005).

From the generic diversity table (Appendix A), taxa were examined for their potential as ark kinds. The result is offered in Table 4. Taxa with fossil occurrences in Lower Eocene or below are considered to have a continuous fossil record (CFR) with the Flood. Since most creation biology studies identify the created kind at the level of the family or above, families with a fossil record occurrence in the Lower Eocene or below are considered candidates for ark kinds. But, since Mesozoic occurrences might represent pre-Flood morphologies not represented on the ark, and some diversification from ark kinds might have occurred by the Lower Eocene, this list of taxa should be considered an exaggerated number. In Table 4 this number is given as the larger number in the range of numbers given for ark kinds.

Taxa lacking fossils in the Lower Eocene or below are considered to have a discontinuous fossil record (DFR) with the Flood. In cases of a DFR family, successively higher taxonomic groups are considered until the fossil record is CFR. The CFR taxon of the lowest taxonomic level is postulated to be an ark kind, and the number of them in a taxonomic group is considered to be a minimum number of ark kinds (the smaller number in the range of numbers given for ark kinds in Table 4). DFR subtaxa in such an ark taxon are postulated to be post-Flood in origin, descendant from that ark taxon. DFR taxa with a spotty fossil record (i.e. Mesozoic subsystems and/or Cenozoic subseries skipped in the stratigraphic range of a group) which get sufficiently close to the Lower Eocene might even be considered ark kinds.

5.7. Discussion

5.7.1. Creation Biosystematics. It is useful to consider how this study compares with basic type and baraminology studies. First, since basic type biology assembles basic types around successful hybridization and other measures of high similarity, it is reasonable to assume that basic types are truly monophyletic. If so, each terrestrial basic type should be descendant from a single ark kind. This means that basic types should all be subsets of the ark kinds identified in this study, and more than one basic type could be included in a single ark kind. Thus far, basic type biology has postulated mammalian basic types only at the level of the family or below (as reviewed by Wood 2008), and each of these is a subset of an ark kind as proposed in Table 4.

Baraminology, in contrast, identifies groups not based upon common descent, but upon similarity and dissimilarity. A monobaramin is a group showing substantial holistic continuity without substantial discontinuity and a holobaramin is a group showing holistic continuity surrounded by discontinuity. By this definition it is likely that on the ark each ark kind would have been holobaraminic. After the Flood, for as long as a given ark kind diversified via more or less uniform morphological steps, it would continue to be holobaraminic (both apobaraminic and monobaraminic) and all subtaxa monobaraminic. On the other hand, if large morphological steps were possible in post-Flood diversification, an ark kind could conceivably have generated multiple post-Flood holobaramins.

Studies which assign monobaraminic status to a taxonomic level of family or below are within and consistent with the ark kinds of this paper. Five baraminological studies by Wood (2008) seem to show inter-familial continuity in ways consistent with the ark kind hypotheses of this paper (Table 4): 1) no statistically significant discontinuity was found between the families Rhinocerotidae and Hyracodontidae, consistent with this paper's suggestion that the superfamily Rhinocerotoidea containing the two families were descendant from a single ark kind; 2) no statistically significant discontinuity was found between the bat families Noctilionidae and Mormoopidae, consistent with this paper's suggestion that the order Chiroptera containing these two families was descendant from a single ark kind; 3) no statistically significant discontinuity was found in the insectivores between the family Dasypodidae and the genus *Vassalia* of the superfamilies Dasypodoidea and Glyptodontoidea, consistent with this paper's suggestion that the order Cingulata containing these two superfamilies was descendant from a single ark kind; 4) no statistically significant discontinuity was found among representatives of two insectivore superfamilies Erinaceoidea and Talpoidea, consistent with this paper's suggestion that the order Erinaceomorpha containing these two superfamilies was descendant from a single ark kind; and 6) continuity was found between the family Hippopotamidae and two genera of the family Anthracotheriidae, consistent with this paper's suggestion that the superfamily Suoidea (containing the family Hippopotamidae) arose in post-Flood times from some other ark kind–most probably one of the superfamilies Anthracotherioidea, Dichobunoidea, or Anoplotherioidea. Unlike the conclusions of this paper, one of Wood's (2008) baraminological studies did not find statistically significant discontinuity among five feliform and three non-phocoid caniform families, whereas this paper posits that the caniforms and feliforms are descendant from different ark kinds (Table 4). Finally, although one of Wood's (2008) holobaramins (the Leporidae) is a subset of the lagomorph ark kind postulated in this paper (Table 4), Wood's analysis included only genus-level taxa from the other lagomorph family, Ochotonidae. A broader study across lagomorph species is needed to determine how holobaramin designations compare with this paper's conclusions.

Wise (2005) suggested that significant rearrangements of higher taxa may suggest a lack of discontinuity between them. According to that criterion, differences in the mammalian classifications of McKenna and Bell (1997) and Wilson and Reed (2005) (see Table 4) suggest continuity between the families Viverridae and Herpestidae (descendants of the same feliform ark kind in this paper), the family Talpidae and the superfamily Soriocoidea (suggesting that the sub-baraminic Talpidae is descendant of the Soricomorpha ark kind, not the Erinaceomorpha ark kind as suggested by McKenna and Bell classification), the superfamilies Loroidea and Lemuroidea (descendants of same strepsirhrini ark kind in this paper) and Phalangeroidea and Vombatoidea (descendants of the same australidelphian ark kind in this paper), and the suborders Sciuromorpha and Myomorpha (suggesting a reordering of McKenna and Bell's infraorders is necessary).

If God endowed an ark kind with the ability to change via steps of substantially different magnitudes, discontinuity might be generated among the descendants of a given ark kind. If such discontinuity were to fully envelop a subtaxon, that group would be holobaraminic. If this happened, although all descendants of an ark kind would still be apobaraminic, one or more subtaxa would be holobaraminic and one or more holobaramins would have been generated from another holobaramin in post-Flood times. Seven baraminic studies seem to evidence holobaramins arising after the Flood: 1) Wood (2008) found some evidence for discontinuity surrounding the order Cingulata, whereas this paper suggests a more inclusive ark kind (magnorder Xenarthra: Table 4); 2) Robinson and Cavanaugh (1998) identified the family Felidae as holobaraminic, whereas this paper suggests a more inclusive ark kind (suborder Feliformia: Table 4); 3) Wood (2008) identified the family Phocidae as holobaraminic, whereas this paper suggests a more inclusive ark kind (suborder Caniformia: Table 4); 4) Wood (2008) found reason to identify the bat family Mormoopidae as holobaraminic, whereas this paper suggests a more inclusive ark kind (order Chiroptera: Table 4); 5) Wood (2008) identified the subfamily Erinaceinae (tribe Erinaceini in McKenna and Bell 1997) as a holobaramin whereas this paper suggests a more inclusive ark kind (superfamily Erinaceoidea: Table 4); 6) Wood (2008) identified discontinuity between the group containing the family Hippopotamidae and two anthracothere genera and the remaining suoids and anthracotheres whereas this paper suggests a more inclusive ark kind (something larger than the superfamily Suoidea: Table 4); and 7) Wood (2008) identified the family Galagonidae (subfamily Galagoninae in McKenna and Bell 1997) as holobaraminic, whereas this paper suggests a more inclusive ark kind (infraorder Strepsirhrini: Table 4).

Perhaps most interesting in these studies is the ambiguity involved in all but the last two: in the first study Wood (2008) did not find the discontinuity surrounding the order Cingulata altogether convincing; the second and third studies, which identified holobaramins within the carnivores, seemed to be contradicted by one of Wood's (2008) studies which failed to find statistically significant discontinuity across the carnivore families; in the fourth and fifth studies Wood (2008) identified discontinuities around the family Mormoopidae and the subfamily Erinaceeinae, respectively, but other analyses in the same work (Wood

2008) these discontinuities were not identified. Wood (2008) suggests that this type of ambiguity may be due to different character selection involved in different taxonomic studies. It doesn't take too much reflection to realize that the choice of certain characters at the expense of others can, on the one hand, separate continuous sequences into discrete (discontinuous) groups, and, on the other hand, unite discontinuous groups into an undifferentiable blur. Although character selection could explain this ambiguity, it also might be true that this ambiguity is characteristic of the type of discontinuity arising within descendants of ark kinds. Either way, further study of such ambiguities should prove enlightening for creation biology.

5.7.2. On the Ark and Off. Aside from humans, only land animals are explicitly listed as intended ark inhabitants (Gen. 6:19-20; 7:2-3), those who entered the ark (Gen. 7:8-9, 14-15), those who died outside the ark (Gen. 7:21-23), those commanded to exit the ark (Gen. 8:17) and those who exited the ark (Gen. 8:19). It is generally assumed that God somehow preserved the water animals outside the ark, and thus were never really 'ark kinds'. What of the mammals that live in the water? What is their status as 'ark kinds'?

First of all, it must be assumed that the water animals also experienced a very large population bottleneck at the time of the Flood. The huge number of fossils of sea creatures in Flood sediments gives direct testimony to the vast number of individuals who did *not* survive the Flood. The excellent preservation of so many fossils testifies to the rapid deposition of huge amounts of sediment which must have been carried in the Flood waters. Sedimentary units of consistent lithology found spread across entire continents suggest that organisms must have been transported at least multiple thousands of miles in sediment-laden water before they were finally buried. This, combined with tectonic turbulence, volcanic heating, and chemical reactions is expected to have been deadly for a vast percentage of the organisms of the sea. This is likely to have produced a bottleneck in not only the number of individuals, but also the number of species in the waters of the world. In fact, survival in such conditions seems so unlikely that it is probably only with God's intervention that any organisms survived at all. Perhaps the diversity of water organisms was reduced comparably to the diversity of land animals.

Secondly, assuming comparable completeness of the fossil record, water kinds which survived the Flood should have left a fossil record continuous with Flood sediments just as the terrestrial organisms did. Similarly, water organisms which arose after the Flood should appear in the fossil record after the Flood and have a fossil record discontinuous with Flood sediments. Since more than one species of a given kind of water organism might have survived the Flood outside the ark, the number of water taxa with a fossil record continuous with the Flood will underestimate the number of water baramins. Nonetheless, the post-Flood taxa with a fossil record discontinuous with Flood sediments should be subbaraminic, whether those organisms are of the land or of the water.

Thirdly, many of the water mammals are only semi-aquatic. Mammals such as otters, beavers, muskrats, and even seals, may have been able to survive on the ark without having to live in water. Finally, some of the animals which are aquatic or marine today may not have been aquatic at the time of the Flood. The marine and sea otters, for example, are members of the mustelid (weasel) family and their aquatic character is likely to have been revealed after the Flood. The whales might turn out to be another example. Only when including the legged archaeocetes (and/or possibly the terrestrial suborder Acreodi) do the whales have a fossil record continuous with the Flood. Vestigial legs and hips in modern whales confirm legged ancestors of the whales existed only a short time ago. It is possible that the purely marine cetaceans of the present were derived from semi-aquatic or even terrestrial ancestors on the ark.

5.7.3 Fossil Record Incompleteness. Biblically we know that humans were not only separately created, but separately represented on the ark from all other organisms. Yet, humans have a discontinuous fossil record with respect to the Flood, so they are included as post-Flood descendants of an anthropoid ark kind. On the other hand, it has been argued (Wise 2002) that humans did not appear earlier in the Cenozoic because of their longevity in immediate post-Flood times. No fossils can be found in an interval where no individuals died, and it's likely that no humans had died before the deposition of the entire Paleogene and part of the Neogene systems. As evidenced by humans, the post-Flood continuity criterion would seriously underestimate the number of ark kinds in taxa with long generation times. The biblical account does not suggest that any other organism had substantially longer generation times, and the rather large diversity and disparity of fossils from the Lower Eocene within just a few years or few decades of the Flood suggests that animals were dying in a wide range of taxa within a short time of the Flood. Thus although the post-Flood continuity criterion did not identify the human ark kind, there is no good reason to expect that it missed other taxa for similar reasons.

It was suggested above that an incomplete fossil record could lead the post-Flood continuity criterion to underestimate the number of ark kinds. However, the fact that such a high disparity and diversity of mammal taxa had already made it half way around the world (to present-day Wyoming) within a few years or decades of the Flood suggests that mechanisms of rapid dispersal and diversification were in operation even for organisms traditionally associated with slow dispersal rates. The only concern, as indicated above, is high number of genera without a fossil record. However, the high number of genera without a fossil record might be an indicator that the group had an origin in the very recent past. And, given that the post-Flood continuity criterion in other taxa most often connects superfamily groups and above, it is most likely that a better fossil record would add less than 30% more ark kinds (see Table 4).

5.7.4. Further Research. A variety of studies can examine this paper's assumptions. For example: 1) The Cretaceous/Paleogene boundary location of the Flood/post-Flood boundary can be examined with further research into Flood/post-Flood boundary criteria; 2) The effect of regional preservability can be examined by comparing stratigraphic ranges of the same taxon in regions having different percentages of subtaxa lacking a fossil record; and 3) The effect of taxonomic preservability can be examined by comparing the continuity of stratigraphic ranges of long-ranging subtaxa in taxa having a high percentage of subtaxa lacking a fossil record. A variety of studies can test the robustness of this paper's conclusions: 1) Alternate mammalian classifications should agree at the level of the ark kind and differ only among sub-baraminic groups; 2) ANOPA and MDS studies should establish discontinuity among this paper's proposed ark kinds and continuity and/or smaller-scale discontinuities among subtaxa; and 3) The subtaxa of ark kinds should appear in sensible bio-geo-strati-graphic sequence.

This paper's method can also be applied to other well-preserved fossil taxa. Although birds and reptiles don't have the best fossil record, their fossil record might nonetheless be informative. Invertebrates with hard parts (e.g. land snails), though, ought to be good candidates. And, given that sub-baraminic groups are identified by exclusively post-Flood occurrences of *any* organism—even if not a terrestrial animal—plants and even sea creatures such as mollusks, echinoderms, brachiopods, and crustaceans should prove to be lucrative areas of study.

5.8. Conclusion

Further research is needed to determine the effect of fossil preservability on the conclusions of this paper. In the meantime, mammal taxa which lack a fossil record from the Lower Eocene or before can be understood to have arisen after the Flood as subtaxa of ark kinds. True morphological discontinuities can also be expected to lie along boundaries between conventionally-defined taxa. Based upon fossil data in McKenna and Bell (1997), mammals accounted for a total of no more than 234 kinds on the ark (300 if the fossil record of mammals is much poorer than this author believes), and perhaps as few as half that number. This brings the number of mammals on the ark and mammals named by Adam to well within space considerations on the ark and time constraints on the sixth day of creation.

The Bible mentions camels in Job's day (Job 1:3, 17; 42:12) and Abraham's day (Gen. 12:16; Gen. 24) and lions in Job's day (Job 4:10-11; 10:16; 28:8; 38:39). Yet, the camel genus does not appear until the Upper Miocene (McKenna and Bell 1997:415) and the lion subgenus does not appear until the Upper Pliocene (McKenna and Bell 1997:233). This suggests that the Paleogene and lower Neogene Systems were laid down in something on the order of two centuries of time (Whitmore & Wise 2008). This in turn suggests a lot of diversification occurred in the space of two centuries. From the original 100-300 ark kinds, over 700 genera were alive by the time Upper Pliocene sediments were deposited (Appendix A), with over 1200 genera and 5300 species today (Wilson and Reeder 2005). The average ark kind has generated 20-50 genera and probably something on the order of 100-250 species (given that there is an average of about 5 species per mammal genus in the present: Wilson and Reeder 2005).

Acknowledgments

I would like to thank Todd Wood and Roger Sanders for helpful comments on an earlier draft of this paper.

References

Austin, S.A., J.R. Baumgardner, D.R. Humphreys, A.A. Snelling, L. Vardiman, and K.P. Wise. 1994. Catastrophic plate tectonics: A global flood model of earth history. In: Walsh, R.E., ed. *Proceedings of the Third International Conference on Creationism*. Creation Science Fellowship, Pittsburgh, PA, pp. 609-621.

Chadwick, A.V. 2007. Megatrends in North American Paleocurrents. http://origins.swau.edu/papers/global/paleocurrents/eng/

Darwin, C. 1859. *On the Origin of Species*. John Murray, London.

Kurtén, B. 1968. *Pleistocene Mammals of Europe*. Aldine, Chicago.

Linnaeus, C. 1735. *Systema Naturæ, sive Regna Tria Naturæ Systematice Proposita per Classes, Ordines, Genera, et Species*. Theodorum Haak, Leyden [1st edition 1735; 12th edition 1766-68].

McKenna, C.M., and S.K. Bell. 1997. *Classification of Mammals above the Species Level*. Columbia University Press, New York, NY.

Sepkoski, J.J. 1981. A factor analytic description of the Phanerozoic marine fossil record. *Paleobiology* 7:36–53.

Snelling, A.A., M. Ernst, E. Scheven, J. Scheven, S. A. Austin, K. P. Wise, P. Garner, P. Garton, and D. Tyler. 1996. The geological column. *Creation Ex Nihilo Technical Journal* 10(3):333-334.

Valentine, J.W. 1970. How many marine invertebrate species? *Journal of Paleontology* 44:410-415.

Whitmore, J.H. and P. Garner. 2008. Using suites of criteria to recognize pre-Flood, Flood, and post-Flood strata in the rock record with application to Wyoming (USA). In: Snelling, A.A., ed. *Proceedings of the Sixth International Conference on Creationism*. Creation Science Fellowship, Pittsburgh, PA and Institute for Creation Research, Dallas, TX, pp. 425-448.

Whitmore, J.H. and K.P. Wise. 2008. Rapid and early post-Flood mammalian diversification evidence in the Green River Formation. In: Snelling, A.A., ed. *Proceedings of the Sixth International Conference on Creationism*. Creation Science Fellowship, Pittsburgh, PA and Institute for Creation Research, Dallas, TX, pp. 449-457.

Wilson, D.E. and D.M. Reader, eds. 2005. *Mammal Species of the World: A Taxonomic and Geographic Reference*. Third Edition. Johns Hopkins University Press, Baltimore, MD.

Wise, K.P. 1991. The fossil record: The ultimate test-case for young-earth creationism. *Opus: A Journal for Interdisciplinary Studies* 1991-92:17-29.

Wise, K.P. 2002. *Faith, Form and Time*. Broadman and Holman, Nashville, TN.

Wise, K.P. 2005. Interspecific hybrids in the Solenaceae. *Occasional Papers of the BSG* 5:17-18.

Wise, K.P. 2008. Baraminology and the fossil record of the mammals. *Occasional Papers of the BSG* 11:10-11.
Wood, T.C. 2008. Animal and Plant Baramins. *CORE Issues in Creation* 3:1-258.

Table 4: Baraminic Status of Mammals. Based upon application of the post-Flood continuity criterion to the generic diversity of mammals in the fossil record (Appendix A).

KEY:

open box : descendants of proposed ark kind (minimizing # ark kinds)
gray box : proposed ark kind for 1B
black box : ark kind if at family level (maximizing # ark kinds)
1B: (proposed as) descendant from 1 ark kind
SB: (proposed as) sub-baraminic
AK: (proposed as the Flood-surviving) ark kind (for the 1B)
NFR: New Fossil Record (i.e. fossil record begins *after* the Flood)
CFR: Continuous Fossil Record (back to the Flood)
DFR: Discontinuous Fossil Record (back to the Flood, but discontinuously)

	# of Ark Kinds
Non-marsupial and non-placental theriomorphs (Mesozoic to lower Tertiary fossils; 51 families; 199 genera; UTr-UEo): 48 families have a CFR or Flood fossil record, so if baramins are defined at the level of the family there are as many as 45 in this group. Alternatively, if baramins are defined at a well-defined taxonomic level above the level of the family, the following 14 groups would be a *minimum* number of baramins:	14-48

the multituberculate Superfamily Ptilodontoidea (2 families; 16 genera; UK-UEoc)
the multituberculate Superfamily Taeniolabidoidea (3 fams; 17 genera; UK-LoEoc)
the multituberculate Suborder Gondwanatheria (2 families; 3 genera; UK-LoPaleo)
the Infraclass Triconodonta (3 families; 17 genera; UTr-UK)
the Superlegion Kuehneotheria (2 families; 3 genera; UTr-LoJ)
the Order Amphidontoidea (1 family; 4 genera; LoJ-LoK)
the Order Spalacotherioidea (3 families; 11 genera; MJ-UK)
the Order Dryolestida (6 families; 5 genera; MJ-UK)
the Order Amphitheriida (1 family; 1 genus; MJ)
the Infralegion Peramura (1 family; 4 genera; MJ-LoK)
the Supercohort Aegialodontia (1 family; 1 genus; LoK)
the Order Deltatheroida (2 families; 5 genera; UK)
the Order Asiadelphia (1 family; 1 genus; LoK-UK)
the Suborder Archimetatheria (2 families; 8 genera; UK-MEoc)
NOTE: Most of these animals probably cohabited with the dinosaurs and probably died out with the remainder of the dinosaur biome soon after the Flood.

Subclass Prototheria (2 families; 6 genera; LoK-R): DFR	1

Of the subtaxa, the Order Tachyglossa (1 family; 2 genera; MMio-R) has a NFR ➔ SB ➔ have to go to the subclass level to get a DFR or CFR

Family Ornithorhychidae (4 genera; LoK-R), w/DFR is the living
taxon of lowest taxonomic level w/DFR or CFR
→ propose: Subclass Prototheria is 1B and descendant from Family
Ornithorhychidae, as AK

Magnorder Australidelphia (23 families; 14 extant families; 152 genera;   1
59 living genera; ~216 extant species; UK-R): CFR   (5)
Of the subtaxa, the Superorder Eometatheria (22 families; 145
genera; UOligo-R) has a NFR → SB → have to go to the
magnorder level to get a CFR
Family Microbiotheriidae (7 genera; spotty UK-R), w/DFR is the
living taxon of lowest taxonomic level w/DFR or CFR (and, in
fact, the *only* family with DFR or CFR)
→ propose: Magnorder Australidelphia is 1B and descendant from
Family Microbiotheriidae as AK.
NOTE: If the high number of genera without a fossil record suggests
range extensions, at most 4 additional ark kinds are possible.

Magnorder Ameridelphia (18 families; 146 genera; LoK-R): 11 families   6-11
have a CFR or Flood fossil record, so if baramins are defined at
the level of the family there are 11 in this group. At *minimum*, the
following are baramins:
Order Didelphimorphia (2 families; 56 genera; LoK-R): CFR
Family Didelphidae (52 genera; UK-R): CFR
Family Sparassocynidae (1 genus; LoEo-UPlio): CFR
The older fossil record of the didelphids, the didelphids known
from Flood sediments, and the CFR of even Subfamily
Didelphinae being CFR (living taxon of lowest taxonomic
level having CFR) → propose: Order Didelphimorphia may
be 1B and descendant from Subfamily Alphadontinae as
AK.
Superfamily Caenolestoidea (4 families; 21 genera; UPaleo-R): since
3 of the families have NFR, the superfamily is the lowest taxon
w/DFR or CFR
Family Sternbergiidae (1 genus; UPaleo): CFR
→ propose: Superfamily Caenolestoidea is 1B and descendant
from Family Sternbergiidae as AK
Superfamily Polydolopoidea (4 families; 12 genera; LoPaleo-
LoMio): CFR:
Family Sillustaniidae (1 genus; LoPaleo): CFR
Family Polydolopidae (8 genera; UPaleo-LoMio): CFR
Family Prepidolopidae (1 genus; LoEo-MEo): CFR
Family Bonapartheriidae (1 genus; LoEo): CFR
Although all 4 families have a CFR, combining the fossil records
yields a smooth fossil record → propose: Superfamily
Polydolopoidea may be 1B and descendant from Family
Sillustaniidae as AK
Superfamily Argyrolagoidea (3 families; 5 genera; MEoc-LoPlio):
NFR (but nearly makes it back to the Flood and is of very low
diversity) → (if it is assumed to be 1B) → it is the lowest taxon
w/DFR or CFR
→ propose: Superfamily Argyrolagoidea is 1B

Superfamily Caroloameghinioidea (2 families; 5 genera; UK-LoEoc):
  CFR
    Family Glasbiidae (1 genus; UK): CFR or Flood fossil record
    Family Caroloameghiniidae (4 genera; LoPaleo-LoEo): CFR
    non-overlapping stratigraphic ranges ➔ propose Superfamily
      Caroloameghinioidea may be 1B and descendant from
      Family Glasbiidae as AK.
Order Sparassodonta (3 families; 39 genera; LoPaleo-Uplio): CFR;
    b/c one family has a NFR, the order is the lowest taxon w/CFR
    ➔ propose Order Sprasodonta is 1B and descendant from one
    of the two following families as AK:
    Family Mayulestidae (1 genus; LoPaleo): CFR
    Family Borhyaenidae (37 genera; LoPaleo-UPlio): CFR

Order Bibymalagasia (1 genus; R): SB?; no fossil record, so this is either   0-1
    a baramin of poor preservation potential or a sub-baraminic   (1)
    group
    NOTE: If the high number of genera without a fossil record suggests
      range extensions, at most 1 ark kinds is possible in this group.

Magnorder Xenarthra (16 families; 221 genera; UPaleo-R): 5 families   1-5
    have a CFR, so if baramins are defined at the level of the family,   (3-7)
    there are 5 in this group:
    Order Pilosa (10 families; 104 genera; MEo-R): NFR ➔ SB ➔ have
      to go to the magnorder level to get a CFR
    Order Cingulata (6 families; 117 genera; UPaleo-R):
      Family Protobradidae (1 family; LoEo): CFR
      Superfamily Dasypodoidea (2 families; 46 genera; UPaleo-R):
        CFR
        Family Dasypodidae (41 genera; UPaleo-R): CFR
        Family Peltephilidae (5 genera; LoEo-UOligo): CFR
      Superfamily Glyptodontoidea (3 families; 70 genera; LoEo-
        UPleisto): CFR; since one of the families has a NFR, the
        superfamily is the lowest taxon w/CFR
        Family Pampatheriidae (4 genera; LoEo-UPleisto): DFR
        Family Palaeopeltidae (1 genus; LoEo-UOligo): CFR
    ➔ propose: Magnorder Xenarthra is 1B and descendant of
      Subfamily Dasypodinae as AK
    NOTE: If the high number of genera without a fossil record suggests
      range extensions, at most 2 additional ark kinds in the Pilosans
      are possible.

Superorder Leptictida (4 families; 32 genera; LoK-UOligo): CFR; all   1-4
    4 families have a CFR or Flood fossil record, so if baramins
    are defined at the level of the family, there are as many as 4
    in this group. Alternatively, if baramins are defined at a well-
    defined taxonomic level above the level of the family, the whole
    superorder would be the baramin.
    Family Gypsonictiopidae (7 genera; LoK-UPaleo): CFR
    Family Kulbeckiidae (1 genus; UK): CFR
    Family Didymoconidae (6 genera; LoPaleo-LoOligo): CFR

Family Leptictidae (10 genera; LoPaleo-UOligo): CFR

Mirorder Macroscelidea (1 family: Macroscelididae; 12 genera; UEo-R): NFR (w/poor fossil record early on + older unassigned genera); does not quite go back to the boundary, but it does have a poor fossil record at the beginning. If it was united with one or more of the 3 families (3; 14; 7 genera) not now assigned to mirorders in the Grandorder Anagalida it would go back to the boundary   1

Order Mimotonida (1 family: Mimotonidae; 3 genera; LoPaleo-LoOligo): CFR ➔ 1B   1

Order Lagomorpha (2 families; 68 genera; LoEo-R): CFR   1
    Family Ochotonidae (26 genera; UEo-R): NFR ➔ SB ➔ have to go to order level to get a CFR
    Family Leporidae (42 genera; LoEo-R): CFR; in fact, the living family of the lowest taxonomic level with CFR
    ➔ propose: Order Lagomorpha is 1B and descendant from Family Leporidae as AK

Order Mixodontia (1 family: Eurymylidae; 12 genera; UPaleo-MEo): CFR ➔ 1B   1

Order Rodentia (53 families; 1169 genera; LoPaleo-R): only 3 of the 5 suborders have a CFR: 12 families have a CFR, so if baramins are defined at the level of the family there are 12 in this group. *Minimally:*   7-12 (13-18)
Family Alagomyidae (2 genera; UPaleo-LoEo): CFR
rodent Suborder Anomaluromorpha (4 families; 4 genera; MEo-R): NFR ➔ SB
    NOTE: If the high number of genera without a fossil record suggests range extensions, at most 1 additional ark kind is possible.
rodent Suborder Hystricognatha (23 families; 227 genera; UEo-R): NFR ➔ SB
    NOTE: If the high number of genera without a fossil record suggests range extensions, at most 4 additional ark kinds are possible.
rodent Suborder Sciuromorpha (10 families; 209 genera; LoPaleo-R): CFR
Family Ischyromyidae (29 genera; UPaleo-LoMio): CFR
Superfamily Aplodontoidea (3 families; 35 genera; MEo-R): NFR ➔ SB
Infraorder Theridomyomorpha (1 family: Theridomyidae; 27 genera; LoEo-UOligo): CFR ➔ 1B
Infraorder Sciurida (2 families; 87 genera; LoEo-R): CFR
    Family Sciuridae (86 genera; UEo-R): NFR ➔ SB; have to go to the infraorder level to get a CFR
    Family Reithroparamyidae (1 genus; LoEo-MEo): CFR

➔ propose: Infraorder Sciurida is 1B and descendant from
    Family Reithroparamyidae as AK
Infraorder Castorimorpha (3 families; 31 genera; LoEo-R): CFR
    Families Castoridae (25 genera; UEo-R) and Rhizospalacidae
        (1 genus; UOligo) are both NFR ➔ SB; have to go to the
        infraorder level to get a CFR
    Family Eutypomyidae (LoEo-MMio): CFR
    ➔ propose: Infraorder Castorimorpha is 1B and descendant
        from Family Eutypomyidae as AK
rodent Suborder Myomorpha (9 families; 644 genera; LoEo-R): CFR
    Infraorder Myodonta (4 families; 513 genera; LoEo-R): CFR
        Superfamily Muroidea (2 families; 473 genera; MEo-R): NFR
            ➔ SB; have to go to the infraorder level to get a CFR
        Superfamily Dipodoidea (2 families; 40 genera; LoEo-R): CFR
            Family Armintomyidae (1 genus; MEo): NFR; have to go to
                the superfamily level to get a CFR
            Family Dipodidae (39 genera; LoEo-R): CFR, being the
                living family of lowest taxonomic level with CFR
        ➔ propose: Infraorder Myodonta is 1B and descendant from
            Family Dipodidae as AK
        NOTE: If the high number of genera without a fossil record
            suggests range extensions, at most 1 additional ark kind
            is possible.
    Infraorder Glirimorpha (1 family: Myoxidae; 45 genera; LoEo-R):
        CFR ➔ 1B
    Infraorder Geomorpha (3 families; 84 genera; LoEo-R): CFR
        Superfamily Geomyoidea (2 families; 46 genera; MEo-R):
            NFR ➔ SB; have to go to the infraorder level to get a
            CFR
        Superfamily Eomyoidea (1 family; 36 genera; LoEo-UPleisto):
            CFR, with Family Eomyidae as the living family of lowest
            taxonomic level with CFR
        ➔ propose: Infraorder Geomorpha is 1B and descendant
            from Family Eomyidae as AK
rodent Suborder Sciuravida (5 families; 72 genera; LoEo-R): CFR;
    4 of the 5 families have a CFR; if baramins are defined at
    the level of the family there are as many as 4 in this group.
    Alternatively, if baramins are defined at a well-defined
    taxonomic level above the level of the family, the entire
    suborder might be descendant from 1 baramin.
    Family Ivanantoniidae (1 genus; LoEo): CFR
    Family Sciuravidae (7 genera; LoEo-UEo): CFR
    Family Chapattimyidae (30 genera; LoEo-LoMio): CFR
    Family Cylindrodontidae (10 genera; LoEo-LoMio): CFR

Order Cimolesta (22 families; 130 genera; UK-R): 20 of the families   10-20
have a CFR; if baramins are defined at the level of the family there are
as many as 20 in this group; the only living family has a NFR and have
to go to the suborder level to get a CFR; Minimally:
    Suborder Didelphodonta (1 family: Cimolestidae 13 genera; UK-
        MEo): CFR ➔ 1B
    Suborder Apatotheria (1 family: Apatemyidae 6 genera; LoPaleo-
        UOlig): CFR ➔ 1B

Suborder Taeniodonta (1 family: Stylinodontidae; 9 genera;
   LoPaleo-MEo): CFR ➔ 1B
Suborder Tillodontia (1 family: Tillotheriidae; 14 genera; LoPaleo-
   UEo): CFR ➔ 1B
Superfamily Bemalambdoidea (2 families; 4 genera; LoPaleo-
   UPaleo): CFR
   Family Harpyodidae (2 genera; LoPaleo-UPaleo): CFR
   Family Bemalambdidae (2 genera; LoPaleo): CFR
Superfamily Pantolambdoidea (6 families; 11 genera; LoPaleo-UEo):
   CFR
   Family Pastoralodontidae (2 genera; LoPaleo-UPaleo): CFR
   Family Titanoideidae (1 genus; LoPaleo-LoEo): CFR
   Family Pantolambdidae (2 genera; LoPaleo-UPaleo): CFR
   Family Barylambdidae (3 genera; UPaleo-LoEo): CFR
   Family Cyriacotheriidae (1 genus; UPaleo): CFR
   Family Pantolambdodontidae (2 genera; UPaleo-UEo): CFR
Superfamily Coryphodontoidea (1 family: Coryphtodontidae; 6
   genera; UPaleo-UEo): CFR ➔ 1B
Suborder Pantolesta (3 families; 34 genera; LoPaleo-Uoligo): CFR
   Family Ptolemaiidae (3 genera; UEo-LoOligo): NFR ➔ SB
   Family Pantolestidae (22 genera; LoPaleo-UOligo): CFR; this is
      the older CFR group
   Family Paroxyclaenidae (8 genera; LoEo-UEo): CFR
   ➔ Suborder Pantolesta is 1B and descendant from Family
      Pantolestidae as AK
Suborder Pholidota (3 families; 21 genera; UPaleo-R): CFR
   Family Manidae (8 genera; MEo-R): NFR ➔ SB
   Family Epoicotheriidae (7 genera; UPaleo-LoOligo): CFR
   Family Metacheiromyidae (4 genera; UPaleo-MEo): CFR
   ➔ Suborder Pholidota is 1B and descendant from Family
      Epicotheriidae or Metacheiromyidae as AK
Suborder Enanodonta (1 family: Ernanodontidae; 2 genera; UPaleo-
   LoEo): CFR ➔ 1B

Order Creodonta (2 families; 61 genera; LoPaleo-UMio): both families   1-2
   have a CFR; if baramins are defined at the level of the family
   there are as many as 2 in this group. Alternatively, if baramins are
   defined at a well-defined taxonomic level above the level of the
   family, the entire order might be descendant from 1 baramin.
   Family Hyaenodontidae (50 genera; LoPaleo-UMio): CFR
   Family Oxyaenidae (9 genera; UPaleo-MEo): CFR

Order Carnivora (16 families; 466 genera; LoPaleo-R): minimally: 2
   Suborder Feliformia (7 families; 134 genera; LoPaleo-R): CFR   (3)
      6 of the 7 families have a NFR ➔ SB
      Family Viverravidae (12 genera; LoPaleo-UEo): CFR
      ➔ propose: Suborder Feliformia is 1B and descendant from
         Family Viverravidae as AK
   Suborder Caniformia (9 families; 182 genera; UPaleo-R): CFR
      Infraorder Cynoidea (1 family: Canidae; 46 genera; MEo-R): NFR
         ➔ SB; have to go to the suborder level to get a CFR
      Family Miacidae (12 genera; UPaleo-UEo): CFR

Infraorder Arctoidea (7 families; 266 genera; UPaleo-R): CFR
    Parvorder Ursida (5 families; 124 genera; MEo-R): NFR ➔ SB;
        have to go to the Infraorder level to get a CFR
    Parvorder Mustelida (2 families; 143 genera; LoEo-R): CFR
        Family Mustelidae (120 genera; LoOligo-R): NFR ➔ SB;
           have to go to the Parvorder level to get a CFR
        Family Procyonidae (23 genera; LoEo-R): CFR
➔ propose: Suborder Caniformia is 1B and descendant from
    Family Miacidae as AK (because it has an older fossil
    record)
NOTE: If the high number of genera without a fossil record
    suggests range extensions, at most 1 additional ark kinds
    are possible.

Grandorder Lypotyphla (20 families; 258 genera; LoPaleo-R): 12   2-12
    families have a CFR; if baramins are defined at the level of the   (4-19)
    family there are as many as 12 in this group. *Minimally*:
Order Chrysochloridea (1 family; 8 genera; LoMio-R): NFR ➔ SB;
    have to go to the grandorder level to get a CFR [NOTE: Wilson
    and Reed (2005) unite this taxon with Tenrecidae into the
    order Afrosoricida. This may suggests that the chrysochlorids
    are post-Flood descendants of the soricomorphs]
    NOTE: If the high number of genera without a fossil record
        suggests range extensions, at most 1 additional ark kind is
        possible.
Family Adapisoriculidae (3 genera; UPaleo-LoEo): CFR
Order Erinaceomorpha (8 families; 111 genera; LoPaleo-R): CFR
    Family Sespedectidae (5 genera; UPaleo-LoOligo): CFR
    Family Amphilemuridae (5 genera; LoEo-LoOligo): CFR
    Family Adapisoricidae (2 genera; UPaleo-LoEo): CFR
    Family Creotarsidae (1 genus; LoEo): CFR
    Superfamily Talpoidea (7 families; 56 genera; MEo-R): NFR ➔
        SB; have to go to the level of the order to get a CFR
    Superfamily Erinaceoidea (1 family: Erinaceidae; 36 genera;
        LoPaleo-R): CFR
Order Soricomorpha (10 families; 135 genera; UK-R)
    Family Otlestidae (1 genus; UK): CFR or Flood fossil record
    Family Geolabididae (4 genera; UK-LoMio): CFR
    Superfamily Tenrecoidea (1 family; 13 genera; LoMio-R): spotty
        NFR ➔ SB?; have to go to the level of the Order to get a
        CFR
    NOTE: If the high number of genera without a fossil record
        suggests range extensions, at most 1 additional ark kind is
        possible.
    Superfamily Soriocoidea (7 families; 115 genera; LoPaleo-R):
        CFR
        Family Micropternodontidae (8 genera; LoPaleo-UOligo):
           CFR
        Family Apternodontidae (3 genera; UPaleo-LoOligo): CFR
        Family Plesiosoricida (6 genera; LoEo-LoPlio): CFR
        Family Nyctitheriidae (17 genera; LoPaleo-Oligo): CFR

Order Chiroptera (21 families; 219 genera; UPaleo-R): 6 families have a
  CFR; if baramins are defined at the level of the family there are as
  many as 6 in this group. *Minimally*:
    Suborder Megachiroptera (1 family; 44 genera; spotty LoOligo-R):
      spotty NFR ➔ SB?; have to go to the level of the order to get
      a CFR
      NOTE: If the high number of genera without a fossil record
        suggests range extensions, at most 1 additional ark kind is
        possible.
    Suborder Microchiroptera (20 families; 175 genera; UPaleo-R)
      Family Archaeonycteridae (2 genera; UPaleo-MEo)
      Family Palaeochiropterygidae (3 genera; LoEo-MEo)
      Family Hassianycterididae (1 genus; LoEo-MEo)
      Infraorder Yinochiroptera (5 families; 23 genera; MEo-R): CFR
        ➔ SB
      Infraorder Yangochiroptera (11 families; 127 genera; LoEo-R)
        Superfamily Noctilionoidea (3 families; 53 genera; MMio-R):
          NFR ➔ SB; have to go to the level of the infraorder to
          get a CFR
        Superfamily Vespertilionoidea (7 families; 73 genera; LoEo-
          R): CFR
          Family Philisidae (2 genera; LoEo-UEo): CFR
          Family Natalidae (2 genera; LoEo-R): CFR

        3-6
        (4-7)

Order Primates (32 families; 279 genera; LoPaleo-R): 15 families have a
  CFR; if baramins are defined at the level of the family there are as
  many as 15 in this group; *Minimally*:
  Family Purgatoriidae (1 genus; LoPaleo): CFR
  Family Microsyopidae (9 genera; UPaleo-MEo): CFR
  Family Micromomyidae (4 genera; UPaleo-LoEo): CFR
  Family Picromomyidae (2 genera; LoEo-MEo): CFR
  Family Plesiadapidae (7 genera; LoPaleo-LoEo): CFR
  Family Palaechthonidae (5 genera; LoPaleo-UPaleo): CFR
  Family Picrodontidae (3 genera; LoPaleo-UPaleo): CFR
  Suborder Dermoptera (4 families; 22 genera; LoPaleo-R): CFR
    Family Galeopithecidae (2 genera; UEo-R): NFR ➔ SB; have to
      go to the level of the suborder to get a CFR
    Family Paromomyidae (8 genera; LoPaleo-MEo): CFR
    Family Plagiomenidae (9 genera; LoPaleo-UOligo): CFR
    Family Mixodectidae (2 genera; LoPaleo): CFR
    ➔ propose: Suborder Dermoptera is 1B and descendant from
      one of the three CFR families above
  Infraorder Strepsirhrini (9 families; 68 genera; LoEo-R): CFR
    Superfamilies Daubentoniidae, Loroidea, and Indroidea are
      NFR; have to go to the level of the infraorder to get CFR
    Superfamily Lemuroidea (2 families; 40 genera; LoEo-R): CFR
      Family Lemuridae (6 genera; R): NFR ➔ SB; have to go to the
        level of the superfamily to get a CFR
      Family Adapidae (34 genera; LoEo-UMio): CFR
    ➔ propose: Infraorder Strepsirhrini is 1B and descendant from
      Family Adapidae as AK

        5-15
        (9-19)

NOTE: If the high number of genera without a fossil record
   suggests range extensions, at most 3 additional ark kinds
   are possible.
Parvorder Tarsiiformes (5 families; 45 genera; LoPaleo-R): CFR
   Superfamily Carpolestoidea (1 family: Carpolestidae; 5 genera;
      LoPaleo-LoEo): CFR
   Superfamily Tarsioidea (4 families; 40 genera; LoPaleo-R): CFR
      Families Afrotarsiidae and Tarsiidae are NFR ➔ SB; have to
         go to the level of the superfamily to get a CFR
      Family Omomyidae (33 genera; LoPaleo-UEo): CFR
      Family Microchoeridae (5 genera; LoEo-UEo): CFR
      ➔ propose: Superfamily Tarsioidea is 1B and descendant
         from Family Omomyidae as AK (b/c of an older fossil
         record)
Parvorder Anthropoidea (7 families; 104 genera; LoEo-R): CFR
   Superfamily Callitrichoidea (2 families; 33 genera; UOligo-R):
      NFR ➔ SB; have to go to the level of the parvorder to get
      a CFR
   Superfamily Cercopithecoidea (3 families; 61 genera; LoEo-R):
      CFR
      Families Cercopithecidae and Hominidae are NFR ➔ SB;
         have to go to the level of the superfamily to get a CFR
      Family Pliopithecidae (11 genera; LoEo-UMio): CFR
      ➔ propose: Parvorder Anthropoidea is 1B and descendant
         from Family Pliopithecidae as AK (NOTE, however, that
         man is in the Family Hominidae)
   NOTE: If the high number of genera without a fossil record
      suggests range extensions, at most 1 additional ark kind
      is possible.

Order Scandentia (1 family: Tupaiidae; 7 genera; MEo-R): NFR (but   0-1
   almost & spotty) ➔ 1B?   (1)
   NOTE: If the high number of genera without a fossil record suggests
      range extensions, at most 1 ark kind is possible.

Order Tubulidentata (1 family; 5 genera; Oligo-R): NFR ➔ SB   0

Order Dinocerata (1 family: Uintitheriidae; 6 genera; UPaleo-MEo):   1
   CFR ➔ 1B

Order Procreodi (2 families; 29 genera; LoPaleo-UEo):   2
   Family Oxyclaenidae (14 genera; LoPaleo-UEo): CFR ➔ 1B
   Family Arctocyonidae (15 genera; LoPaleo-LoEo): CFR ➔ 1B

Order Condylarthra (6 families; 59 genera; LoPaleo-UOligo):   6
   Family Hyopsodontidae (21 genera; LoPaleo-LoOligo): CFR ➔ 1B
   Family Mioclaenidae (15 genera; LoPaleo-UPaleo): CFR ➔ 1B
   Family Phenacodontidae (5 genera; LoPaleo-MEo): CFR ➔ 1B
   Family Periptychidae (13 genera; LoPaleo-LoEo): CFR ➔ 1B
   Family Peligrotheriidae (1 genus; LoPaleo): CFR ➔ 1B

Family Didolodontidae (4 genera; UPaleo-UOligo): CFR ➔ 1B

Order Arctostylopida (1 family: Arctostylopidae; 9 genera; UPaleo-   1
LoEo): CFR ➔ 1B

Order Cete (29 families; 282 genera; LoPaleo-R): 4 families have a   4
   CFR; if baramins are defined at the level of the family there are as   (7)
   many as 4 in this group. *Minimally*:
   Suborder Acreodi (3 families; 27 genera; LoPaleo-LoOligo): CFR
      Family Triisodontidae (5 genera; LoPaleo-MEo): CFR
      Family Mesonychidae (15 genera; LoPaleo-UEo): CFR
      Family Hapalodectidae (5 genera; UPaleo-UEo): CFR
   Suborder Cetacea (26 families; 255 genera; LoEo-R): CFR
      Infraorder Autoceta (23 families; 231 genera; LoOligo-R): NFR·
        ➔ SB; have to go to the suborder level to get a CFR
      Infraorder Archaeoceti (3 families; 22 genera; LoEo-UMio): CFR
        Families Basilosauridae and Remingtonocetidae have a DFR
          ➔ SB; have to go to the level of the infraorder to get a
          CFR
        Family Protocetidae (12 genera; LoEo-MEo): CFR
   ➔ propose: Suborder Cetacea is 1B and descendant from Family
      Protocetidae as AK
   NOTE: If the high number of genera without a fossil record
      suggests range extensions, at most 3 additional ark kinds
      are possible.

Suborder Suiformes (18 families; 248 genera; LoEo-R): 6 families have   3-6
   a CFR; if baramins are defined at the level of the family there are
   as many as 4 in this group. *Minimally*:
   Family Raoellidae (6 genera; LoEo-MEo)
   Superfamily Suoidea (4 families; 69 genera; UEo-R): NFR ➔ SB
   Superfamily Oreodontoidea (2 families; 50 genera; MEo-UMio):
      NFR ➔ SB
   Superfamily Entelodontoidea (1 family; 7 genera; MEo-LoMio): NFR
      ➔ SB
   Superfamily Dichobunoidea (4 families; 49 genera; LoEo-UOligo):
      CFR
      Family Helohyidae (8 genera; MEo): NFR ➔ SB; have to go to
        the superfamily level to get a CFR
      Family Dichobunidae (36 genera; LoEo-UOligo): CFR
      Family Cebochoeridae (3 genera; LoEo-LoOligo): CFR
      Family Mixtotheriidae (1 genus; LoEo-UEo): CFR
      ➔ propose: Superfamily Dichobunoidea is 1B and descendant
        from one of the 3 families as AK
   Superfamily Anthracotherioidea (2 families; 45 genera; LoEo-
      LoPleisto): CFR
      Family Anthracotheriidae (37 genera; MEo-LoPlio): NFR ➔ SB;
        have to go to the superfamily level to get a CFR
      Family Haplobunodontidae (8 genera; LoEo-UEo): CFR
      ➔ propose: Superfamily Anthracotherioidea is 1B

Superfamily Anoplotherioidea (3 families; 17 genera; LoEo-MMio): CFR
Families Anoplotheriidae and Cainotheriidae are NFR ➔ SB; have to go to the level of the superfamily to get a CFR
Family Dacrytheriidae (5 genera; LoEo-LoOligo): CFR
➔ propose: Superfamily Anoplotherioidea is 1B and descendant from Family Dacrytheriidae as AK

Suborder Tylopoda (4 families; 66 genera; MEo-R): None of the families has a fossil record that goes quite far enough back, although 3 of the 4 get close and go equally far back: 3?
Family Xiphodontidae (4 genera; MEo-LoOligo): NFR (but close) ➔ 1B?
Superfamily Cameloidea (2 families; 49 genera; MEo-R) : NFR (but close) ➔ 1B?
Family Oromerycidae (7 genera; MMio-UMio): NFR ➔ SB
Family Camelidae (42 genera; MEo-R): NFR (but close) ➔ 1B?
Superfamily Protoceratoidea (1 family: Protoceratidae; 13 genera; MEo-LoPlio) : NFR (but close) ➔ 1B?

Suborder Ruminantia (15 families; 390 genera; LoEo-R): CFR; only 1 family has a CFR in this group   1
Family Amphimerycidae (2 genera; LoEo-LoOligo): CFR
Superfamilies Cervoidea, Giraffoidea, and Bovoidea are NFR ➔ SB; have to go to the level of the suborder to get a CFR
➔ propose: Suborder Ruminantia is 1B and descendant from Family Amphimerycidae as AK

Mirorder Meridiungulata (26 families; 251 genera; UK-R): 20 families have a CFR; if baramins are defined at the level of the family there are as many as 4 in this group. *Minimally*:   9-20
Family Perutheriidae (1 genus; UK): CFR or Flood fossil record
Family Amilnedwardsiidae (2 genera; Lo Eo): CFR
Order Litopterna (5 families; 50 genera; UPaleo-UPleisto): CFR
Family Protolipternidae (1 genus; UPaleo): CFR
Superfamily Macrauchenioidea (3 families; 27 genera; UPaleo-UPleisto): all families go back far enough:
Family Macraucheniidae (18 genera; UPaleo-UPleisto)
Family Notonychopidae (1 genus; UPaleo)
Family Adianthidae (8 genera; LoEo-MMio)
Superfamily Protorherioidea (1 family: Prototheriidae; 18 genera; UPaleo-Uplio): CFR ➔ 1B
Order Notoungulata (14 families; 167 genera; UPaleo-UPleisto): CFR
Suborder Notioprogonia (2 families; 11 genera; UPaleo-MEo): CFR:
Family Henricosborniidae (4 genera; UPaleo-LoEo)
Family Notostylopidae (5 genera; LoEo-LoOligo)
➔ propose: Suborder Notioprogonia as 1B and descendant from Family Henricosborniidae as AK (b/c the older fossil record)

Suborder Toxodontia (5 families; 84 genera; UPaleo-UPleisto):
      CFR
   Families Leontiniidae, Toxodontidae, and Homalodotheriidae
      are NFR ➔ SB; have to go to the level of the suborder
      to get a CFR
   Family Isotemnidae (12 genera; UPaleo-UOligo): CFR
   Family Notohippidae (17 genera: LoEo-UMio): CFR
   ➔ propose: Suborder Toxodontia as 1B and descendant from
      Family Isotemnidae as AK (b/c the older fossil record)
Suborder Typotheria (5 families; 37 genera; UPaleo-Mpleisto):
      CFR
   Family Mesotheriidae (10 genera; MEo-UPleisto): NFR ➔ SB;
      have to go to the level of the suborder to get a CFR
   Family Archaeopithecidae (2 genera; LoEo): CFR
   Family Oldfieldthomasiidae (8 genera; UPaleo-MEo): CFR
   Family Interatheriidae (15 genera; UPaleo-UMio): CFR
   Family Campanorcidae (1 genus; LoEo): CFR
   ➔ propose: Suborder Typotheria as 1B and descendant from
      Family Oldfieldthomasiidae as AK (b/c the older certain
      fossil record)
Suborder Hegetotheria (2 families; 20 genera; UPaleo-LoPleisto):
      CFR
   Family Hegetotheriidae (11 genera; MEo-LoPleisto): NFR ➔
      SB; have to go to the level of the suborder to get a CFR
   Family Archaeohyracidae (4 genera; UPaleo-UOligo): CFR
   ➔ propose: Suborder Hegetotheria and descendant from
      Family Archaeohyracidae as AK
Order Astrapotheria (3 families; 16 genera; UPaleo-UMio): CFR
   Family Eoastrapostylopidae (1 genus; UPaleo): CFR
   Family Trigonostylopidae (3 genera; UPaleo-MEo): CFR
   Family Astrapotheriidae (10 genera; LoEo-UMio): CFR
   ➔ propose: Order Astrapotheria is 1B and descendant from
      Family Eoastrapostylopidae or Trigonostylopidae as AK (b/c
      older fossil record)
Order Xenungulata (1 family: Carodniidae; 2 genera; UPaleo): CFR
      ➔ 1B
Order Pyrotheria (1 family: Pyrotheriidae; 6 genera; LoEo-UOligo):
      CFR ➔ 1B

Order Perissodactyla (14 families; 244 genera; UPaleo-R): 8 families   5-8
      have a CFR; if baramins are defined at the level of the family there
      are as many as 4 in this group. *Minimally*:
   Suborder Hippomorpha (2 families; 44 genera; LoEo-R): CFR
      Family Equidae (32 genera; LoEo-R): CFR
      Family Palaeotheriidae (12 genera; LoEo-LoOligo): CFR
   Suborder Ceratomorpha (12 families; 198 genera; LoEo-R): CFR
      Infraorder Selenida (4 families; 63 genera; LoEo-UPleisto): CFR
         Superfamily Brontotherioidea (2 families; 46 genera; LoEo-
            LoOligo): CFR
            Family Anchilophidae (3 genera; MEo-UEo): NFR ➔ SB;
               have to go to the level of the superfamily to get a
               CFR
            Family Brontotheriidae (43 genera; LoEo-LoOligo): CFR

➔ propose: Superfamily Brontotherioidea is 1B and
descendant from Family Brontotheriidae as AK
Superfamily Chalicotherioidea (2 families; 17 genera; LoEo-
UPleisto): CFR
Family Chalicotheriidae (9 genera; UEo-UPleisto): NFR ➔
SB; have to go to the level of the superfamily to get
a CFR
Family Eomoropidae (7 genera; LoEo-UEo): CFR
➔ propose: Superfamily Chalicotherioidea is 1B and
descendant from Family Eomoropidae as AK
Infraorder Tapiromorpha (8 families; 135 genera; LoEo-R): CFR
Superfamily Rhinocerotoidea (2 families; 99 genera; LoEo-R):
CFR
Family Rhinocerotidae (72 genera; MEo-R): NFR ➔ SB;
have to go to the level of superfamily to get a CFR
Family Hyracodontidae (26 genera; LoEo-UMio): CFR
➔ propose: Superfamily Rhinocerotoidea as 1B and
descendant from Family Hyracodontidae as AK
Superfamily Tapiroidea (6 families; 36 genera; LoEo-R): CFR
Families Deperetellidae, Lophialetidae, and Tapiridae are
NFR ➔ SB; have to go to the level of the Superfamily
to get a CFR
Family Helaletidae (6 genera; LoEo-UOligo): CFR
Family Isectolophidae (4 genera; LoEo-MEo): CFR
Family Lophiodontidae (4 genera; LoEo-UEo): CFR

Order Uranotheria (19 families; 108 genera; LoPaleo-R): CFR   4-6
Suborder Hyracoidea (2 families; 22 genera; LoEo-R): CFR
Family Procaviidae (5 genera; LoMio-R): NFR ➔ SB; have to go
to the level of the suborder to get a CFR
Family Pliohyracidae (16 genera; LoEo-LoPleisto): CFR
➔ propose: Suborder Hyracoidea is 1B and descendant from
Family Pliohyracidae as AK
Suborder Embrithopoda (2 families; 5 genera; LoPaleo-LoOligo):
CFR
Family Arsinoitheriidae (3 genera; MEo-LoOligo): NFR ➔ SB;
have to go to the level of the suborder to get a CFR
Family Phenacolophidae (2 genera; LoPaleo-UPaleo): CFR
➔ propose: Suborder Embrithopoda is 1B and descendant from
Family Phenacolophidae as AK
Suborder Tethytheria (15 families; 81 genera; UPaleo-R): CFR
Infraorder Sirenia (3 families; 31 genera; LoEo-R): CFR
Family Trichechidae (3 genera; MMio-R): NFR ➔ SB; have to
go to the level of the infraorder to get a CFR
Family Prorastomidae (1 family; LoEo-UEo): CFR
Family Dugongidae (22 families; LoEo-R): CFR
➔ propose: Infraorder Sirenia is 1B and descendant from
Family Prorastomidae or Dugongidae as AK
Infraorder Behemota (12 families; 50 genera; UPaleo-R): CFR
Parvorder Desmostylia (1 family; 6 genera; UOligo-UMio):
NFR ➔ SB; have to go to the level of the infraorder to
get a CFR

Parvorder Proboscidea (11 families; 44 genera; UPaleo-R):
   CFR
   Family Anthracobunidae (5 genera; LoEo-MEo): CFR
   Family Numidotheriidae (2 genera; UPaleo-LoEo): CFR
   Superfamilies Mammutoidea and Elephantoidea have NFR
         → SB; have to go to the level of the parvorder to get
         a CFR
→ propose: Infraorder Behemota is 1B and descendant from
      Family Numidotheriidae as AK (b/c with an older fossil
      record)

TOTAL: 97-203
                                                               (123-234)

Appendix A.

Available as supplemental data at
http://www.bryancore.org/issues/number_5.html

-goes against Darwin (symbiosis)
-considered an exception
-serial theory

6. Symbiosis, Relationship and the Origin of Species

JOSEPH W. FRANCIS
THE MASTER'S COLLEGE

found everywhere

6.1. Introduction

Interaction among living organisms is a ubiquitous biological phenomenon. Even seemingly solitary creatures like a single-celled pond organism or the elusive mountain lion interact with prey or the pervasive microbes which attach to and thrive with every organism in all ecosystems. The interaction among living organisms can be fleeting and short lived or involve long term relationship. Sustained interaction of living organisms is often referred to as symbiosis, which is more formally defined as; long term association involving protracted contact between two or more different kinds of organisms (Margulis 2002).[1] *long time*

The purpose of this paper is to examine the role that symbiosis plays or has played in the origin of species from both evolutionary and creation biology perspectives. The idea that the fusion of two or more different kinds of living organism can lead to a new species (symbiogenesis) is foreign to Darwin's much more conservative individualistic and gradual theory of speciation, i.e. single species are modified slowly by slight modification to form new species. Interestingly, even with evidence supporting a possible role for symbiosis in the generation of species, symbiosis as a driving force for evolution is considered an exception to the rule rather than the rule (Sapp 1994). The serial endosymbiotic theory (SET) which proposes that eukaryotic cells and their corresponding organelles were derived from mergers of prokaryotic cells (Margulis 2002, Frank 2002), is widely accepted, and is thought to explain the origin of the eukaryotic Kingdoms, but is regarded by many evolutionary biologists as an unsatisfactory explanation for the origin of new individual species.

make new

slow

modify

---

1   Definitions of symbiosis which are more inclusive are used by biologists and have incorporated a wide variety of cooperative relationships, for example, pollinators and their respective plants. However, the more narrow definition above is commonly used and it is the definition we will typically use in this paper although the concepts of the more inclusive definition may also be noted.

examine symbiosis and relationships

There is, however, a small but growing number of evolutionary biologists (symbiologists) who propose that the processes of natural selection and mutation, although active in the speciation process, are not adequate to create the novelty required for formation of new species. They suggest that a more radical genetic plasticity which permits genome merger in contrast to small mutational change is the key to promotion of speciation and fits better with the data which shows saltational rather than gradual speciation events in the fossil record.

Recent work in creationism also suggests that post creation speciation events are consistent with both the scientific data and biblical data (Wood 2008, Wise 2002). This view of creationism explains how the earth could contain a vast diversity of living things developed from an original set of created organisms which diversified during several epochs of rapid speciation. Natural selection and mutation, although woven into the fabric of creation, would not have enough time based on our current understanding of evolutionary mechanisms to produce the rapid speciation events required by these new theories in young age creationism (Wood 2002). Therefore, it is interesting to note that non-Darwinian mechanisms of speciation are of interest to both creation and evolutionary biologists.

Although some creationists have tended to overlooked the importance of symbiotic phenomenon in nature because of a narrow focus on the problems inherent in SET, I believe that creationism may provide a better framework for explaining the phenomenon of symbiosis and symbiosis induced speciation than other model systems for the following reasons. First, because of the prevalence and the importance of the concept of relationship in Scripture, creationists should anticipate and expect that symbiotic relationships will be prevalent and persistent throughout the living world. Secondly, because some living organisms were created to serve others, the persistence of relationships where only one partner benefits from symbiotic-like association, would be predicted and explained within creation biology.[2] Thirdly, theories of symbiogenesis imply but tend to gloss over the fact that the genetic or morphological novelty that arises during symbiosis-induced speciation is enhanced by the association of disparate creatures or disparate genomes. This effect would be relatively small in non-theistic origin of life theories because common descent presumably would generate fairly uniform initial life forms. In contrast, since creation biology posits high discontinuity and disparity among the first life forms, symbiogenesis-induced novelty could be very high. In order to explore these concepts more thoroughly in this paper we will review the classification system of symbiosis, consider a

---

2   The origin of unequal mutualism and non-mutualistic relationship can be explained within the evolution model since mutualism is widely held to be derived from parasitic relationships. However, it may be more problematic for evolutionary biology to explain the long term persistence of such relationships.

brief history of symbiosis; and then examine the concept of symbiogenesis in the context of both creation and evolutionary biology models.

6.2. Classification of Symbiotic Relationships

Various criteria are used to classify symbiotic relationships. There are three basic forms of symbiosis which are widely recognized; 1) mutualism, 2) commensalism 3) and parasitism. Mutualism is defined as an association which involves a benefit supplied to both symbiont partners; in nature it is typically observed as an unbalanced relationship with one partner receiving more benefit than the other (Law and Dieckman 1988). Commensualism as originally described by van Beneden is defined as an organism which shares the table scraps of another organism (Van Beneden 1876). According to Atlas and Bartha, commensualism involves one symbiont or population which benefits from a relationship "while the other remains unaffected" (Atlas 1998).[3] Parasitism is defined as a long term relationship with one partner being harmed by the relationship.

It is difficult to classify individual symbiotic relationships as being strictly mutualistic, commensualistic or parasitic since many relationships demonstrate aspects of some or all of these modes of living. For instance, the relationship between the oyster-crab (*Pinnotheres ostreum*) and its host oyster (*Crassostrea virginica*) appears at first glance to be a good example of a commensualistic relationship, in that the oyster receives "table scraps" from the crab which lives in its partners shell. However, the crab can be viewed as invading its host but also benefits from the protection of the clam shell, so in fact this relationship also displays parasitism and mutualism (Howe 2002). The lichen relationship, one of the oldest documented symbiosis which typically involves a partnership between algae and fungi, appears to be mutualistic. However, this partnership also demonstrates some aspects of parasitism because the fungus invades the algae cells and some are harmed and destroyed by the invasion.

The broad classifications mentioned above can be broken down into subcategories that more succinctly define the relationship. These subcategories typically involve some aspect of the structural location of the symbiotic partners with respect to one another and the functions provided by each symbiont.[4] I propose, for the sake of simplicity, that the structural classification of symbionts involve two broad categories:

---

3   This phenomena will also be referred to in this paper as unequal mutualism.
4   Ahmadjian and Paracer, include structural classification within their framework for classifying symbionts (Paracer 2000). Their scheme is a modification of the one developed by Starr and includes the following categories; location of symbiont, persistence of symbiosis, dependence of symbiosis, specificity of symbiosis, and symbiotic products (Starr 1975). However, these authors do not suggest a mechanism for how to classify symbiosis and some of the categories seemed seldom used or impractical.

Structural categories [handwritten]

location (exosymbiotic vs endosymbiotic vs endocytobiotic) and dependence (obligate vs facultative). An obligate symbiont is one that cannot live apart from its partner and a facultative symbiont can live in a "free" or "associated" symbiotic state. The "location" classification category can be subdivided into the following three subcategories based on the work of Nardon and Charles (Nardon 2002):

Exosymbiosis: The symbiotic partners are external to each other. For instance, lichens would be included in this category even though one partner can partly invade the other.

Endosymbiosis: One symbiont in the relationship thrives in the internal spaces of the partner but remain extracellular.

Endocytobiosis: One symbiont is found inside the cells of the partner, but can often exist extracellularly for part of its life history.

Each location category can be subdivided further to indicate the size of the symbionts-namely macro-organisms (defined as multicellular) versus microorganisms (typically defined as unicellular) (Table 1). It is interesting to note that two subcategories, namely the macro-macro-endocytobiosis and micro-micro-endosymbiosis may have few if any examples. However, bacteria typically promote the formation of large multicellular structures and essentially create inner-spaces which could harbor endosymbionts, therefore this relationship may indeed fulfill the criteria for micro-micro-endosymbiosis. In the case of macro-macro-endocytobiosis, multicellular parasites can invade individual cells of metazoans so it is also possible for this arrangement to occur. As mentioned, symbionts can also be classified according to the function they provide to their partner. Since this classification tends to flow from the creation model we will discuss the functional classification in a later section of the paper.

6.2.1. More about endosymbiosis. Endosymbiosis is a widespread phenomenon in nature and the most documented symbiotic phenomenon. For instance, viruses are ubiquitous in nature and are predicted to be found in the cells of all organisms, therefore endosymbiosis and endocytobiosis may be the most common biological phenomena in the biosphere (Frank

	macro/macro	macro/micro	micro/micro
exosymbiosis	X	X	X
endosymbiosis	X	X	?
endocytobiosis	?	X	X

Table 1. This table shows the subdivisions of the location category of structural classification of symbiosis. There are many examples of symbiosis in each category (X. with exception of the macro/macro endocytobiosis and micro/micro endosymbiosis categories.)

2007). Endocytobiosis, which is often referred to as endosymbiosis, is of interest to evolutionary cell biologists because it is widely held to be an innovative mechanism which caused the derivation of eukaryotic cell organelles from prokaryotes; the central concept of SET (Margulis 1975 1981). Creationists have been critical of this theory and some aspects of the theory remain obscure and unexplained, however, this does not change the fact that endosymbiosis is a widespread phenomena in nature and therefore worthy of study by creation scientists (Bergman 1998).

Microbes and viruses are the primary symbionts involved in endosymbiotic phenomena. They are also abundant as exosymbionts and have been observed as exosymbionts and endosymbionts on the same host cell.

6.3. A Brief History of Symbiosis

Mutually beneficial relationships were described in written stories circulated among the ancients including, Aristotle, Cicero, Aelian, Herodotus and Pliny (Sapp 1994). One of the more popular tales among these authors was that of the Egyptian plover and the Nile crocodile. Herodotus claimed that "The plover ate leaches from the crocodile's mouth." (Egerton 1973). In their discourse on mutualism the ancient authors pointed out that qualities like friendship could be observed and learned from nature (Egerton 1973).

More thoroughly documented theoretical and scientific studies of symbiosis occurred in the 18th and 19th centuries and originated from four different groups and disciplines; 1) Russian biology and social Darwinism, 2) cell biology, 3) natural theology and early creationists and 4) botany.

6.3.1. Russian biology and social Darwinism. The idea of cooperation among living organisms was a dominate theme among Russian biologists of the 19th century (Todes 1989; Sapp 1994). Many of them along with the social Darwinists rejected the concept of mutual struggle and the Malthusian-based Darwinism prevalent in England and instead viewed the relationship among organisms as more beneficial than detrimental. One of their most vocal proponents was Peter Kropotkin, an anarchist geologist who proposed that mutual aid was more prevalent in nature than mutual struggle (Kroptkin 1915). This ideology would lay the groundwork for Russian cell biologists to view the cell as an entity constructed of several different organisms. Not all English scientists were opposed to the idea of cooperative relationship, authors Geddes and Thompson in their book, *The Evolution of Sex*, emphasized that association of species in the context of "love and sociality and cooperation and sacrifice" as exemplified in sexual reproducing organisms, was an important force in evolution equal or superior to competition. However, many contemporaries of these early advocates of symbiosis were not convinced that true symbiotic relationships existed. They suggested that symbiotic associations at their core were nothing more than parasitic or slave-like relationships.

Herbert Spencer, a leading thinker and spokesman for social Darwinism in the 19th and 20th centuries was an advocate of the "survival of the fittest" view of life and thus he also would have supported the view that parasitism was a common feature of organismal interaction (Spencer 1899). However, he also noted that competition among organisms was balanced by the existence of beneficial symbiotic relationships and that over time peaceful competitive relationships would dominate ecosystems. He viewed nature as an organic whole or superorganism, and viewed human society as an organism which could progressively improve via cooperation and social evolution aided by institutions such as education. Strikingly, some of Spencer's views appear creationistic, for instance, Spencer was enamored with the wide disparity and discontinuity between plants and animals which he referred to as "that widest contrast which the higher organic world presents." He also marveled at their interdependence and observed that some symbiotic creatures were constructed of both "vegetal and animal" elements. The interdependence of plants and animals would be a common theme among the early symbiologists. It is no surprise then to note that Spencer was influenced by the creationist writings of van Beneden (Sapp 1994)

6.3.2. Cell Biology. Spencer's ideas of the superorganism and mutual dependence were prevalent in the writings of cell biologists of the late 19th century. The concept of the "cell-state", "cell commonwealth" or "cell republic" formed the basis of cell theory espoused by German cell biologists such as Virchow, Haeckel and Hertwig (Sapp 1994). Cells were viewed as obligate members of a collective; an interdependent society which made up the individual multicellular creature.[5] The idea of the collective would also be applied to the subcellular level, and many biologists of this time period suggested that cells were constructed of smaller transferable living entities; "physiological units" (Herbert Spencer), "gemmules" (Darwin), "biophors" (Weisman), and "pangenes" (Hugo de Vries). Even though these entities were never proven to physically exist the ideas would serve as the forerunner of the "endosymbiosis" theories popularized in the late 20th century by Lynn Margulis and others.

6.3.3. Natural theology and early creationists. The influence of theology on symbiosis can be traced back to the natural theologians of the 17th-19th centuries. The works of Linnaeus and the French zoologist Pierre-Joseph van Beneden, in particular stand out, Linnaeus (1781) primarily commented about general ecological relationships whereas van Beneden (1876) concentrated on the study of individual mutual relationships.

---

5   Fascinatingly, in Germany, these views were prevalent in other disciplines including social engineering and politics and the idea of the "good" of the collective whole versus the selfish needs of the individual would be a dominate theme in German politics for the first half of the 20th century.

It is obvious from Linnaeus's work that he was heavily influenced by both Aristotle's great chain of being and the Bible. In the *Oeconomy of Nature*, Linnaeus described all living creatures as being connected "to produce general ends and reciprocal uses." Linnaeus commented on the design of grasses and trees and how they were ubiquitous in nature, "The great Author and Parent of all things, decreed that the whole earth should be covered with plants." Linnaeus commented about creation of individual plant types for certain purposes. For instance he noted the ability of grasses to grow in diverse places and how this was consistent with their creation as food for cattle and other domestic farm animals and he pointed out that trees were designed to provide sustenance for non-domestic creatures because their leaves were not readily accessible by lowly cattle (Linnaeus 1781).

Although Linnaeus did not write extensively about individual mutualistic relationships, he did mention the relationship between the shell-fish *Pinna* and its live-in partner, the oyster crab. Both Aristotle and van Beneden were also smitten by the oyster crab's ability to live in the dark chamber of shellfish and share its spoils as well as offer its blind partner an early warning system for lurking predators (Sapp 1994, Van Beneden 1876). In his book *Animal Parasites and Messmates* van Beneden described a variety of different animal relationships and, like Linnaeus, focused on how creatures were designed to interact with one another and provide the basic necessities of life, i.e., food and shelter. Van Beneden introduced the term "mutualism" in a lecture in 1873 and believed that all "mutual adaptations were pre-arranged" by God and that the earth was prepared to promote relationships among living things. "...we cannot divest ourselves of the idea that the earth has been prepared successively for plants, animals, and man" (Sapp 1994, Van Beneden 1876).

6.3.4. Botany. Athough a zoologist introduced the concept of mutualism, it was a botanist who is credited with the first use of the term symbiosis. Botanist Albert Frank coined the term "symbiotisumus" in 1877 while studying lichens, which are constructed of partners from two different kingdoms (Sapp 1994; Frank 1877). Some lichens can also include a bacterial partner, and thus be composed of creatures from three different kingdoms. Frank along with many other lichenologists of his time felt that even though the lichen relationship looked in part to be detrimental to the algae, parasitism did not adequately describe the relationship which characterized lichens.

Anton de Bary, a well known botanist and lichenologist used the term symbiosis in a speech in 1878, and despite Frank's work, he is typically cited as the person who introduce the concept of symbiosis. de Bary defined symbiosis as "the living together of unlike named organisms" (Sapp 1994; De Bary 1879) There is good evidence to suggest that Anton de Bary was heavily influenced by van Beneden and his writings describing mutualism. De Bary also noted that there were many different gradations of symbiosis recognized among the diverse lichens. He was also open to the idea that symbiosis involved many different kinds of associations including both parasitism and those involving organisms which don't live in close proximity (e.g., the relationship between pollinating insects and flowering plants). De Bary also suggested in his work that symbiosis might be a source of evolutionary innovation. Thus his ideas preceeded by decades the more modern evolutionary endosymbiosis theories.

The symbiologists who immediately followed Frank and de Bary primarily focused their work on the association of animals with plant-like cholorophyll-containing organisms such as the symbiosis involving the green hydra and its algal symbiont. Thus one of the common themes evident in the early history of symbiosis is the focus on the relationship between plants and animals. Many of the early "symbiologists" were fascinated by this relationship but also struggled with how to classify the relationship given the taxonomic disparity between the symbionts, and the fact that the animal partner appeared to parasitize the plant.

6.3.5. Contemporary views of symbiosis. Not much is recorded about symbiosis during the early 20th century as more scientists turned their attention to models of competition and the discoveries in molecular biology shifted the focus from organisms to nucleo-centric genetics (Sapp 1994). However, one U.S. scientist entertained the idea that mitochondria were symbionts living inside cells. In the 1920's Ivan Wallin suggested that acquired bacteria (mitochondria) were the source of new genes and evolutionary novelty and wrote a text with the title, *Symbionticism and the Origin of Species*. Wallin's ideas were an extension of those of de Bary and Merezhkowsky (1905) who viewed the nucleus and cytoplasm as symbiotic partners. Another biologist who thought along these lines was Félix d'Herelle who suggested that bacteria which harbor viruses were "microlichens" and mentioned in his writings that he believed that symbiosis was a major driving force of evolutionary novelty (d'Herelle 1926). Ivan Wallin tried in vain to isolate and grow mitochondria apart from cells but his work inspired another American scientist Lynn Margulis, to promote a revival of the "cell collective" or endosymbiosis concepts in the 1960's and 70's. Margulis's work was met with skepticism but decades of persistence resulted in wide acceptance of SET (Margulis 1975). Even so, the idea that organismal fusion or gene transfer among disparate life forms can lead to speciation is today not widely recognized among mainstream evolutionary biologists. For instance in his seminal work of over 1400 pages, *The Structure of Evolutionary Thought*, Stephen J. Gould did not once refer to symbiosis (Sapp 2007) and in *Wonderful life* he referred to SET as "quirky" evolution (Gould 1990).

more 17th–19th
century

6.4. Symbiogenesis, Speciation and Evolutionary Biology

Symbiologists insist that symbiosis has played a major role in the evolution of life on earth, although they represent a minority voice among evolutionary biologists. They build their case for this view by showing that natural selection and mutation, are wholly inadequate to create the genetic or morphological novelty required to create new species. Margulis comments:

> "Never, however, did that one mutation make a wing, a fruit, a woody stem or claw appear. Mutations in summary tend to induce sickness, death or deficiencies. No evidence in the vast literature of hereditary change shows unambiguous evidence that random mutation itself, even with geographical isolation of populations, leads to speciation. Then how do new species come into being? How do cauliflowers descend from tiny, wild Mediterranean cabbagelike plants, or pigs from wild boars?" (Margulis and Sagan 2002, p. 29).

> "Speciation, whether in the remote Galapagos, in the laboratory cages of the drosophilosophers, or in the crowded sediments of the paleontologists, still has never been directly traced. The closest science has come to observing and recording actual speciation in animals is the work of Theodosius Dobzhansky in *Drosophila paulistorium* fruit flies. But even here, only reproductive isolation, not new species, appeared." (Margulis and Sagan 2002, p. 31).

The concepts of mutation and selection are not totally abandoned by advocates of this model; they are considered processes of refinement (Margulis and Sagan 2002). In addition, although symbiologists appear to reject the idea of mutation as a driving force for speciation, and therefore distance themselves from neo-Darwinism, the argument may be based more on semantics than true differences of opinion because the symbiologists propose a more radical form of mutation involving genome merger or gene transfer which promotes a rapid change in organismal biology in contrast to gradual change induced by single-nucleotide mutation. John Maynard Smith takes a middle position and suggests that evolutionary novelty can be produced by both gradual Darwinian and symbiotic mechanisms, but he also expressed in his early writings on the subject that symbiogenesis did not directly lead to the derivation of multicellular plants or animals (Smith 1991). In his later writings, however, he suggested that endosymbiosis did play a role in major evolutionary transitions (Szathmáry 1997).[6]

6.4.1. Speciation via Endosymbiosis (SET theory). The data presented by symbiologists in support of symbiosis-induced speciation (symbiogenesis) often involve contemporary examples of the SET theory, i.e. speciation by acquired bacteria or viruses. There are few if any examples where the fusion of multicellular genomes leads to speciation but speculative models do exist. We will consider several examples of symbiogenesis.

Lynn Margulis and fellow symbiologists infer that symbiogenesis is a proven fact because it is responsible for the origin all of the major animal kingdoms readily observable on earth. Margulis comments:

> "The creative force of symbiosis produced eukaryotic cells from bacteria. Hence all larger organisms–protoctists, fungi, animals and plants–originated symbiogenetically. " (Margulis and Sagan 2002 p. 56).

Thus Margulis relies heavily on the natural history of cellular origins to show that symbiogenesis is a major force of evolution and speciation. Margulis also suggests that it was more than just the acquisition of mitochondria which led to the formation of eukaryotic cells; symbiologists now postulate that cholorplasts, nuclei, cilium, and cytoskeletal components were derived from the acquisition of microbes (Margulis and Sagan 2002). The discovery of DNA in mitochondria and chloroplasts supports Margulis theory that these organelles were once free living microbes. In addition, the fact that the mitochondrial genome is inadequate for supporting the mitochondrion outside the cell without expression of nuclear genes provides support for the idea that genome merger and genome interaction is an important part of symbiogenesis. Margulis also claims that symbiogenesis can be observed today and cites several examples of speciation in her text, including the speciation of: the plants, *Ardisia* and *Abutilon*, the ciliate *Euplotidium*, the rice weevil *Sitophilus oryzae* and termites *Macrotermes*. Correspondingly, it is interesting to note that Margulis relies heavily on the idea that speciation occurs via the acquisition of genomes and genome integration provides the source of "heritable novelty" which promotes speciation. Margulis comments:

> "Organisms also gain new hereditary traits by accumulation of viruses, or of plasmids or other short pieces

---

6   Smith referred to seven major transitions in evolution, for example the prokaryote to eukaryote transition. In a majority of these transitions he suggested that smaller entities combined to make larger entities.

of DNA. They acquire long pieces of new DNA, many genes at once, by bacterial mating and by legitimate sexual mating with distant relatives–that is, by hybridization...taken together these means constitute a strong case that Darwin's dilemma is solved. Science now knows the major source of evolutionary novelty."

"When a gene of one organism enters and remains within *ex.* the genes of another, for example when a gene is passed from a free-living bacterium to the nucleus of a plant, integration is complete. No greater intimacy is known than the permanent harboring of your partner's genes. By the time this level of intimacy occurs, the chance is great that behavioral, metabolic and gene-product integrations are already in place." (Margulis and Sagan 2002, p. 101)

However, in the examples of speciation cited in her text, little hard *- no genome* data is presented to show how genome acquisition actually influenced the symbiosis or speciation events. Instead, in the examples given, speciation is occurring most likely because the acquired symbionts provide a survival advantage to the host organism; it is not clear whether genome integration or interaction plays any role at all in the speciation events described. *Ardisia*

Let's consider each example individually. *Ardisia* is a tropical flowering plant in the family Myrsinaceae. Bacterial endosymbionts *are thriving* live within the tissues of *Ardisia* and promote a fluted morphology in the leaves.[7] The bacterial symbiont is transferred via the plant seed and the plants are severely crippled and non-reproductive without the endosymbiont. (Reid 2007). There are over 30 species of Ardisia and it is predicted that they all contain their own unique species of obligate endosymbiotic bacterium. Margulis suggests that these 30 species of *Ardisia* would not exist without endosymbionts and therefore this is an example of endosymbiosis-induced speciation. Although it is very possible that the bacteria promote the survival and speciation of this plant, there is no indication that genome interaction is involved in this speciation event (Margulis 2000).

Euplotidium The surface of the ciliate *Euplotidium* harbors an exosymbiont *external* bacterium. This unusual and fascinating bacterium contains a coiled ribbon which is shot out of each bacterium when *Euplotidium* is threatened by predators. All six species of *Euplotidium* contain the ribbon-shooting exosymbionts and they are very susceptible to predation without the exosymbionts. Margulis suggests that this is another example *new to me*

---

7   These bacterial symbionts are true endosymbionts and not endocytobionts because they are not found inside the cells but instead are found within the tissue structure of the leaves.

no genome

of symbiosis induced speciation, but again, there is no reference or data presented which shows that there is genome sharing or integration in this system.

Margulis also suggests a role for endosymbionts in the speciation of rice weevils and termites but no genome integration events are presented in these models. In both the weevils and termites, the endosymbionts provide vital nutrients such as vitamins, growth factors and enzymes, and thus it could be claimed that the genome of the symbionts is indirectly involved in the speciation process. However, scientists who study the weevil symbiosis admit that there is no evidence of true genome sharing (Nardon and Grenier 1991). They do, however, suggest that the endosymbiont assisted speciation in rice weevils may be induced by sexual isolation since the hybrids resulting from mating of two weevil sibling species produced sterile offspring.[8] — *maybe*

Margulis does describe at least one example of genome integration. The flowering maple *Abutilon pictum* can be infected with a virus which promotes differential color patterns involving stripes or spots in the leaves of this plant (Reid 2007). Viral modulation of organisms typically involves genetic interaction which can include viral gene expression and genome integration. However, it is not clear how this coloration pattern influences speciation outside of the fact that human gardeners have selected this plant for its coloration patterns. Nonetheless this is an example of a "Lamarckian-like" inheritable trait that originated via genome acquisition.

There is at least one example of symbiogenesis which has been observed in the laboratory. Kwang Jeon isolated a bacterium-infected strain of *Amoeba proteus*, (xD amoeba), after he noted that his pure cultures of *Amoeba proteus* were dying from infection. Jeon painstakingly isolated the infected survivors and propogated them over a number of months and years, and noted over time that although they demonstrated slow growth compared to the wildtype, the xD amoeba became dependent on their bacterial symbiont (Margulis 1989; Ryan 2002; Jeon 1972). In this case there is some evidence of genome interaction but it appears to be very limited and involves the endosymbiont deactivation of one host gene with the subsequent activation of a redundant back-up gene. It is important to note that the xD amoeba is less hardy than its wild type counterpart and is easily killed by very small changes in feeding parameters and temperature (Jeon 1972). It is doubtful that this laboratory strain could survive in the typical habitat populated by *Amoeba proteus*. Richard law suggests that this is an example of the evolution of a non-mutualistic symbiosis whereby organisms can grow dependent on one

8   The mechanism of sexual isolation in insects in postulated to involve nucleocytoplasmic incompatability which has been demonstrated to be induced in a variety of insect species by endosymbionts.

another without providing or receiving benefits from one another (Law 1998). It is interesting to note that this example of speciation stands in stark contrast to the previous mentioned speciation events which clearly show that the endosymbiont provides a survival advantage to its host. Jeon comments:

> "On the basis of the structural and physiological changes brought about by endosymbionts in xD amoeba...one could consider the symbiont-bearing xD strain a new "species" of *Amoeba*. However, until evidence for genetic differences between D and xD amoeba is obtained, it would be more prudent to treat xD amoeba as belonging to a variant strain." (Jeon 1991, p. 118)

Jeon is clearly more conservative than Margulis with respect to what constitutes speciation.

Is there an example of endosymbiotic-induced symbiogenesis with evidence of both genome alteration and promotion of host survival in the wild? Frank Ryan in his text Darwin's Blind Spot suggests that the viral endosymbiont-induced speciation of Australian Rock wallabies might satisfy these criteria. Multiple species of Rock wallabies live close to one another and have undergone rapid speciation. Evolutionary biologists studying this phenomenon have noted that the speciation is much too rapid to be accounted for by natural selection and mutation alone. It appears that during hybridization of these animals, the centromeres of the gamete chromosomes become unusually susceptible to gene rearrangement and gene insertion. In many cases endogenous retroviruses (KERVs) have been found at the centromere locations. Thus, it appears that endosymbiont-induced speciation by genetic alteration is occurring in this organism. However, this scenario presents several problems for the theory of symbiogenesis. One is that the new populations may not be considered truly new species by some species definitions because there is not true reproductive isolation. Secondly, the endogenous retroviruses may have always been part of the animal genome and may not be true viruses or symbionts. Nonetheless, it appears that rapid speciation is occurring in this group of animals.

Chromophytes represent another possible example of speciation by endosymbiotic genome acquisition. In these chimeric organisms an algae-like symbiont appears to have been engulfed by a flagellated protozoan. The genome of the algae is highly reduced and is called a nucleomorph. The enslaved alga contains a chloroplast which is surrounded by up to four membranes, suggesting that the alga was once engulfed by the protozoan (Douglass 2001). The protozoan host provides proteins which the algal symbiont uses for its metabolism and the nucleomorph contributes to the functioning of the chloroplast. Although the acquisition of the algae has not been observed in this type of endocytobiosis, recently the acquisition of a green algae symbiont by a protozoan has been described. The protozoan *Hatena engulfs* an algae which loses its cytoskeleton and flagellum and induces its host to switch to autotrophic nutrition and perform phototaxis using an eyespot (Okamoto, N. and Inouye 2005).

6.4.2. Speciation by Genome Merger in Multicellular Organism.

Although sexual reproduction within a species and hybridization of similar species is readily observed, there are few if any studies which show that merger or genome acquisition has occurred among widely disparate metazoan species. Williamson (2007) has developed and proposed an intriguing larval transfer theory which suggests that many larva have been transferred into their present day lineages from other distantly related animal groups by cross-fertilization. He suggests that the larval stage of development and the subsequent adult stage of development represents the sequential expression of two different ancient merged genomes. Williamson presents some interesting ideas and has performed some laboratory experiments but crucial experiments involving genome analysis have not yet been performed to any great extent and several scientists have attempted to reproduce his work without success.[9]

Despite the fact that genome merger has not been demonstrated in many cases of symbiogenesis, it cannot be ignored that symbiosis is a ubiquitous and important formative process in organismal biology. The evaluation of symbiogenesis as a process of innovation from an evolutionary biology perspective leads to a number of conclusions: 1) symbiotic relationships are primarily derived from parasitism which involves invasion and cell and organismal death as part of the trial and error process involved in the establishment of such relationships, 2) although symbiosis provides a source of variation at the genetic or morphology level upon which natural selection and mutation can act, symbiosis does not explain where the initial source of variation comes from, 3) symbiosis can promote survival and reproductive isolation of organisms to help establish new species, 4) although natural selection should theoretically tend to promote symbiotic relationships where both partners receive a benefit many relationships persist where primary benefit comes to only one partner, 5) The involvement of genome acquisition in speciation appears to be limited to endosymbiosis events involving bacteria and viruses and 6) barriers to genome acquisition may prevent widespread genome acquisition among metazoan species.

---

9   For more on this topic the reader is referred to Williamson, D.I., and S.E. Vickers. 2007. The Origins of Larvae. *American Scientist* 95:509-517. Also see letters to the editor in the *American Scientist* 96:91, 2008.

It is interesting to note that symbiotic phenomena fulfill the criteria of two major species concepts: symbionts promote reproductive isolation (biological species concept) and in some instances they promote profound changes in morphology (morphological species concept) (Margulis 2002).

6.5. Symbiosis and Creation: Beneficial Relationship as the Origin of Symbiosis

6.5.1. Biblical concepts which provide a framework for understanding relationships evident in nature. The natural theology of van Beneden and Linnaeus and other early creationists clearly had an influence on the early formulations of symbiosis theory. However, an in-depth analysis of Scripture is not evident the writings of either van Beneden or Linnaeus. In fact, van Beneden's writings reveal that he was influenced by the political and social climate of his day perhaps just as much as he was influenced by scriptural principles (Sapp 1994). More recently, several creationists have noted the interdependence of living creatures within ecosystems, (Zuill 2000) but an in-depth analysis of biological relationships from a biblical perspective is lacking.

6.5.2. Biology and the Bible. Scriptural concepts which support symbiosis are abundant. In fact, relationship among organisms is very consistent with how Scripture portrays biology. Some aspects of physiology and anatomy are described in Scripture, however, it is the relationships among organisms which appear to be the main message portrayed by the Bible in reference to biology. For example, in the Bible there is an emphasis on the relationship between plants and animals (Genesis 1:30), between animals themselves (Isaiah 11:6-7), between man and plants (Genesis 1:29; Jonah 4:6) and between man and animals (Genesis 2:19-20). Many symbiotic relationships, evident within the living creation, are characterized by intimacy and sacrificial giving, and provide a picture of the eternal attributes of relationship demonstrated within the Godhead and demonstrated by the redemptive relationship between God and man.

6.5.3. Relationship a foundational biblical concept. The concept of relationship is prevalent in the biblical text and is evident both within the God-head and created realms described in Scripture. For example, relationship among the members of the Trinity is an eternal attribute of the Godhead and it can be described as exhibiting both hierarchical and non-hierarchical attributes (Deut 6:4). For instance, Christ subjected himself to the Father's authority yet he maintained his position within the Godhead (Matt 28:19, Matt 3:16-17, 2 Cor 13:14, John 10: 18, 30). These relationships which show both hierarchical structure and equality are reflected within the created order. For instance, many animals which live in social groups exhibit an authority structure but also demonstrate equality among the "working" class individuals. A closer examination of the God-head relationships and those built into the fabric of creation as described in Scripture, shows that there are at least three main categories of relationship; (1) interpersonal, one on one relationship, (2) headship, relationship and (3) community, relationship among members of a group.

6.5.4. One on one interpersonal relationship. Interpersonal relationship is abundant in the living creation and in most all cases is characterized by long-term intimate personal contact. For instance, Christ's relationship with the Father and his relationship with the Church is mirrored in both the marriage relationship and salvation relationship (Ephesians 5:23; Rev 19:9, 21:9; John 3:29). Romans 7:4 states that we are "joined with God" upon salvation. In all these cases physical contact or intimate communication occurs. Aspects of the marriage relationship are also readily observed among living things; many monogamous relationships are observed in the animal kingdom among male and female partners. It is also interesting to note that Adam who was surrounded by living creatures in a beautiful garden was declared by God to be "alone." (Genesis 2:18) Thus it is clear that God did not create organisms to live in seclusion; interpersonal relationship is a fundamental part of creation. Ecclesiastes states that it is not good for man to live and work alone and there is strength in companionship; "Two are better than one...", "...woe to him who is alone when he falls...," "A threefold cord is not quickly broken." (Ecclesiastes 4;8-12)

Many aspects of one-on-one relationship are observed in nature and within symbiotic relationships. For instance, there is close and intimate contact between the fungal and algal partners in the lichen (Howe 2002). In fact, the fungus invades the algal cells, yet this relationship, which appears pathogenic and parasitic in many ways produces a novel creature with a distinct morphology, unique ecological niche and potentially increased lifespan. One-on-one relationships also display specificity since in many cases individuals in monogamous relationships can detect their partner against the background of similar-looking individuals. Therefore, creationism would predict that because symbionts were created to interact with certain partners many symbionts will display specificity at the level of partner recognition. This type of specificity has been documented in a variety of symbiotic relationships. For instance, the "leafcutter" ants eat as their primary food source a fungus which they grow on leaves procured for this purpose (Currie 2003). The fungus which survives because the ants grow and protect it is a pure strain specific to each leafcutter ant species. In another example, specificity is also demonstrated in the relationship between the Hawaiian bobtail squid and *Vibrio fischeri*, a light producing bacterium. The squid possesses an elaborate light organ specifically designed to interact with only *Vibrio fischeri* and uses mechanisms to eliminate other bacterial species (Nyholm 2004).

6.5.5. Headship relationship. Scripture illustrates this relationship principle most vividly by references to human social structure and the interaction of humans with nature. For instance, man was created not only to interact and enjoy the beauty and fellowship of plants and animals but he was also to name them and exercise dominion over them (Psalm 8; Genesis 2:19, 7:2). This does not imply destruction, but instead stewardship as man is to cultivate, interact and study the creatures in the garden (Psalm 8). This headship relationship is also described in Scripture within the family structure (Ephesians 5:38, 6:1-5), the Trinity (John 10:18), the church (I Tim 3:1-15; Ephesians 5:23; I Cor 12:28), the business world (Luke 19:12-13; John 2:14), and government (Romans 13). Christ himself illustrated this principle as the head of the church and as the "good" shepherd (Ephesians 5:38; John 1:11). This kind of relationship could be considered mutualistic since the practice of headship or leadership benefits both the leader of the group and individuals in the group.

Headship relationship is also demonstrated in animal societies many of which demonstrate a hierarchical pecking order; the alpha male or female leader, or queen in the social insects for example. In addition, this kind of relationship is evident in symbiotic group dynamics involving multiple species. Ants which farm aphids[10] and obtain sugary secretions from them would be an example as well as the many invertebrates which uptake algae and allow it to grow within their cells or body cavities and harvest the energy captured by photosynthesis.[11] In a majority of these cases, one species tends to dominate and appears to control the relationship. In addition, in many relationships involving bacterial symbionts the bacteria receive little to no benefit. For instance, the light producing *Vibrio fischeri* bacteria previously mentioned appears to receive little benefit from the Hawaiian Bobtail squid (Nyholm 2004).[12] Nor does it appear to benefit directly from its own light production. Thus, many mutualistic relationships in nature appear to be one-sided or unequal; one partner is dominant and receives more benefit from the relationship. The persistence of unequal mutualism is explained better by creationism since creationism might predict that some organisms may be specifically designed to be head partners and other organisms as providers of nutrients or other benefits. In contrast, a strict evolutionary biology view would expect natural selection to choose mutual over non-mutual symbiotic relationships.[13]

---

10   Ants farm several different kinds of insects including aphids, scale insects, and mealy bugs.
11   Some invertebrate sea creatures literally strip the chloroplasts from algae and incorporate the chloroplasts into their own tissues.
12   Many Vibrio species appear to flourish as free-living aquatic bacteria.
13   Evolutionary biologists do posit that non-mutualistic partners can originate from parasitic relationships. However, they also suggest that the long term persistence of non-mutualistic partners is doubtful since the selection process eventually leads to a degradation of the partner which contributes less to the relationship.

6.5.6. Community relationship. This scriptural principle is most dramatically demonstrated by the imagery of the church as a functioning body (I Cor 12:12-27). In this model the biblical author draws an analogy between human body parts and the individuals who make up the church; each part/individual has a vital role to play in maintenance of the church. In essence, the individuals work together to promote the functioning of a superstructure or superorganism; a concept also explored by the early pioneers of symbiosis. Community relationship was instilled into creation during the creation week as Adam was commanded to interact and name the animals and plants and animals were designed to interact for nutritional purposes (Genesis 2). The fact that vegetation is generally designed to be non-motile is consistent with most animals being drawn together during feeding times.

The individual symbionts involved in community relationships tend to display incomplete mutualism, i.e. they are unlikely to have all their nutritional requirements fulfilled by a single partner and therefore require multiple connections with a variety of organisms. Balanced two-party mutualisms are more likely to promote relationships which persist independently of other organisms because all their needs are met by their partner. Modern ecological principles are thus consistent with biblical concepts of organismal inter-relationship and incomplete mutualism. This includes the observation that there is a highly coordinated flow of energy through ecosystems as animals consume but do not exhaust, their food source.

Consider the ant-aphid example. This mutualism which appears to be an exclusive relationship between ant and aphid actually involves several other partners; the aphids are dependent on both vascular plants and bacterial symbionts for nutrition (Offenberg 2001). (The ants do not supply nutrition to the aphids and may operate primarily as agents of refuse removal and guardians.) The bacterial symbionts live in specially designed cells within the aphid and provide amino acids not supplied by the plant sap. Viral symbionts are most likely also involved because bacterial symbionts of insects have also been shown to possess viral symbionts which in turn influence the bacteria-insect relationship (Bordenstein 2006). Thus, community relationship involves a network of interdependent mutualistic relationships and it is highly likely that all organisms are part of intricate community networks.

Community relationship is most dramatically demonstrated within bacterial colonial group dynamics. In nature, bacteria live in large community groups and secrete polysaccharides which form an intricate biofilm structure (O'Toole 2000). Biofilms have been shown to involve bacteria and other microbes living in an elaborate symbiotic community structure which involves division of labor and complex structures which benefit the community as a whole.

We can draw several conclusions and predictions about intra-organismal symbiotic relationship in nature from analysis of these general scriptural principles: (1) All living organisms possess design features which promote their interaction with other organisms including features which foster the establishment of symbiotic relationship, (2) incomplete or unequal symbiotic relationships would be expected in the creation model for two reasons; (a) many organisms were created to serve other organisms without receiving a benefit in return[14] and (b) this type of relationship fosters a community relationship because of the mutiple interactions which take place among living organisms, (3) some symbiotic relationships would be expected to show some attributes of parasitism because incomplete mutualism typically causes one symbiont to dominate the other and, (4) although it would not be expected to be a primary source of symbiotic relationship, some contemporary instances of symbiosis may be tertiary derivations from parasitic activity.

6.5.7. Classifying symbiotic relationship according to the function provided by the symbiont. As discussed, a biblical view of symbiotic relationship suggests that symbionts will provide a beneficial function for their partner(s). Beneficial functions provided by symbionts are likely to increase the survival of organisms, and thus they are likely to indirectly participate in mechanisms of speciation. The beneficial functions provided by symbionts fall into several categories. This type of classification schema has a biblical basis; many organisms were described as belonging to a certain structure or functional group during the initial creation events documented in Genesis. For instance, some organisms were classified as flying or creeping things, and others, by inference as swimming creatures (Genesis 1:19, 24,25). In addition, some organisms were categorized as food providers, and some as protectors of the garden (Genesis 1:29; 3:24). Symbiotic relationships can be placed into functional categories based on the roles played by the symbionts which include, nutrition provision, metabolism alteration, reproduction control, host defense, thermotolerance, behavior modification, genetic repair, manipulation of morphology, and influence on genetic constitution.

Understanding, studying and categorizing symbiotic relationships in terms of their function will help inform the biology creation model. For instance, symbionts can induce profound changes in the physiology and anatomy of their hosts. This may have implications for how creationists view and study speciation or the fossil record. We will explore below examples of several of these functional categories and the implications for creation biology.

6.5.8. Symbiosis-induced morphology change. Morphology change seems to be a common phenomena among symbionts. Lichens provide perhaps the most dramatic illustration of morphology change.

---

14   The Christian concepts of service and sacrifice involve non-reciprocation.

Over 13,000 species of lichens have been documented and their total numbers may exceed 20,000 species, yet less than 40 algae species participate in the symbiosis. Each lichen species displays a plant like morphology which the symbionts alone do note resemble. In addition, the lichen morphologies allow the lichen to grow and thrive in places where the individual symbionts cannot. The morphologies can appear highly developed such that the lichen can display plant-like structures including roots, leaves, stems and reproductive structures. In another case of dramatic morphological change, the sea lettuce alga forms a multicellular lettuce leaf-like structure only in the presence of a bacterial secretion product. Without the presence of the bacterium and the secreted product the algae displays no multicellular structure (Matsuo 2005). The morphology of fungal symbionts can also be dramatically influenced by insect symbionts which grow fungus as food. When grown in the lab, the fungal symbionts typically look very similar and display primarily a nondescript hyphal structure. In the presence of the insect, the fungal symbionts can take on many different and unique morphologies seldom viewed in sterile laboratory cultures.

It appears that the most dramatic morphology changes take place in the micro-micro-symbiosis category. However, there are examples of macro-symbiont morphology alteration. Consider for example the ant-mite symbiosis. Mites are common residents of ant colonies and some ants suffer from the attachment of mites to the end of their legs in what appears to be a degradatory parasitic relationship, yet remarkably, the mite acts like a leg component and coordinates its body movement with the ant leg movement. For instance, some ants form ant "bridges" by joining their leg appendages together. During the bridge formation the leg-attached mite has been observed moving its appendages to assist in connecting ants during the bridge building (Hölldobler 1998). In addition, the mite can also make the ant appear taller, allowing the ant to exhibit dominance when confronted with a foreign ant. In mammals, intestinal symbiotic bacteria are very important to intestinal health. Removal of symbionts can cause under-development of intestines and can cause disease. This could certainly lead to stunted growth and smaller skeletal frames and could be one factor in the variety of human form noted in the fossil record.

Organogenesis and alteration of organ morphology can also be induced in multicellular organisms by symbionts. For instance, root nodules in plants are induced by fairly complex signaling pathways between the bacterial symbiont and the host plant. The nodules are complex structures which harbor the bacteria. Also, the root nodule bacteria undergo dramatic morphology changes in cell size and shape. Many invertebrates including perhaps a majority of insects also grow complex organs which harbor bacterial symbionts (Buchner 1965). In some cases, for example, in the light organ of the Hawaiian bobtail squid, the organ morphology can be shaped by the presence of the bacterial symbiont (Nyholm 2004).

Symbiosis-induced morphology should be of interest to creationists for several reasons. The observation that morphology can be induced rapidly without a long development time may offer an explanation for the sudden appearance of novel morphologies in the fossil record and it is consistent with the concept of rapid diversification.

6.5.9. Nutrition provision and symbiosis. Provision of nutrition, compared to other symbiotic-induced functions, has received the most attention in the symbiosis literature and was a primary observation made by the early zoologists (Paracer 2000; van Beneden 1876). Symbiotic nutrition provision is widespread in nature and can be observed on a large scale. For instance, mychorrizae are fungal root structures which provide nutrients for many plants (Allen 1991). In fact, it is now predicted that most or all plants in ecosystems are connected underground by vast networks of mychorrizae. Henry Gee referred to this as an underground "internet" connecting many plants in a vast network (Simard 1997). This is consistent with what we have previously mentioned regarding how unequal or incomplete mutualism tends to promote connections among many species in a given ecosystem. Thus, in this instance we see unequal mutualism promoting an interconnected hidden foodweb underlying the more visible foodweb associations. Relatedly, creationists have also noted that bacteria which are symbiotic with many multicellular organisms, are also involved in cycling nutrients in biogeochemical cycles. Thus it appears that bacteria and other microbes are designed to provide an interface between biological organisms and mineral cycles (Francis 2003). We would expect then to find microbes involved in connecting these two realms. Indeed many microbes have complex mechanisms to mine elements from rocks.

In some cases organisms possess digestive systems which appear to be entirely dedicated to obtaining nutrition from microbial symbionts. For instance the tube worm *Riftia pachyptila* possesses a trophosome which is a digestive organ dedicated to obtaining nutrition from bacteria supplying the bacterial symbionts with nutrition in the form of a heme-like protein (Cavanaugh 1994).

6.5.10. Genetic constitution and symbiosis. Microbial symbionts possess complex mechanisms which allow them to obtain and transfer genetic components. Many viruses and bacteria appear designed to deliver genetic components to microbes and multicellular creatures. For example, they possess mobile genetic elements which often include elaborate and elegant mechanisms of genetic exchange among organisms. Relatedly, many multicellular creatures possess genetic signatures within their genomes consistent with microbial transfer of mobile genetic elements.

184 Genesis Kinds

Creationists have hypothesized that mobile genetic elements may have participated in baraminic diversification events (Wood 2003). In addition, bacteria and viruses appear to possess mechanisms which foster short term epigenetic alterations in organisms, including the delivery of protein and membrane components which can alter or manipulate biochemical pathways and cell architecture. The study of symbiotic-induced genetic alteration should provide many fruitful avenues of research for creationists as they seek explanations for baramin and species diversification events.

6.5.11. Reproduction control and symbiosis. Consistent with the observation that symbionts interface genetically with organisms is the observation that bacterial and viral symbionts colonize reproductive tracts of insects, mollusks and echinoderms and most likely other animal groups. The reproductive organs of many insect species appear to harbor bacterial symbionts. In fact the bacterium *Wolbachia* is estimated to colonize over six million different insect species, and it is estimated to infect up to 75% of the total insect population within any given ecosystem (Johanowicz 1998). *Wolbachia* colonize eggs and reproductive tracts of insects and have a number of different effects on reproduction, including overriding chromosomal sex determination, selective killing of males, and cytoplasmic incompatibility. All of these functions involve a direct influence on reproduction and can modulate reproduction under certain circumstances. From an evolutionary biology perspective, *Wolbachia* infection looks in many ways like parasitism. However, from a creationist perspective, it appears that *Wolbachia* may be involved in reproduction control. Creationists have an interest in reproduction control since it is postulated that some control mechanism would need to be in place in the pre-Fall environment.

Bacteriophages are viruses which infect bacteria. Many bacteriophages lyse their host, thus essentially performing a form of population control.[15] Several investigators have noted the population control mechanism of bacteriophages in nature. For instance, *Vibrio cholera* populations appear to be held in check in natural waterways by bacteriophages (Faruque 2005; Francis 2006). Medical researchers are also interested in phage therapy of bacterial infections and the control of cancer cells via eukaryotic viruses (Kim 2007). Phage and virus research should be another fruitful avenue of creation research into population control mechanisms.

6.5.12. Host defense and symbiosis. Host defense is commonly found in symbiotic relationships and occurs within the macro and micro-symbiosis classifications. For instance, both the oyster crab and clown fish are vigilant in their protection of their respective hosts, the oyster

---

15 If we think of bacteria as extracorporeal tissues or organs, then the viral control of bacterial reproduction would be analogous to the cell reproduction control which occurs within the tissues of an organism.

and anemone respectively (Godwin 1992). In turn the sea anemone with its stinging tentacles protects its fish or crab host partner. In fact, some hermit crabs carry sea anemones as a mobile host defense system on their shells. The leaf-cutter farmer ants carry an antibiotic-producing bacterium within elaborate designed crypts on their cuticles, complete with secretion glands to protect their fungal farms from microbe invaders (Currie 2006). A variety of different birds have formed partnerships with ants in a behavior called "anting" (Facklam 1989). In this case birds pick up formic-acid producing ants or allow them to crawl up their spread wings where they produce formic acid and kill parasites residing in their feathers. It is not known whether the ant benefits from such an association. In another relationship involving toxins, several fish species live underneath jellyfish such as the deadly man-o-war. The fish which are immune to the jellyfish venom serve as "bait" attracting fish for the jellyfish to sting and consume in return for their protection (Mansueti 1963). Several birds ride the backs of herding animals such as cattle and oxen. One of these birds, the oxpecker, not only removes ticks and other parasites from the ox, but can also provide an early warning system to the herd of advancing predators.

One of the most intricate and fascinating "host defense" relationships involves the symbiotic intestinal bacteria found in the mammalian gut. The microbes which make up the normal flora of the gut live in a microcosm which involves hundreds of bacterial and viral species. The normal flora of the gut represents the densest, most populated ecosystem on earth. The normal symbiotic bacterial flora is so important to health that scientists are proposing that the immune system and symbiotic bacteria work together to provide host defense in this vital organ system (Kitano 2006). The immune system near the intestines continuously samples the bacteria of the gut and can distinguish between normal flora and invasive disease causing bacteria (Kraehenbuhl 2004). Many diseases may be caused by a decrease or sub-optimal dose of normal flora bacteria.

Symbiosis-induced host defense appears to be somewhat problematic to explain within a creationist model. Creationists would predict that since disease was not part of the pre-Fall world that host protection mechanisms would not be needed. Therefore host defense mechanisms should bear the hallmarks of secondary post-Fall adaptations to the environment rather than primary designed mechanisms. In some of the examples mentioned above, the adaptations do appear to be rather simple secondary adaptations to the environment, (e.g., the parasite eating birds). However, in other cases, the mechanisms appear designed, e.g., the elaborate antibiotic crypts of the ant or the exquisite mammalian immune system. One explanation for the existence of elaborate host defense systems in a pre-Fall environment is that they were initially designed to select and procure complementary microbial symbionts by filtering them from a biosphere teeming with literally millions of microbes.[16]

6.5.13. Endosymbiosis and the organosubstrate. As discussed, endosymbiosis is one of the most well documented biological phenomena yet it is largely ignored within the field of creation biology. Endosymbiosis is abundant and ongoing in nature and is anticipated and expected within the creation model for several reasons. One is that as we have noted, relationship is a fundamental aspect of God's living creation and endosymbiosis is one form of relationship. In contrast, the evolution of eukaryotic cells via an endosymbiotic mechanism would not be anticipated or expected within the creation model because eukaryotic cells are integral structural building blocks of fully formed metazoan baramins. However, endocytobiosis involving the presence of microbe like organelles within cells would be anticipated by the organosubstrate concept. In this creation concept, microbes are viewed as vital links between essential minerals and living organisms (Francis 2003). Microbes are positioned at important interfaces between the abiotic and biotic realms where they participate in biogeochemical cycles and the uptake of nutrients into biotic reservoirs. Their ubiquity within the biosphere is consistent with this role. Because microbes possess mechanisms which allow them to deliver nutrients to living organisms it would be expected that we would find them in many environments including those inside living organisms and inside cells. In some cases they would have the ability to move in an out of biological organisms and in some cases they would be fixed. Thus we could view mitochondria and choloroplasts as fixed, intracellular, nutrient-gathering and distributing microbe-like organelles. And correspondingly, microbes which live outside cells would be considered as fixed or mobile nutrient gathering and distributing extracellular organelles.

6.5.14. Symbiogenesis and Baraminology. A monobaramin is typically viewed as a single unique entity, yet all monobaramins contain symbionts which also may in fact be considered baramins. How then should this influence our view of what a baramin is? In the case of humans microbial symbionts live in association with the human body in abundance and contribute to its physiology in many ways. It is becoming increasingly clear that the human body should be considered as part of a larger human metabiome or metagenome. Therefore baramins were most likely created with symbionts *in situ* (although organisms also appear designed to acquire baramins). In many cases microbial endo-or exo-symbionts could be considered as a body part or tissue in the original baramin. This would leave the baramin concept largely intact. However, some

---

16   This is dramatically displayed in the Hawaiian bobtail squid-*Vibrio fischeri* symbiosis. The squid filters out the Vibrio symbiont from dilute waters by using an inflammation process which involves trapping, killing and expulsion of non-symbionts using immune system components.

symbionts contribute to major morphological and physiological changes in their host. They play a much more dramatic role than a body part or tissue. Consider lichens for example. This symbiosis is a radical departure from the solitary free living lifestyle of the individual symbionts which compose the lichen. Should the component organisms be considered as separate baramins, or should the intact lichen be considered a single baramin or should we consider the system a chimeric baramin? Or is it possible that the lichen was the originally created baramin, and that at the Fall, breakdown of the lichen association led to the free living lifestyles of its component partners? These questions among others represent some interesting challenges for baraminology.

6.6. Summary and Conclusions

All living organisms are predicted to be involved in symbiotic relationships.[17] Many symbiotic relationships involve multiple partners which may or may not provide benefit to their associated partners within the relationship. In fact, many symbiotic relationships display aspects of parasitism or unequal mutualism where one partner benefits at the expense of the other partner. Since the evolutionary model predicts that symbiosis is derived from parasitism, it is expected in this model that mutualistic relationships may show some aspects of parasitism.

One of the most abundant unequal mutualisms which may be difficult to explain within the evolutionary biology model is the nutritional-based relationship between plants and animals; a common relationship observed by many symbiologists. Plants persist in the environment and are typically not eliminated by selection even though they receive little to no benefit from animals. From a creationist perspective, the symbiotic relationship between two disparate creatures which appears in some ways to be parasitic, can be predicted as well as explained. For instance, creationism would predict that because plants were created to provide food for animals that they would be designed to live in close proximity to animals and designed to be partially consumed. This is reminiscent of Linnaeus's emphasis on the design of plants as food for animals and is also noted in more recent creationist literature (Zuill 2000). In addition, creationism would predict that plants would be designed to persist in ecosystems so that they could continue to provide food while resisting elimination. The end result of this design is a creature which associates with animals in long term relationship while possessing regenerative capabilities to provide long-term nutrition.

Relatedly, the unequal relationship which typifies many symbiotic phenomena, is characterized as involving multiple partners for each

---

17   There is possibly one known exception to this prediction because a recent study involving genomic analysis claims that a single bacterium species lives solitarily in a sterile environment deep within the earth (Chivian 2008).

individual symbiont because each symbiont requires multiple inputs to supply its needs. This design fosters community development and is also consistent with the scriptural concept that community structure was designed into the fabric of the living creation.

Symbionts, perform many different functions within their community including promotion and induction of speciation. The process of speciation is a major concept in both the creation model and evolutionary biology models. In the evolutionary model symbiogenesis is postulated to have caused several major transitions, e.g. the prokaryote to eukaryote transition. In the creation model symbiogenesis is of interest as a mechanism for rapid species diversification and there are several documented instances of symbiont-induced rapid speciation. The variation required for symbiogenesis is derived from the disparity of the partners which merge to create the novel species. If the partners are similar or identical they would theoretically produce less variety in the new species compared with the variation produced by disparate partners. Creation biology would therefore offer a better explanation for the derivation of symbiogenesis-induced novelty since creation biology postulates that a discontinuous set of organisms were created in the beginning.

Speciation promoted by symbionts appears to be limited to the acquisition of a microbial partner and there are natural barriers to speciation by genome fusion of disparate metazoans. Microbial symbiont induced speciation can involve either a slow or rapid speciation process. In the slow speciation process, microbes promote survival of organisms which can then be modified by classical evolutionary mechanisms; the rapid speciation process involves the hybridization of similar species and promotion of genetic novelty by a microbial symbiont which associates with one or both species. The natural barriers to speciation among disparate organisms and the rapid speciation of organisms within a created kind or baramin, would be expected in the creation model, since it would be postulated that a mechanism to preserve the discontinuity between created kinds would exist. In addition, the derivation of baramins by rapid diversification within a kind is consistent with the character of a Creator Who made a sustainable creation.

References

Allen, M.F. 1991. *The Ecology of Mycorrhizae.* Cambridge University Press, New York.

Atlas et al. 1998. *Microbial Ecology: Fundamentals and Applications.* Benjamin Cummings, Menlo Park, pp. 60.

Bergman, J. 1998. The unabridgeable chasm between prokaryotes and eukaryotes. In: Walsh R.E., ed. *Proceedings of the Fourth International Conference on Creationism.* Creation Science Fellowship, Pittsburgh, pp. 67-77.

Bordenstein, S.R. et al. 2006. The Tripartite associations between Bacteriophage, Wolbachia, and Arthropods. *PLoS Pathogens* 2:384-393.

Buchner, P. 1965. *Endosymbiosis of Animals with Plant Microorganisms.* Interscience Publishers, New York.

Cavanaugh, C.M. 1994. Microbial Symbiosis: Patterns of Diversity in the Marine Environment. *American Zoologist* 34:79-89.

Chivian, D., E.L. Brodie, E. Alm, D. Culley, P. Dehal, T. DeSantis, T. Gihring, A. Lapidus, L. Lin, S. Lowry, D. Moser, P. Richardson, G. Southam, G. Wanger, L. Pratt, G. Andersen, T. Hazen, F. Brockman, A. Arkin, and Onstott T. 2008. Environmental Genomics Reveals a Single-Species Ecosystem Deep Within Earth. *Science* 322: 275-278.

Christensen, A.M. and J.J. McDermott. 1958. Life history and biology of the Oyster Crab *Pinnotheres ostreum* Say. *Biological Bulletin* 114: 146-179.

Currie, C.R. 2003. Ancient Tripartite Coevolution in the Attine Ant-Microbe Symbiosis. *Science* 229:386.

Currie, C.R. et al. 2006. Coevolved Crypts and Exocrine Glands Support Mutualistic Bacteria in Fungus-Growing Ants. *Science* 311:81-83.

D'Herelle, F. and G.H. Smith, trans. 1926. *Bacteriophage and its behavior.* Balliere. Tindall and Cox, London.

De Bary, A. 1879. *Die Erscheinung der symbiose.* Verlag Trubner, Strassburg, pp. 1-30, 21-22.

Douglass, S., S. Zauner, M. Fraunholz, M. Beaton, S. Penny, L. Deng, X. Wu, M. Reith, T. Cavalier-Smith, and U. Maier. 2001. *Nature* 410:1091-1096.

Egerton, F. 1973. Changing concepts of the balance of nature. *Quarterly Review of Biology* 48:322-350.

Facklam, M. 1989. *Partners for Life: The Mysteries of Animal Symbiosis.* Little, Brown and Co., Boston.

Faruque, S.M. et al. 2005. Self-limiting nature of seasonal cholera epidemics: Role of host-mediated amplification of phage. *PNAS* 102:6119.

Francis, J. 2003. The organosubstrate of life: A creationist perspective of microbes and viruses. In: Ivey, R.L ed. *Proceedings of the Fifth*

190   Genesis Kinds

International Conference on Creationism, pp. 433.

Francis, J. 2006. The role of virulence factors in the establishment of beneficial ecological relationships of *Vibrio cholera* and *Vibrio fischeri*. *Occasional Papers of the BSG* 8:7.

Frank, A.B. 1877. Ueber die biologischen Verhältnisse des Thallus einiger Krustenflechten. *Beiträge zur Biologie der Pflanzen* 2:123-200.

Geddes, P. and J.A. Thomson. 1911. *Evolution*. Williams and Norgate, London.

Godwin, J. 1992. Defense of host actinians by anemonefishes *Copeia* 3: 902-908.

Gould, S.J. 1990. *Wonderful Life: The Burgess Shale and the Nature of History*. Norton, New York.

Hölldobler, B. and E.O. Wilson. 1998. *Journey to the Ants: A Story of Scientific Exploration*. Belknap Press, Cambridge, MA.

Howe, G.F. et al. 2002. Lichens: A Partnership for Life. *Creation Research Society Quarterly* 39:81.

Jeon, K. 1972. Development of cellular dependence on infective organisms: Microurgical studies in amoebas. *Science* 176:1112.

Jeon K. 1991. Amoeba and x-bacteria: Symbiont acquisition and possible species change. In: Margulis, L. and R. Fester, ed. *Symbiosis as a Source of Evolutionary Innovation*. MIT Press, Cambridge, MA, pp. 118–131.

Johanowicz, D.L. et al. 1998. The manipulation of arthropod reproduction by wolbachia endosymbionts. *The Florida Entomologist* 81: 310-317.

Kim, L. 2007. Viral attenuation (reduction of pathogenicity) and its link to innate oncolytic potential: Implications of a perfect original creation. *Occasional Papers of the BSG* 10:17.

Kitano, H. et al. 2006. Robustness trade-offs and host–microbial symbiosis in the immune system. *Molecular Systems Biology* 2:2006.0022, doi:1 0.1038/msb4100039.

Kropotkin, P. 1915. *Mutual Aid: A Factor of Evolution*. William Heinemann, London.

Kraehenbuhl, J.P. et al. 2004. Keeping the gut microflora at bay. *Science* 303:1624-1625.

Law, R., and U. Dieckmann. 1998. Symbiosis through exploitation and the merger of lineages in evolution. *Proc. R. Soc. Lond.* B 265:1245-1253.

Linnaeus, C. 1781. Oeconomy of Nature. F.J. Brand, trans. In: *Selected dissertations from the Amoenitates Academicae*. Robinson and Robson, London.

Mansueti, R. 1963. Symbiotic behavior between small fishes and jellyfishes, with new data on that between the stromateid, *Peprilus alepidotus*, and the scyphomedusa, *Chrysaora quinquecirrha*. *Copeia* 1:40-80.

Margulis, L. and R. Fester. 1991. *Symbiosis as a Source of Evolutionary Innovation: Speciation and Morphogenesis*. MIT Press, Cambridge, MA.

Margulis, L. and D. Sagan. 1997. *Microcosmos: Four Billion Years of Microbial Evolution*. University of California Press, Berkeley.

Margulis, L. and D. Sagan. 2002. *Acquiring Genomes: The Theory of the*

Origin of Species. Persues Press, NewYork.

Margulis, L. 1975. Symbiotic theory for the origin of eukaryotic organelles: Criteria for proof. *Symposia of the Society for Experimental Biology* 29: 21-38.

Margulis, L. 1981. *Symbiosis in Cell Evolution*. W.H Freeman, New York.

Matsuo, Y. et al. 2005. Isolation of an algal morphogenesis inducer from a marine bacterium. *Science* 307:1598

Nardon, P. and A.M. Grenier. 1991. Serial endosymbiosis theory and weevil evolution: The role of symbiosis. In: Margulis, L. and R. Fester, eds. *Symbiosis as a Source of Evolutionary Innovation*. MIT Press, Cambridge, MA, pp. 154-169.

Nardon, P. and H. Charles. 2001. Morphological aspects of symbiosis. In: Seckbach J. ed. *Symbiosis: Mechanisms and Model Systems*. Kluwer Academic Publishers, Dordrecht, pp. 13-46.

Nyholm, S.V., and M. McFall-Ngai. 2004. The winnowing: establishing the squid-vibrio symbiosis. *Nature Reviews Microbiology* 2:632.

Offenberg, J. 2001. Balancing between mutualism and exploitation: the symbiotic interaction between Lasius ants and aphids. *Behavioral Ecology and Sociobiology* 49:304-310.

Okamoto, N. and I. Inouye. 2005. A Secondary Symbiosis in Progress? *Science* 310:287.

O'Toole, G., et al. 2000. Biofilm formation as microbial development. *Annual Review of Microbiology* 54:49.

Paracer, S., et al. 2000. *Symbiosis: An Introduction to Biological Association*. Oxford University Press, New York.

Reid, R. 2007. *Biological emergences: Evolution by Natural Experiment*. MIT Press, Cambridge, MA.

Ryan, F. 2002. *Darwin's Blind Spot: Evolution Beyond Natural Selection*. Houghton Mifflin Books, New York.

Ryan, F. 2007. Viruses as symbionts. *Symbiosis* 44:11-21.

Sapp, J. 1994. *Evolution by Association: A History of Symbiosis*. Oxford, New York, pp.18-19.

Sapp, J. 2007. The structure of microbial evolutionary theory. *Studies in History and Philosophy of Biological and Biomedical Sciences* 38:780.

Simard, S.W., et al. 1997. Net transfer of carbon between ectomycorrhizal tree species in the field. *Nature* 388:579.

Smith, J.M. 1991. A Darwinian view of symbiosis. In: Margulis, L. and R. Fester, ed. *Symbiosis as a Source of Evolutionary Innovation*. MIT Press, Cambridge, MA, pp. 26-39.

Spencer, H. 1899. *The Principles of Biology*. D. Appleton and Co., New York.

Starr, M.P. 1975. A generalized scheme for classifying organismic associations. In: Jennings, D.H. and D.L Lee, eds. *Symbiosis: Symposia of the Soc. for Experimental Biology* 29:1-20.

Stoodley, P., et al. 2002. Biofilms as complex differentiated communities. *Annual Review of Microbiology*,56:187.

Szathmáry, E. and J.M. Smith. 1997. From replicators to reproducers: the first major transitions leading to life. *Journal of Theoretical Biology* 187: 555.

Todes, D.P. 1989. *Darwin without Malthus: The Struggle for Existence in Russian Evolutionary Thought.* Oxford University Press, New York.

Wise, K. 2002. *Faith, Form and Time.* Broadman & Holman, Nashville.

Wood, T.C. 2002. The AGEing process: Rapid post-Flood intrabaraminic diversification caused by Altruistic Genetic Elements (AGEs). *Origins* (GRI) 54:5.

Wood, T.C. 2003. Perspectives on AGEing: a young-earth creation diversification model. In: Ivey, R.L ed. *Proceedings of the Fifth International Conference on Creationism.* Creation Science Fellowship, Pittsburgh, pp. 479-489.

Wood, T.C. 2008. Species variability and creationism. *Origins* (GRI) 62:6-25.

Van Beneden, P.J. 1876. *Animal Parasites and Messmates.* Henry S. King, London.

Williamson, D.I., and S.E. Vickers. 2007. The origins of larvae. *American Scientist* 95:509-517.

Zuill, H. 2000. Ecology biodiversity and creation. *CEN Technical Journal* 14:82-90.

CORE Issues in Creation

Established in 2005, the CORE *Issues* monograph series presents high quality scholarly work from or related to a young-age creation perspective. This monograph series is not for the publication of scholarly critiques of alternative positions (other venues exist for that kind of publication). Rather, CORE *Issues* has been created to publish any monograph in any discipline (philosophy, theology, physics, geology, biology, archaeology, linguistics, etc., etc.) which substantially contributes to the systematic development of a positive, young-age creation model. Original monographs will thoroughly review the conventional and creationist literature on the subject, offer a constructive interpretation of the subject's data, integrate well with other disciplines as the model is constructed, and advance creation model development. Other monographs offer reprints, compendia, or translations of significant historical works that are currently unavailable. CORE *Issues* is peer-reviewed and will strive for the very highest scholarship standards. CORE *Issues* is a joint publication of the Center for Origins Research at Bryan College and Wipf & Stock Publishers.

CORE *Issues* does not publish works written only by Bryan College faculty but encourages outside submissions. Researchers may submit monograph proposals (full manuscripts are not accepted) to CORE either electronically at info@bryancore.org or by regular mail:

CORE *Issues* editor
Bryan College 7802
721 Bryan Drive
Dayton, TN 37321

Previous Volumes in the **CORE Issues** Series

1. A Creationist Review and Preliminary Analysis of the History, Geology, Climate, and Biology of the Galápagos Islands, by Wood (2005)
2. Johannes Buteo's The Shape and Capacity of Noah's Ark, trans. by Griffith & Monette (2008)
3. Animal and Plant Baramins, by Wood (2008)
4. Christian Perspectives on the Origin of Species, edited by Garner (2009)

CHRIST ABOVE ALL
BRYAN
COLLEGE

CORE
CENTER FOR ORIGINS RESEARCH